WHEN MISS EMMIE
WAS IN RUSSIA

When Miss Emmie was in Russia

English governesses before, during and after the October Revolution

HARVEY PITCHER

London

First published by John Murray in 1977

This paperback edition published in
the United Kingdom by Eland Publishing Ltd
61 Exmouth Market, London EC1R 4QL in 2011

Copyright © Harvey Pitcher 1977

ISBN 978 1 906011 49 9

Cover: October 17th, 1905 (oil on canvas)
by Ilya Repin (1844–1930)
State Russian Museum, St Petersburg, Russia
The Bridgeman Art Library

Printed in Spain by GraphyCems, Navarra

*To my mother and
in memory of my father*

Contents

PART THREE

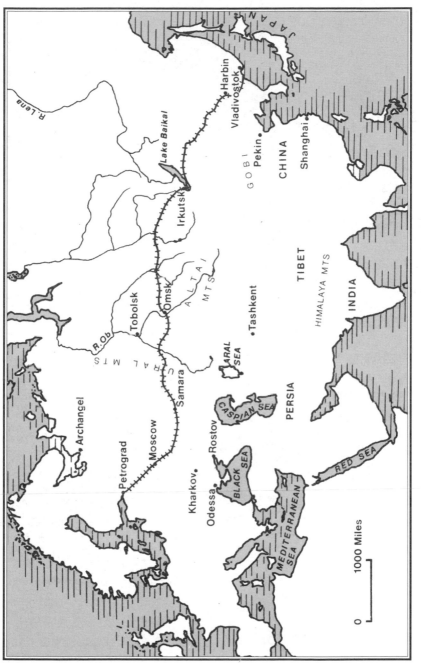

Map of the Trans-Siberian Railway, 1917

Map of European Russia showing places mentioned in this book

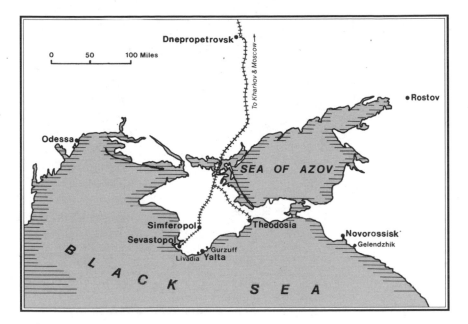

Map of the Crimean Peninsula

Introduction

'Of course, I never *intended* going to Russia! I was going to be a teacher!'

But Emma Dashwood did go to Russia, setting off from Tilbury Docks in the autumn of 1911 with another girl in her early twenties; and instead of the promised year, it was two and a half years before she returned to England in June 1914. Among her fellow passengers on the boat home was a Mr Stephens, who worked for a shipping company and lived with his family in Moscow.

'Oh, you'll be back all right,' he said to her, when she explained that she was probably returning to England for good. 'They all come back to Russia. They always do. You must give me a ring when you're next in Moscow.'

A few months later she did so.

'God bless my soul!' was all the astonished Mr Stephens could manage to say on hearing her voice again. For in the meantime the First World War had broken out, and travel between England and Russia had become difficult and dangerous. On this occasion, instead of the promised year, it was four and a half years before she finally returned to England in May 1919, still cheerfully unperturbed in spite of having lived through two revolutions and their aftermath.

In the Russian families where she was employed, Emma Dashwood was known as 'Miss Emmie'. But this book is not just the story of a single governess. The Miss Emmie of the title is also meant to be representative of the surprisingly large number of 'Miss Emmies' who went out as English governesses—and by English is meant English-speaking, for the Scots and Irish were always very prominent in the movement. Their total numbers must be reckoned in thousands rather than hundreds, for it was much less unusual to find a girl from Britain working as a governess in Russia before the Revolution than it might seem to us today. Their story lasts almost exactly a hundred years. It begins soon after the Napoleonic Wars and breaks off abruptly in 1920, and it tells how the English governess gradually became established as a familiar institution in upper-class Russian society. Its final chapter is dramatic: for in the period from 1917 to 1920, quite unexpectedly, our governesses found themselves unwilling but active participants in the turbulent life of Revolutionary Russia.

It is fortunate that governesses, like clergymen, always seem to live to a ripe old age, and that like elephants, they never forget. How surprising it was to meet Miss Dashwood for the first time and to find in her someone who had not only seen and lived in 'Old Russia', but could vividly recall so many of the interesting little domestic details of her life there; her memories were still in mint condition for the simple reason that no one had ever questioned her at length about Russia before, and she was not therefore recalling memories of memories.

But I feared that Miss Dashwood, born in 1889, might be a lone survivor of her generation, and was further surprised when enquiries soon brought me into contact with a number of other ladies who had been in Russia in the years from 1910 to 1920, and whose varied experiences provided an excellent foil for Miss Dashwood's simple story. There was Mrs Bangham (Edith Kerby), the only one who had been born and brought up as a member of the resident British community in Russia; Mrs Thomson (Marguerite Bennet or Scottie, as she is referred to in the book), taking on jobs that 'no Englishman in Russia then could have done at all'; the reluctant chaperone, Louisette Andrews; Mrs Dawe (Rosamond Dowse), only two weeks past her eighteenth birthday when she arrived in Russia as a governess in May 1914; and the loyal Mrs Whitley (Helen Clarke).

The English governesses in Russia were unassuming people. None of them would have seen anything admirable, let alone heroic, in the actions they performed on behalf of their Russian families during the years of Revolution. Nor would they have imagined that their stories might be fascinating in themselves, open our eyes in a new way to Russian society in those critical years, and often be more lively and amusing than the memoirs of the soldiers and diplomats. These first-hand accounts have been rescued just in time, for it goes without saying that former English governesses in Russia are no longer very numerous. At the time of writing all the ladies mentioned above are alive and well with the exception of Mrs Thomson, who died on July 24th, 1975, at the age of ninety-two. Since for all of them age has become a matter for self-congratulation rather than concealment, I can reveal that Miss Andrews and Mrs Whitley are both ninety-four, Miss Dashwood eighty-six, Mrs Bangham eighty-four, while Mrs Dawe, not yet quite eighty, is probably the youngest survivor of that generation of young girls who went out to Russia.

It has been a great pleasure in writing this book to meet and correspond with a very large number of helpful and friendly people. I shall postpone my acknowledgements of help received and of sources used until the end of the book, by which time they will be more meaningful to the reader, but I take the opportunity here of thanking Mrs Osyth Leeston for her very helpful advice on editorial matters.

Cromer, March 1976   H. J. P.

I

Setting Off

It all began with the Sinclairs.

The Sinclairs were a large family and lived in Gloucester Street, Norwich. When his first wife died, Mr Sinclair married again, but Edith, the eldest of his nine children, did not take to her new step-mother. Family tradition has it that she was an attractive, strong-willed young girl with red hair, who ran away from home while still in her teens and found herself a job as a nanny with a family living in Scarborough. This must have been some time in the late 1890's; and when changing circumstances took her Scarborough family to Russia, young Edith Sinclair went with them.

At first she was miserable and longed for home. She was sitting on a tram one day in St Petersburg, feeling particularly homesick and dabbing at her eyes with a handkerchief, when an English lady spotted her and guessing she was from England, began talking to her. Edith poured out her woes to this new acquaintance, who suggested that she come to live with her for a while, and look for more interesting jobs in good Russian families. The offer was accepted, and it was in one of these jobs, several years later, that she was taking some Russian children out for their usual Sunday morning walk. Before they could enter the park, they were turned back by a group of mounted soldiers armed with rifles. A huge procession of workers, led by an Orthodox priest, was on its way to Palace Square to present a petition to the Tsar. But the petition was never handed over. Troops fired on the crowd and more than a hundred workers were killed on that 'Bloody Sunday' in January 1905. And it was in another of her jobs that she first met Dmitri Kovalsky, a well-to-do young Russian naval officer and the son of an admiral. Kovalsky's family disapproved strongly of his association with the unknown English governess with the red hair, but Edith had little to fear from her family: Norwich was a long way off. Kovalsky retired from active service in the navy and married the attractive Miss Sinclair—married her twice, in fact, in Russia and in England.

As an Englishwoman married to a Russian with good social connections, Edith Kovalsky was in a unique position to act as a kind of unofficial employment agency in Russia for relatives and friends from England. No less than three of her sisters came out to stay in Russia. First, in 1904 or early 1905, before Edith's marriage, came May Sinclair, for whom Edith found a job as governess in the distinguished Vereshchagin family, whose most famous member, the painter Vasily Vereshchagin, had died only a short time before. The estate was in the north-eastern part of European Russia, some two days' journey by train from St Petersburg. There really were bears roaming in the huge forests that surrounded the house and provided the main source of income for the estate, and May Sinclair and her pupils were never allowed to go out far on their own, especially in severe weather. She learned the language quickly: no one in the household could speak a word of English! But life in Russia seems to have suited her. Though engaged to be married to an Englishman from her home town, she did not return to Norwich until 1907—her husband-to-be having finally put his foot down—stopping off for a few days at St Petersburg on her way back to buy most of her trousseau.

Next came sister Gertie, whose husband, a mining chemist, had taken a job in Russia, and last of all, in about 1910, came Katie Sinclair, who was also engaged. Katie seems to have been a more timid soul than her enterprising elder sisters. Many years later she used to complain that she had not been well treated in Russia. People were always trying to take advantage of her, she claimed, and she often reminded her listeners of one unpleasant *nouveau riche* family where they had made her sleep on a camp bed in the hall whenever guests arrived, and she was quite sure that large rats used to scamper across her face during the night.

It seems certain, however, that Katie never mentioned the rats when she wrote home to her great Norwich friend, Gertie Kirby. There was a vacancy for an English governess in a family not far from Katie in St Petersburg, and she was most anxious that Gertie should come out and join her. But by this time Edith Kovalsky had children of her own, and she too was in need of a young English girl to help look after and teach her small son. When old Mrs

Sinclair, now apparently on good terms with her stepdaughter, met Gertie Kirby one day in Norwich with her friend Emma Dashwood, she immediately turned to Emmie and said: 'Why don't *you* go out and stay with Edith?'

Emma Dashwood was twenty-one, a year younger than Gertie. To be a teacher had always been her greatest ambition. She had met Edith Kovalsky once before on Unthank Road—'looking very smart and wearing one of those great big picture hats that were just coming into fashion'—when Edith and her son, Tolya, were visiting Norwich. But Emmie had never in her life been as far as London, let alone abroad, let alone to Russia. Needless to say, there was much discussion in the family. Emmie's father, a master baker and confectioner in Norwich, had died some years before, and her Quaker uncle was very much opposed to the whole scheme. It was a strange country, the language was obviously impossible, and what about the dreadful Russian winter? But Emmie's friend and teacher, Mrs Nash, who was preparing her to enter the teaching profession, thought the visit would be an excellent way of enabling her protégée to broaden her horizons. There was also the financial consideration. Mrs Dashwood had three daughters younger than Emmie. A girl's wages in England at that time were scarcely enough to keep her. In Russia Emmie would be earning her keep and also saving a little money to send home. In any case, it was only to be for a year, Emmie would not be travelling alone but with Gertie Kirby, and she would not be going to an entirely strange Russian household but to the Anglo-Russian home of Edith Kovalsky. And behind all these pros and cons there was the simple fact that she *wanted* to go, and was thrilled by the idea of this exciting new adventure.

Gertie and Emmie left Norwich late one Friday afternoon in November 1911. Gertie's family, Emmie's family and old Mrs Sinclair were at Thorpe Station to see them off. In London they were met by relatives of Gertie's, who accompanied them to the docks. There was a very thick fog that evening, and all the foghorns were blaring. They were booked to travel on a small German cargo boat, and because of the superstition that it was bad luck to start a voyage on a Friday, the boat was not due to leave until just after midnight. The two girls settled down in their cabin, and when Emmie woke early the next morning, she was relieved to find herself feeling quite normal. 'Gertie, we're good sailors after all!' she shouted down from her upper berth. 'I feel all right, don't you?'

Gertie agreed. Not until some time later did they realise that because the fog had not lifted, their boat was still firmly anchored in Tilbury Docks. When they did finally get under way, it was a very different story. . . . But by the time they reached the smooth waters of the Kiel Canal they had begun eating again, and as they approached St Petersburg, they were both feeling positively cheerful. A number of small boats had been trapped by the ice and were waiting for an ice-cutter to free them.

'I was so *thrilled*,' Miss Dashwood now recalls, 'to watch our boat cutting its way through the ice, I was afraid I might tumble over the front of the boat in my excitement.'

She didn't fall over the front, of course, and for the moment we can safely leave Emma Dashwood, about to arrive at St Petersburg in the autumn of 1911, and travel still further back into the past.

2

Pioneers

There is a sense in which the story of Miss Dashwood in Russia does not begin with the Sinclairs, but forms part of the final chapter of a very much longer story which begins with the first English governesses in Russia. Not all of them approached St Petersburg with the same expectant cheerfulness as Gertie and Emmie. 'Every spring,' writes an engaging German observer, J. G. Kohl, who was in Russia in the 1830's,

from the same ships that have brought out the new fashions and new books from London, Paris, and Lübeck, many young ladies may be seen landing with torn veils and ruffled head-gear. These are the lovely and unlovely Swiss, German, French, and English women destined to officiate in Russia as priestesses of Minerva, in fanning the flame of mental cultivation. Exhausted by sea-sickness, saddened by homesickness, frightened by the bearded Russians who greet their eyes in Cronstadt, and pierced through and through by the chill breath of a St Petersburg May, they issue from their cabins, pale, timid, and slow, anxiety and white fear upon their lips, and despair in their eyes.

And there was worse to come!

Unwillingly the fair strangers leave the ship. . . . Their entrance into a rich and distinguished house is a new stage of suffering: and if the rude voices, long beards, and filthy clothing of the barbarous population of the harbour terrified them, here the glitter of unwonted luxury alarms their bashfulness. The loud tumultuous life of a great house in Russia, where no one comprehends their feelings in the slightest degree, is enough to overwhelm them; and, quartered in an apartment with the tribe of children intrusted to their care, they have scarcely a corner to themselves where they can weep out their grief.

But with time comes experience and the strangers 'learn to assume, by day at least, a decorous mask of cheerfulness, and thus contrive in the end to put a good face on the matter, even should the pillow be tear-moistened at night'.

The financial rewards for foreign governesses and tutors, who were more highly regarded and better paid than their counterparts in the rest of Europe, did, however, go a long way towards compensating for their discomforts. 'The cities of Montbeillard, Lausanne, Neufchatel, and some others, the nurseries for governesses for all Europe,' writes Kohl, 'are full of small capitalists of both sexes, who have accumulated their little fortunes in Russia.' But not every governess returned to her native country. Those who were tolerably pretty and agreeable could 'scarcely fail to entangle the heart of some young adjutant or colonel'; while others

contrive to accommodate themselves so thoroughly to the Russian element as to exchange their own national peculiarities for those of Russia, and prefer remaining for life where they have spent the better part of it. In many Russian families are to be found such after-growths of super-annuated English nurses, Frenchwomen, and Germans, who have adhered to the family till they are considered regular parts of it, and enjoy all the privileges of adoption accordingly.

It is clear that Kohl regarded governesses from England as less common than those from Switzerland, Germany and France, though 'the bonnes, or nursery-maids, for the younger children in St Petersburg, must be English, who, by general consent, are pronounced better suited for the office than those of any other nation'. (A *Russian* governess, of course, was unthinkable: the Russian nobility spoke French among themselves, using Russian—and that often imperfectly—only when addressing social inferiors.) A certain Miss Esterly, travelling in France with the Russian family of Davydoff in 1815 and described as 'a poor, quiet, little personage who seems estimable, but very miserable', may well, as Bea Howe suggests in *A Galaxy of Governesses*, claim the distinction of being the first recorded English governess with a foreign family abroad; while Russia's great national poet, Alexander Pushkin, first introduced the English governess, in the person of 'Miss Jackson', into Russian fiction in one of his prose *Tales of Belkin*, written in 1830. A minor figure and something of a caricature, this forty-year-old spinster is heavily powdered, tightly corseted and remarkably well paid for 'dying of boredom in this barbaric Russia'. That the English governess was still a rare phenomenon is suggested by the fact that Pushkin refers to her as 'Madame Miss Jackson' and makes her employer an eccentric Anglophile, whose grooms are dressed as English jockeys and who addresses his daughter in English as 'my dear'.

One very unusual English governess in Moscow from 1824 to 1828 was Claire Clairmont. She had previously been the mistress of Lord Byron, a secret which she kept strictly to herself in reactionary Moscow, and had borne him a daughter, Allegra. It was grief at the sudden death of Allegra (whom she had surrendered to Byron and had not seen before the child's unexpected death) and at the drowning of her one friend, Shelley, that made her abandon Italy and travel across Europe to the alien land of Russia. Among the dowdy governess sparrows Claire Clairmont stands out like some exotic bird of plumage, but there is one characteristic that she does share with her more run-of-the-mill colleagues: longevity. She was ninety-one when she died in Florence in 1879. The American novelist, Henry James, was told all about Miss Clairmont's legendary past when he visited Florence, and of how a young American traveller was said to have infiltrated himself into the Clairmont household as a lodger in the hope of discovering forgotten 'literary remains': a story which gave James the idea for his famous novel, *The Aspern Papers* (1888).

From the worldly and enigmatic Miss Clairmont it is a far cry to those young English girls, Quakers and Methodists, who went out to Russia as governesses in the 1830's. The 'clearing-house' for these girls was the home in Moscow of a Mrs Scott, whose son, Alexander, married a Russian girl who was the aunt of the novelist, Nikolai Leskov (1831–95). In 1857 Leskov resigned from the Russian civil service and joined the British firm of Scott & Wilkins, of which his uncle by marriage was a director. Thanks to his aunt, who herself eventually joined the Society of Friends, he had always been interested in the Quakers, and in his novel, *The Vale of Tears* (1892), he portrays a Quaker governess who shows such skill in helping the Russian peasants during the famine of 1840 that she comes to be regarded as a kind of saint.

That the English governess was able to obtain posts at the very highest level during the early years of her 'Russian century' is apparent in the case of Helen Pinkerton.

Helen was a Scot, born in Edinburgh in 1818. It seems likely that she was a relative, perhaps a niece, of the Rev. Robert Pinkerton, who in 1805 arrived at Karass, a missionary post among the Tartars in the North Caucasus, set up three years before by the Edinburgh Missionary Society. Pinkerton was to become well known as the author of a book published in 1833, based on his wide travels all over Russia from 1812 to 1825 on behalf of the Russian Bible Society, an offshoot of the British and Foreign Bible Society.

In 1835, when she was only seventeen, Helen married a man twice her age, Ludwig Marguardt, a citizen of Saxony employed by the Russians as a landscape gardener and botanist. A year later the wife of Tsar Nicholas I gave birth to her third son, named after his father, and in due course Helen Pinkerton, while still only in her twenties, was appointed English governess to the young Grand Duke Nicholas. This Grand Duke survived until 1929 and it was his son, Grand Duke Nicholas the younger, who commanded the Russian armies during the early part of the First World War. Helen herself, a widow for many years, lived on until 1905, having been granted a grace and favour flat in the Grand Duke's palace in St Petersburg and a pension from the privy purse.

Beyond this point information about her becomes fragmentary: a scrap of paper preserved by chance and a story handed down through the generations. The scrap of paper, shown to me by Helen's great-granddaughter, consists of a note dated June 6th, 1886, and addressed by Helen to her great friend, the Rev. Little, chaplain to the English Church in St Petersburg. 'I should be pleased to see you this evening,' she writes and one imagines the note being handed to the house-porter or *dvornik* to be taken round to the chaplain's house. As for the story, that takes us right back to the eighteenth century, to the time of the French Revolution. Because of the discrepancy in years between Helen and her husband, the visitors to their house covered a wide age span. Among them was an elderly Frenchman. One day, when her older sons were still quite young, Helen sent for them to be brought to the drawing-room while he was there. It was the fashion at that time for small boys to wear loose silk shirts and on this occasion they were wearing red ones. The old gentleman took one look at them and threw up his arms in horror.

'*Mais Hélène !*' he exclaimed in tones of the deepest reproach; for the sight of those red shirts had evoked in him vivid memories of the jailers in the Bastille where he had been imprisoned as a young man.

A governess of a different kind, who went out to Russia in 1849 and must have moved in more humble circles, was Miss Handcock.

There had been a prosperous British trading community in Russia ever since Elizabethan times. By the 1840's the British colony in St Petersburg was sufficiently large and thriving to support its own church—started in 1753 and re-built in 1815, with a seating capacity of five hundred—and its own boarding school for girls. It was on a visit to the offices of the Governesses' Benevolent Institution (the G.B.I.) in London, hunting for governesses of more recent vintage, that I was fortunate enough to discover letters written in 1849 relating to the appointment of a new governess for the English girls' school in St Petersburg. The G.B.I. had been started in 1841. In 1843 a remarkable Victorian philanthropist, the Rev. David Laing, was asked to act as Honorary Secretary, and from 1845 one important function of the Institution was to compile a register of posts for governesses.

The letters are written by Dr Edward Law, who had been chaplain to the English Church in St Petersburg for twenty-nine years since 1820. In December 1825, according to Mrs Disbrowe, wife of the British Minister Plenipotentiary to the Court at St Petersburg, he 'gave us a most impressive sermon on Sunday, and passed a beautiful eulogium on the late monarch': the Emperor Alexander I, who had just died. The task of finding a new governess must have been entrusted to Dr Law by the school committee before he left on a visit to England in the summer of 1849. 'Our school at St. P.,' he writes on July 14th in a letter to be forwarded to the Rev. Laing,

is established, with slight variations, upon the National System. We have a *large* House, consisting of 3 Stories, of which one is appropriated to the Master & Mistress, Mr & Mrs Watkins, the assistant, or Governess, & the Girls who are *Boarders*, in number between 30 & 40. The duties of Miss H. would be to assist Mrs W. during the School Hours, a part of which is employed in needle work, & taking Lessons in Russ & German in an adjoining room—to walk out with the Girls, to exercise such general superintendence as may be deemed necessary. She will be provided with a furnished room (but must bring her own Sheets, blankets, & Towels,

& pay for her own washing) fuel & candles—dinner with the Master & Mistress, who are most excellent people, & will do everything in their power to promote her comfort—bread, & sugar—but must provide her own tea & coffee, unless she may choose to partake of the meals of the children, viz bread & milk, for breakfast & Supper.

The fixed Salary is £50 pr an: but it is not impossible that an addition may be made hereafter should we find our School prosper, & Miss H. a thoroughly competent person; but her friends may rest assured that she will find herself associated with those who will be disposed to act kindly & liberally towards her. Should the engagement be completed I am authorized to pay Miss H. £15 for her travelling expences to St. P—& £10 as an advance of her Salary, the date of which will be reckoned as commencing from the day on which she leaves England.

Having outlined the duties that would devolve upon Miss Handcock, Dr Law goes on to put 'a few Queries' of his own. 'What,' he asks, 'is Miss Handcock's age?' (Here someone has inserted in pencil: '24, governess to Col. Brandeth's children'.)

Has she previously filled any similar situation,—where—& how long,— & can she procure Testimonials to that effect?—(This would, of course, be very satisfactory to me, as acting Member of an absent Comittee.)— It is presumed that Miss H. is a conscientious Member & Communicant of the Church of England, & capable of instructing the younger children in the rudiments of their religion.—Does she speak her own language correctly?—Is she capable (with the assistance of books) of instructing children in the Elements of Grammar Arithmetic Geography, & English & Sacred History?

Does she enjoy good health, & is she blessed with patience & good temper?

He concludes by saying that he will be obliged to hear from the Rev. Laing at the latter's 'earliest convenience, as I have received a recommendation of a Governess for our School from another quarter'. The plain truth, no doubt, coming from a doctor of divinity; but looking back at the previous paragraphs of his letter, one cannot help feeling that Dr Law was more anxious to secure the services of Miss Handcock than he is willing to admit:

Though a resident in a foreign country Miss H. will find herself so completely surrounded with her own countrymen that she will scarcely be aware of the change.

The Climate, with common prudence, I have found remarkably healthy, & I speak from the experience of 29 Years.

Scarcely be aware of the change? A remarkably *healthy* climate? The *Russian Year Book* for 1911, in its section on 'General Information for Travellers', declares: 'There is no more treacherous climate in the world than one meets with in St Petersburg'!

Entirely scrupulous, however, in matters of postage, Dr Law 'as in honesty bound encloses Postage Stamp for this Letter which is to be sent to Mr Laing'.

The latter replied promptly, for on July 20th Dr Law writes:

. . . Your statement concerning Miss Handcock I consider perfectly satisfactory in every point, & she may depend upon her position in society being in every way respectable, & upon every attention being paid towards rendering her comfortable & agreeable. Mrs Watkins, our Head Mistress, was for some years a Governess previous to her marriage, & will not fail to treat Miss H. with kindness & consideration.

When the mother of Miss H. has given her consent in the matter, I shall hope to receive from you a few lines to that effect, & I shall then consider the settlement as conclusive, & send you all due directions, & a Draft on my Banker for £25 as stated in my former Letter.

The maternal consent being given, Dr Law was able to 'enter into further particulars as to obtaining a Passport, engaging a Passage etc.—& to name a few articles which it will be desirable for her to take out, as being cheaper in England than in Russia'. A month later he writes again to the Rev. Laing:

August 27, 1849

Revd & dear Sir,

I was glad to find that Miss Handcock has started per Camilla, & trust that she may have a prosperous voyage. It was not without reason that you cautioned her against her Revd Compagnon de Voyage, the first appointed Master of our School at St P, but whom, as well as his Wife (par nobile)* our Comittee was obliged to dismiss at the end of 3 Months! They caused us serious inconvenience & expence.

Mr M to whose care I confided Miss H. will probably have given her some insight into his character.—I am well acquainted with Dr Leighton —& also with Lady Stuart de Rothesay, who is an excellent person.

* *par nobile fratrum*, a noble pair of brothers.

The last time I came to England, 5 years ago, with one of my daughters (at whose house I am now staying) we accompanied L^d & Lady S. from St P. to Southampton in a Government Steam Frigate, the Sydenham.

I expect to start from Hull on my return to St P. about the 25th of October. Trusting that Miss H. will find her new situation answer her expectations, & assuring her friends that both Mrs. E. Law & myself will do everything in our power to aid & assist her in every way, I remain

Rev^d & dear Sir,

Yours very faithfully,

Edward Law

The Revd D. Laing
26 Mornington Road
London

Who was this clerical reprobate with the equally unprincipled wife, and what sins had they been guilty of? Did they fortify themselves too liberally against the Russian cold? Alas, we shall probably never know. Miss Handcock, however, approaching St Petersburg in the summer of 1849, appears to be in safe hands, though it would be reassuring to learn that her future breakfasts and suppers consisted of something more substantial than bread and milk with the children.

3

Settling In

When Gertie Kirby and Emmie Dashwood arrived at St Petersburg in November 1911, Edith Kovalsky was not there to meet them, but they did not mind as it meant spending extra time together on the boat. Edith arrived next morning. As they disembarked, were they 'pale, timid and slow', and was there 'anxiety and white fear upon their lips, and despair in their eyes'? I find it hard to imagine. A little apprehensive, no doubt, and very relieved that Edith was there to talk Russian to the Customs officials. The rhubarb roots that Emmie had brought out for Edith's kitchen garden escaped attention, as did her Christmas crackers from Caleys of Norwich, and the material which Gertie had brought out for Katie Sinclair. To avoid suspicion, Gertie had carefully nailed the material round the sides of her trunk; Katie was furious when she discovered the nail marks.

They hired a sledge and were taken to the apartment where Gertie was to start her new job. Then Edith and Emmie were driven some miles out of St Petersburg to Peterhof, to the home of Edith's father-in-law, Admiral Kovalsky, and his wife, where they were to spend the weekend. The Kovalskys had by now become reconciled to their new English daughter-in-law, though they could never come to terms with her name, which they pronounced as 'Eddis'. The house had the English name of the 'Villa Rest', and the Kovalskys' daughter, Ariadne, who had been presented at Court, addressed Emmie in excellent English (so Uncle had been wrong in thinking that no one in Russia would be able to speak English properly!) It was Ariadne who gave Emmie the first present she received in Russia: a navy and white warm woollen jacket to be worn underneath a coat. Emmie was thrilled and wrote off home about it straight away.

Peterhof was famous for its magnificent Imperial parks and palaces, and Emmie was taken by Ariadne on a whirlwind sight-seeing tour by sledge. Then, after lunch on Sunday, Edith took

Emmie outside to have a good look round the Kovalskys' house and garden—and it was here that she had her first real shock in Russia. As they were returning to the house, she caught sight of Mme Kovalsky sitting by a window—and she was knitting, knitting on a Sunday! Emmie was flabbergasted, and said so. Edith, who must have been taken aback by this reaction, explained that such behaviour was quite acceptable in Russia and that on *no* account was she to let the Kovalskys see that she found it shocking.

From the 'Villa Rest' they had a long journey by train followed by a sledge drive through the country. The sledge glided smoothly over the country roads, which were covered with fine powdery snow. 'What a lot of cowsheds,' exclaimed Emmie. 'They appear to be dotted all over the countryside.' Edith had to explain that these were not cowsheds, but the log huts in which the peasants lived. They drove through a village: two long rows of huts, each one bearing a sign-board—a painting of a bucket, shovel or whatever the occupant was expected to produce instantly in the event of a village fire. Sturdy peasant women were each carrying two buckets of water on poles from a river some distance away. Their sheepskin coats and rough brown felt boots looked sensible, but the thinness of their kerchiefs and their cotton skirts was surprising in that sharp frosty weather.

As a *zemsky nachalnik* (president of the *zemstvo* or local rural council) Mr Kovalsky had been provided with a comfortable wooden house or *datcha*, painted an attractive shade of pale blue. Just what he *did* in his job Emmie never really found out, though she remembers finding the entrance hall packed with strange peasants one morning and being told that Mr Kovalsky was presiding over a session of the local court. The session took place in a large reception-room where the family's Christmas tree had stood, and when it was over, the smell left behind by the peasants' sheepskin coats was so pungent that the room was unfit to enter for the rest of the day.

In contrast to other governesses, like Gertie, who were pitch-forked straight into a Russian household where no English was spoken, and who must often, as Kohl puts it, have been over-whelmed at first by 'the loud tumultuous life of a great house in Russia, where no one comprehends their feelings in the slightest degree', Emma Dashwood's initiation into life in Russia could not have been gentler. No wonder that she often went round the house singing! The work was easy: elementary instruction and supervision of Tolya, and helping Edith generally about the house; and her salary, though small, enabled her to send home by money order ten roubles (one guinea) a month. The practical Edith was always there to give advice. A large pack of envelopes was immediately prepared, with Emmie's new address written out in Russian characters, and sent off to Mrs Dashwood in Norwich for the use of family and friends. The Kovalskys lived comfortably, though modestly by the standards of their class. They employed a coachman, who was fond of smoking very strong-smelling cigarettes and who later in the year distinguished himself by setting fire to the stables to which he had retired for his usual smoke and a nap; a housemaid (the coachman's daughter), to whom Emmie endeared herself by the gift of an old cloth skirt, the first cloth indoor garment the girl had ever possessed; a nursemaid who looked after the Kovalskys' infant daughter, Roxana; and a cook. This cook, with her funny little freckled face and ginger hair, was a constant source of amusement to Edith and Emmie. They never tired of watching from the window as she fed the chickens, scattering the grain with a shrill cry of *tseep! tseep! tseep!* and stooping down so close to the ground that she looked exactly like a big mother hen fussing over her chicks.

Acquiring a suitable outdoor wardrobe was one of Emmie's first tasks on arrival. She had earlier been promised by Edith the gift of a heavy winter coat or *shooba*, which to judge by its venerable appearance had already seen good service with more than one Sinclair sister; but at least it was warm and saw her through that first winter. Then she also acquired a swansdown hood lined with white Jap silk to wear over the fur turban she had brought from England, long woollen trousers that strapped underfoot, and beautifully made beige and white soft felt boots (*valenki*) that fitted up to the knee. They never got dirty because the snow was so powdery. Goloshes would not be needed until later on, when the thaw began.

The language was not a great problem either. Mr Kovalsky spoke good English, and Emmie could see little point in studying Russian seriously during her year there; especially since she was receiving a regular supply of English books to study from her Norwich teacher, Mrs Nash, which she often read lying on her bed in the afternoons, as Edith insisted she should rest each day. She soon picked up a working knowledge of Russian from the servants, learning for example how to ask Cook for an egg—'Madame says I can have one'—which she used for washing her hair. This working Russian was given its first real test the following spring. With the finer weather, Edith took Emmie out for long walks in the nearby woods, and encouraged Emmie to go out walking on her own. She was now able to wear her green spring coat from England with the long velvet roll collar. When she was out walking alone one day, a group of gipsies came along singing—she had met them before with Edith, who sometimes gave them ribbons. The gipsies began talking to her:

Of course I couldn't understand a *word* they were saying. They didn't ask for money. I had long thick plaits in those days, tied up with ribbon. They began fingering the ribbons and saying *chudny! krasivy!* how lovely! Then they began stroking the velvet collar and obviously wanted me to give them the coat.

'No, no,' I said, 'English coat. *English!* You know lady there'—and I pointed in the direction of the house—'she is kind to you. She gives you things. Come tomorrow. *Tomorrow!*'

They were charming people really, but was I thankful to get away!

Looking back now on the time that she spent with the Kovalskys, what stands out in Miss Dashwood's memory is the firm way in which Edith trained her to behave correctly in polite Russian society—training that was to prove invaluable later on. Emmie accompanied Edith everywhere and learned as she went along. 'Watch all the time' was Edith's advice. 'Watch other people just as I had to. Wait and see what they do and then do the same.' So Emmie watched, and learned, for example, to wait for her chair to be pushed under her before sitting down at table; to crack the two very lightly boiled eggs—served in a napkin on her side plate at lunch—into her glass with a spoon, scoop out the white into the glass, add salt and drink it all down; to cut up the meat with her knife, place the knife on the knife-rest, and eat with a fork only; and always to leave something on her plate, otherwise the servants would think that she needed a second helping. Edith also insisted that she should learn how to officiate at the samovar. Instead of sitting uncomfortably at the table unable to take any part in the conversation, she would feel more at ease doing something useful and exchanging a few Russian words, however limited in scope, with the visitors. The nickel samovar would be brought in and placed in front of her. The charcoal used for keeping the water on the boil all the time could be seen at the bottom glowing a bright red, while the boiling water inside hissed and whined in a cheerful singsong. On top, keeping warm, stood a small teapot containing very, very strong China tea. There was quite an art in judging when to fill up the teapot and how long to let it stand, while at the same time trying to make polite if stumbling conversation with a visitor.

Emmie also learned from Edith the art of tobogganing. Dragging her toboggan through the huge garden and orchard and up the far side of the frozen river, she would choose her direction carefully and go zooming down the bank, across the river and up the bank again on the near side. On one occasion her aim was faulty and she went straight into a tree-trunk: turban went flying and hat-pin too. She had been taught how to roll clear and did not hurt herself, but the hat-pin was lost for good.

As soon as the snow disappeared, warm weather seemed to arrive immediately. The river now was full of activity. Emmie loved to watch the endless stream of logs that floated past, and to listen to the songs of the lumberjacks who lived in little huts on the log-rafts. Her year of adventure in Russia was passing pleasantly if uneventfully. Katie Sinclair came out from St Petersburg to stay with her elder sister; Emmie accompanied Edith to St Petersburg; and Emmie and Gertie Kirby (with an 'i') paid a visit—as it later proved, a very important visit for Emmie—to members of an old-established English family in St Petersburg, the Kerbys (with an 'e').

Then came the bombshell. The Kovalskys announced that in the autumn they would be moving to Vladivostok and invited Emmie to go with them. Vladivostok! It was the terminus of the Trans-Siberian Railway, almost six thousand miles from Moscow. If St Petersburg was far enough away from Norwich, then Vladivostok was the other end of the world. Urgent letters arrived from home, telling her not to dream of accompanying the Kovalskys, but to return to England well before their departure. It looked as if Emmie's year in Russia was about to end in a disappointing anti-climax after all.

4

Britishers

About the year 1875 a young English couple began their married life in St Petersburg. They were Henry William Kerby and his wife, Teresa Rachel (*née* Otten), and their parents had also lived and known one another in Russia.

Henry William was employed by the City of St Petersburg New Waterworks Co. Ltd., a British-owned company registered in 1874 and granted a concession for forty years from 1877. In 1893, by which time the waterworks was functioning very successfully under British supervision, the Municipality of St Petersburg exercised its right to purchase the works by making the company regular payments until the concession expired in 1917; and it must have been in 1893 that Henry William was given the opportunity of exchanging his modestly paid job as works manager for the much more lucrative post of company director. The invitation, it seemed, could not have come at a more opportune time, for the Kerbys by now had a large family to support—Edith, born in 1892, being their seventh child.

But they had reckoned without H. W. Kerby. Henry William turned the offer down flat, and for one very simple reason. If he accepted the directorship, he was expected to renounce his British nationality and become a Russian citizen—and that was a sacrifice which this very principled, very middle-class, Victorian Englishman was just not prepared to make. Bad enough that he and his wife should renounce their nationality, but to allow his children to become foreigners was quite unthinkable! During all his time in Russia he never learned the language properly, as if fearing that to do so would be to compromise his identity as an Englishman. He refused to send his children to a Russian *gymnasium* or high school, on the grounds that he did not consider such schools sufficiently moral. And he was absolutely indignant when his eldest daughter insisted on her right to go out alone to Pekin to marry her fiancé, a

Frenchman whom she had met while working in a bank in St Petersburg—even though the engagement had already lasted seven years!

In 1905, at the time of the abortive revolution, a curious incident took place in the life of the Kerbys that was not unconnected with their Britishness. The family, then living in a third-floor flat in St Petersburg, woke one morning to find the whole house completely surrounded by police. Later they learned that the empty flat downstairs had been used as a secret headquarters by the revolutionaries, who must have hoped that the house occupied by this uncompromising Britisher would be above suspicion.

Unlike their parents and their grandparents, the third generation of Kerbys, to which Edith belonged, had been born and brought up entirely in Russia. The younger children had never even set foot on English soil. They seized upon visitors from England as avidly as Chekhov's three sisters, isolated in the provinces, seized upon a visitor from Moscow. England was their dream, their promised land, and everything English acquired in their minds a special magic. One of Edith's most vivid childhood memories is of getting ready to go to the British Embassy in St Petersburg in 1902 for a gala celebration of King Edward VII's coronation. Her boots had been polished and polished until she was convinced that they had become 'real English Patent Leather shoes'. Imagine her envy and disappointment when on arriving at the Embassy she discovered that some of the other English children had got *their* shoes 'straight from England'! Disappointment was short-lived however. The Kerby children took part in all the games and won prizes. Edith won the sack race and scrambled up on to the platform to receive her prize from the British Ambassador. Then came her second disappointment. She was presented with a very elegant and complicated folding fishing rod. She burst into tears, saying that she wanted a ball and not 'this thing'! The request was granted, and one small boy ran off with the fishing rod, scarcely able to believe his good fortune.

Whereas their father spoke Russian hardly at all, and their mother only imperfectly, all the children had acquired four languages with comparative ease by the age of eight. They spoke English at home and were given lessons by an English teacher from the University. German was spoken at school. Had he accepted the directorship, H. W. Kerby might well have followed the example of a number of

British fathers in Russia, and sent his sons, if not his daughters, back to boarding school in England. As it was, he decided that rather than expose them to what seemed to him the doubtful morals of a Russian *gymnasium*, his children should attend one of the German church schools, the Annenschule (the resident German community in St Petersburg being even larger than the English one). Both boys and girls were taught at the Annenschule, but in different parts of the building. A compulsory second language at the school was French, and the Kerbys also had French teachers coming to the house. The fourth language, Russian, was learned from their dear old maid, who was with them for thirty-five years and whom they taught to read and write.

In the uncomfortably hot summer months all those families who could afford to do so disappeared from St Petersburg—either to German spas or the south of France, to their country estates, to fashionable Russian seaside resorts like Yalta in the Crimea, or more modestly, to a rented summer *datcha* within easy reach of the city. The Kerbys also disappeared from St Petersburg but they did not go very far—only to Lakhta, a humble little fishing village on the Finnish Gulf about six miles from the capital; and the kind of life they led there could not have been further removed from the pampered existence of the well-to-do Russian summer holidaymaker. During those three months the English family came fully into its own—no longer a part of Russian life but free to express its own vigorous personality. No one minded sleeping on springless beds that consisted of flat boards covered by a thin biscuit mattress. One of the combined family tasks each summer was to repick one or two of these mattresses, wash them, dry them in the sun and sew them up again. Every morning the children, barefoot, would comb the beach in search of driftwood, as this was the family's only fuel for cooking. Then they would bake their own real English bread, which tasted quite different from baker's bread. They even made their own soap. When autumn came there were bilberries, cranberries and wild raspberries to be picked and turned into sixty to eighty pounds of jam. After that came the mushrooming season, when the mushrooms were carefully dried over the stove and stored for use during the winter in soups and stews. And finally, before they returned to urban civilization, all the family would go out into the pine woods to gather large baskets of moss. At the flat the moss would be placed in between the double windows before they were sealed up for the winter—providing a touch of colour during the long drab St Petersburg winter, and a cheerful reminder of the summer just past and of holidays still to come.

In winter too they made their own amusements. Toys were always manufactured at home. At the waterworks their father had a patch of ground flooded which the children could use for skating. In later years the boys made their own ice yacht and zipped about the Finnish Gulf at speeds of up to forty miles an hour, while the others, tied on by ropes, skimmed breathlessly and sometimes dangerously along behind.

This peculiarly British spirit of self-help and self-reliance expressed itself most strongly in Edith's eldest brother Harry (Henry). When he was sixteen, he asked permission from his father to emigrate to Canada. H. W. Kerby gave permission but warned his son that he must stand on his own feet and not expect any money from him. To this Harry replied: 'I shall come back when I have got a frock coat, a top hat and a trunk load of presents for my mother and sisters.' He sailed direct to Montreal on a cargo boat, in a black sateen shirt intended to disguise his youthfulness and to save frequent washing. His first dollar, earned carrying bricks on Montreal quayside, was carefully wrapped up and sent to his father to show that he meant business. There followed a series of long letters to his family, describing how he had acquired from the Canadian Government a tract of virgin land which would become his if he made good within three years, how he had broken in a wild horse and bought a pig (which he named after his old German Maths. master at the Annenschule) and some time later, two oxen. He did not believe in treating Indians differently from white people, so once when he came across an Indian lying ill on the prairie, he immediately slung him over his shoulder and took him back to their camp. This created a great impression among the Indians and they became good friends.

A few years later Harry persuaded his best English friend, whose father was manager of one of the Coats cotton mills near St Petersburg, to come out to join him. On the night of his friend's arrival he built up a huge log fire in the shack and they celebrated the great event by having a good supper, smoking pipes and singing the good old songs of an England they scarcely knew. Eventually they settled down to sleep but were suddenly roused by the dog tugging at their bedclothes. The cabin was all ablaze. They were just in time to scramble clear and put out their blazing clothes by lying down and rolling in the snow. The shack was burned to the ground, but Harry and his friend were given refuge and clothing by his friends, the Indians.

At last, after seven years, the family received a wire asking them to come and meet his boat. 'I remember that arrival,' recalls Edith,

as if it was yesterday. A taller, heavier-built, bronzed man, but still with a radiant boyish face, stepped forward in a tall silk hat, in a long black coat and striped trousers, and with several huge trunks. He kissed us all first; then he took off his hat and handed it to one of his sisters, then he took off his coat and handed it to another sister, and in shirt sleeves set about handling his own luggage, refusing porters. He came back loaded with presents and with money saved. I can see my father, a reserved Englishman of the old school, reduced to tears of joy and happiness. . . .

Handling one's own luggage, of course, was a thoroughly unconventional, almost a revolutionary, thing to do in Tsarist Russia, where no gentleman ever dreamed of making any effort to help himself if there was a servant to do the job for him, and many a lady might claim that she had never had to dress herself in her life.

In 1909, when she was seventeen, Edith passed her matriculation and left the Annenschule. 'Throughout my adolescence I was obsessed with a religious mania,' she recorded later. 'All my spare time was taken up with the study of Pitman's shorthand. I sent to London for a complete series of textbooks and carefully taught myself.' A religious mania about *shorthand*? No, the motive behind this remarkable labour of love was to be able to take down sermons and transcribe them into piles of notebooks. These sermons had made a great impression on Edith's youthful mind. They were given at the British & American Chapel by the Rev. Orr, with whom Edith had fallen secretly in love, even though he was twice her age. Not long after, he did marry—another member of his congregation; but the knowledge of shorthand that she had gained as part of her devotion to him was to be important in Edith's life in a way she could never have guessed.

Then in 1911 her father, H. W. Kerby, died at a comparatively early age. Fortunately she had been earning her own living ever since leaving school, either by giving English lessons or by going out as an English-speaking companion to Russian girls in aristocratic or well-to-do families. Rosy-cheeked Miss Kerby, a typically healthy outdoor English girl, who was at home in several languages and always excelled at games and sports (ever since her childhood success in the sack race at the British Embassy?) was always welcome in the great houses of St Petersburg. In winter the daughter of the family would be enticed away from the hothouse atmosphere of boudoir or salon and go out with Miss Kerby to the skating rink, or for long walks, or to concerts in the evening. In summer, instead of daily visits, Edith would accompany the families to their estates and live in, sometimes travelling hundreds of miles into the Russian interior. Here there would be boating and bathing, riding, fishing and shooting, tennis and croquet, and often dancing and moonlight picnics in the late summer evenings. Food was always very plentiful—young sucking pigs were a great delicacy—and the people always perfectly charming; yet one cannot help suspecting that she still hankered after the more Spartan summers of her childhood. But for Edith this life was only a means to an end: that end being to save enough money to enable her to spend a long holiday in England.

*   *   *

But to return to the spring of 1912 and to that first occasion on which Emma Dashwood was taken by Gertie Kirby (with an 'i') to visit members of the Kerby family in St Petersburg. They went to see the Miss Kerbys. But Edith and her sisters were not the only Miss Kerbys living in St Petersburg at that time. Far from it! There were also the unmarried sisters of the late H. W. Kerby, who shared an apartment of their own. They were the Kerby aunts, or as Gertie and Emmie came to think of them: the Aunts. And there were five of them.

The Aunts were middle-aged and had lived in St Petersburg for most of their adult lives. Whereas H. W. Kerby and his wife, conscious of a duty to their children, had tried to lead the life of a self-sufficient English family, bringing up their children in the English way and finding their amusements either as a family or among English friends, the Aunts had been brought into closer contact with Russian life through their occupations. Unlike their brother and his wife, they all spoke English and Russian with equal facility. The eldest sister, Aunt Annie, had been for many years a teacher of English, visiting her pupils daily during the winter and staying with them on their estates during the summer. Aunt Susan was clever with her hands and something of an artist, who received commissions from Russian clients; while Jane, more domesticated than the others, was the Aunt who stayed at home and looked after everything, helped by the maid-of-all-work, Polya, who spoke only Russian. Then there was Aunt Kate, always immaculately dressed in greys and blacks, as befitted her position as companion to the young Princess Beloselsky-Belozersky; and lastly there was the youngest sister Amy, who gave English lessons at home in what was called 'the study' and contained a bureau, but was actually a part of Aunt Annie's bedroom, carefully screened off.

The way of life adopted by the Aunts seems to be a mixture of the Russian and the English. There was not very much space in the flat—two bedrooms had to be shared between four of the aunts—and there must have been a great deal of coming and going, but they seem to have developed the Russian capacity for living harmoniously at close quarters without getting on one another's nerves or demanding privacy. Yet there was also a very English sense of discipline about the flat: everything was always neat and tidy, and the Aunts had a weekly rota for household duties. In appearance too the flat was very English, its atmosphere reminding Emmie of a cosy English cottage. Many of the items of furniture had been taken out to Russia from England by the Aunts' parents. In the evening there was always a welcoming glow from the old-fashioned spirit lamp that stood in the middle of the cloth-covered oval table in the sitting-room, and reminded Emmie of the lamps she used to see in her childhood.

Though far from rich, the Aunts were enormously hospitable to their English friends and acquaintances. Gertie and Emmie were certainly not the first young English governesses to have benefited from the open-hearted 'Russian' hospitality of these English Aunts, and who had been made to feel that here at least were people who would always make them welcome, and to whom they could turn in case of need. The Aunts had taken Gertie under their wing from the start, and on hearing that she was not happy in her first job, made sure that she changed it for a better one.

So it was that in the spring of 1912, Gertie had no hesitation about taking Emmie to spend an evening with the Aunts at their flat on Krónverksky Prospect. Emmie thoroughly enjoyed herself, and the Aunts invited her to spend a few days with them later in the year. When on this second visit Aunt Annie heard from Emmie of the Kovalskys' impending departure for Vladivostok, she immediately decided to take the situation in hand and suggested that Emmie come and stay with them to look for a post as governess with a good Russian family. Aunt Annie, never one to let obstacles stand in her way, herself wrote off to Norwich, pointing out that Emmie had not yet had the experience of living in a thoroughly Russian family, and that it was a pity for her not to do so; and adding that she would make herself personally responsible for Emmie's welfare during the rest of her stay in Russia.

This letter must have done the trick, and in the late autumn of 1912 Emma Dashwood arrived with her luggage at the Aunts' flat. She was to share a bedroom with Aunt Annie, who dubbed her 'my little partner'.

On Sunday they all attended morning service at the British & American Chapel. It was here that Emmie first met Edith, her sisters and their mother, who was still in mourning for her husband. For many years previously a Kerby family crocodile might have been seen every Sunday morning, wending its way decorously along the streets and embankments of St Petersburg. This British & American Congregational Chapel is not to be confused with the English (Anglican) Church of St Mary & All Saints. The English Church seems always to have had a somewhat upper-class character: in the 1840's Dr Edward Law had been well acquainted with Lord and Lady Stuart de Rothesay and had accompanied them from St Petersburg to Southampton. It catered for members of the British Embassy and for the well-to-do British mill-owners and their families, who lived in considerable style in the suburbs outside St Petersburg, though there was also an English Governesses' Club Room attached to the Church. The Kerbys had given up worshipping there ever since the Chaplain had refused to turn out in very severe weather to baptise one of the Kerby children, whereas the minister from the British & American Chapel had been quite willing to come to the house. Aunt Annie, however, still attended the English Church from time to time to take communion.

The British & American Chapel was more solidly middle-class.

Apart from the minister—the Rev. Orr by this time having been replaced by the Rev. Clare—it had a permanent organist and a regular choir of elderly and musically ungifted English ladies. But the Chapel was not just a place of worship. It was more like a social club, a focal point in the life of the British community; it was, in Edith Kerby's words, 'my second home'. English governesses and tutors, cut off during the week in their Russian households, flocked to it in great numbers. At the Chapel arrangements were made, invitations issued, and picnics and outings organised; many a romance must have been started there; and at the Chapel, too, different branches of a family, like the Kerbys, could be sure of meeting one another at least once a week. The Aunts made all their own hats and dresses, and young Edith, who preferred reading serious books and doing things to making herself look fashionable, was known to giggle at the sight of the five of them standing together in their pew, each striving to wear an even more flamboyant hat than her neighbour.

In the vestibule they handed over their outdoor garments, and Aunt Annie, who was very short, raised herself on tiptoe to look in the mirror and check her appearance before they entered the spacious chapel, plainly decorated and furnished in the typical Congregational style. A Russian was employed to pump the organ but was liable to doze off, and then the sound of the organ would grow fainter and fainter until someone roused him to renewed efforts. After the service the Kerbys all congregated in the vestibule. There was much hugging and kissing between the Aunts and their sister-in-law and nieces, followed by an exchange of news. Edith's friend, a governess from Ireland called Miss Ash, had heard of an opening for an English governess which sounded just right for Emma Dashwood. It was in Moscow, not St Petersburg, but Aunt Annie had English friends in Moscow who would be able to keep an eye on her. Two Russian ladies were actually then in St Petersburg looking for some-one, so there was no time to be lost. Arrangements were made for Emmie to go with Aunt Annie for an interview the following evening, after Annie had finished teaching for the day.

Emmie borrowed a smart winter coat from Aunt Amy, as Edith Kovalsky's much-worn old *shooba* was certainly not good enough for the occasion. She and Aunt Annie were shown up to a comfort-able hotel room where two young Russian ladies had just finished dressing for the theatre. Emmie could not help staring with fascination at their beautiful long evening dresses and elaborate coiffures, piled high with artificial curls. Aunt Annie, bright and business-like as usual, talked freely in Russian and English, and it was clear that the Russian ladies, who were obviously sisters, had been much impressed by her. They were surprised to find that Miss Dashwood looked so *very* young—'I don't know what my husband's going to think about this,' remarked one of the ladies with a smile—but the boy she would be looking after was only six and might well take more readily to someone who could easily pass for his elder sister. Miss Dashwood was engaged. The Russian ladies wanted her to leave with them for Moscow the very next day, but Aunt Annie insisted in her usual forthright manner that Emmie be allowed a week's sightseeing in St Petersburg first.

The pastrycook's was still open as they neared Kronverksky Prospect. Well, why not? They bought a good selection of cakes and went home to celebrate.

5
Half-a-Century of Governesses

It was indeed a triumph worth celebrating—more so than Emma Dashwood realised at the time. For the boy that she had been engaged to teach came from a very distinguished family: generals were two-a-penny on his mother's side, while his father was a Marshal of Nobility, the son of a general, and owner of a large and prosperous estate.

But first to return to the wider story of the English governess in Russia during the previous half-century. The Crimean War of 1854–56 and the humiliating peace treaty that the Russians were forced to accept by the Allies, soured Anglo-Russian relations for several years to come. One of those who took part in and vividly described the Crimean campaign was Tolstoy, then in his late twenties. By 1866, after the birth of his second son, Ilya, Tolstoy had overcome his anti-English feelings sufficiently to engage as nursery governess for his three small children a young English girl, Hannah Tracey. He himself had had French and German tutors in the 1830's and 40's. Hannah, who according to Tolstoy's eldest son, Sergei, in *Tolstoy Remembered*, was the daughter of a gardener at Windsor Castle, exemplifies that attitude of 'fresh air and common sense', which was the hallmark of the British nanny and governess abroad. Her nationality, writes Cynthia Asquith in *Married to Tolstoy*, was at first inconvenient to Sonya (Tolstoy's wife),

who had to follow her about, dictionary in hand. But she soon became very fond of this pretty young girl, who, bright and determined, promptly insisted on introducing her own ideas on cleanliness and hygiene. To the horror of the old Russian nurse, she washed the children—the house boasted one bath-tub—in completely cold water, and took them out in all weathers.

The children loved her, and when homesick Hannah began tearfully to warble 'Home Sweet Home', little Tanya would pick up the tune and sing and weep with her. Hannah was with the family for six years, but then in the autumn of 1872 they noticed that she had begun to cough and lose weight. Consumption was diagnosed, and a warmer climate recommended. The Tolstoys' relatives, the Kuzminskys, had recently moved south to the Caucasus, and here Hannah joined them as governess to their children. But the story appears to have had a happy ending, for in the spring of 1874 the Tolstoys heard that Hannah had married the Georgian Prince Matchudatze and would be staying on in the Caucasus permanently: neither the first nor the last English governess to marry well in Russia. Other English governesses succeeded her in the Tolstoy family, teaching all the children from the age of three to nine; but none of them ever came to occupy the same place in the family's affections as Hannah.

About this time the English governess in Russia not only appears more frequently in Russian literature, but also makes her début—as a concept at least—in English fiction. 'To be a governess in Russia,' wrote Mrs Gaskell in *Wives and Daughters*, the novel which she had all but completed at the time of her sudden death in 1866, 'was the equivalent of taking the veil or a lady-like form of suicide.' Her heroine, Cynthia Kirkpatrick, confides:

> I'm getting very much into despair about everything, Molly. I shall try my luck in Russia. I've heard of a situation as English governess at Moscow, in a family owning whole provinces of land, and serfs by the hundred. I put off writing my letter till I came home; I shall be as much out of the way there as if I was married.

Mrs Gaskell's, or Cynthia's, history is at fault here, since serf-owning had been abolished in 1861. Is Cynthia's mind really made up? 'It is quite made up,' she replies. 'I am going to teach little Russian girls; and am never going to marry nobody'—a threat which, needless to say, she has not the least intention of carrying out.

The 1860's was in fact the period of the great foreign expansion of the English governess. A whole army of Englishwomen—or, as Bea Howe colourfully puts it in *A Galaxy of Governesses*, 'a gigantic fifth column operated by a devoted body of genteel ladies and apple-cheeked nannies, which was to exercise enormous power and disseminate the traditional English way of life through European society'—spread across the globe. Paris had long been a happy hunting-ground for the English governess, while after 1870 Vienna became another favourite centre. But even Russia seems tame when compared to some of the exotic places that were reached by these intrepid Victorian ladies. In 1866 Emmeline Lott published *The English Governess in Egypt and Turkey*, based on her experiences as governess to the infant son of the Viceroy of Egypt. In 1870 there came an even greater sensation: the publication by Mrs Anna Leonowens of *The English Governess at the Siamese Court*, followed three years later by *Siamese Harem Life*. When Anna, the young widow of an officer in the Indian Army, accepted an invitation in 1862 from King Mongkut of Siam to become governess to the numerous royal offspring, she little guessed that she had taken the first step on the path to becoming the most glamorous English governess of all time.

What made these genteel Englishwomen uproot themselves and travel to such remote corners of the world? Was it a thirst for adventure? A little, perhaps. But the main driving force seems to have been obvious enough: economic necessity, the search for a respectable living. From at least the 1830's the same cry is repeatedly heard in England: too many governesses, too few jobs! 'By 1845,' writes Bea Howe, 'a governess had never been so easy to distinguish with her pale, depressed look. . . . During the 1840's, over one hundred governesses advertised daily in *The Times* for a situation. . . By 1850, 21,000 refined gentlewomen were registered as belonging to the most despised profession in Victorian England.' In 1859 an article in the *Saturday Review* discussed a typical advertisement in *The Times* for a governess, to which there had been no less than one hundred and forty replies.

Where did they all come from, these refined gentlewomen, and why was their profession so grossly overcrowded? It was overcrowded because it was the *only* respectable occupation open to a gentlewoman in Victorian England who needed to earn her own living, and who did not want to lose caste. (Ladies did not work; women did.) They came from all parts of polite society, linked only by their poverty and their good breeding. Daughters of poor clergymen—like the three Brontë sisters—with those unfortunately large Victorian families, were early prominent among the ranks of the governesses, rubbing shoulders with the daughters of army officers who had lived beyond their means, or with young ladies from noble families fallen on hard times. Any sudden family impoverishment was likely to produce new recruits to the ranks. The head of the family dies prematurely; there are no pension schemes or Welfare State to catch those who are left behind; widow and daughters must immediately start earning their own living. Or the breadwinner becomes incapacitated; or else, very commonly in Victorian England, his business fails and he is declared bankrupt. And the ranks grew and grew, for only an occasional governess succeeded in escaping; once a girl had become a governess, her marriage prospects immediately plummeted.

Their gentility was needed by the newly affluent in Victorian society, but because they were so numerous, they had no bargaining power. They bartered their good breeding for a roof over their heads and a derisory salary.

The plight of the governesses did not however go entirely unnoticed. The publication in 1847 of *Jane Eyre*, in which Charlotte Brontë had drawn on her own earlier governess experiences, created an image of the governess as a gentle soul, meek, downtrodden and long-suffering, and very much deserving of sympathy. The Governesses' Benevolent Institution had already started a few years before. Its object was 'to raise the character of Governesses as a class, and thus improve the tone of Female Education; to assist Governesses in making provision for their old age; and to assist in distress and age those Governesses whose exertions for their parents or families have prevented such a provision'. From the start the Institution attracted influential patrons, and at its first annual dinner, held in April 1844, the guest speaker was Charles Dickens, who spoke eloquently on behalf of the governess, 'her eyes red with poring over advertisements in search of a new situation', and whose salary in a household was lower than the wages paid to the cook, or the butler, or the lady's maid, and 'even lower than those paid to liveried footmen'. His speech was received with 'continued cheering'.

One root cause of the trouble was that governesses were ignorant and ill-equipped for their work. They needed the opportunity to acquire a proper teaching qualification. Accordingly, the Institution's Founder and Honorary Secretary, the Rev. Laing, persuaded some of the professors at King's College in the new University of London to give lectures to them, and in 1847 a building was bought for the purpose in Harley Street. Thus Queen's College came into being, with no less a patron than Victoria herself. The College was an immediate success. Its early students included three girls who later achieved great renown as headmistresses: Dorothea Beale of the Cheltenham Ladies' College, Elizabeth Day of the Manchester High School, and Frances Mary Buss, who became headmistress of the North London Collegiate School at the age of twenty-three; while other former students broke new ground by entering professions that had previously been closed to women.

In 1853 Queen's College became independent of the G.B.I., yet ironically the very success of the College meant that the days of the old-fashioned governess were numbered. Thanks to the pioneering work of women like Miss Buss and Miss Beale, the last three decades of the nineteenth century saw, in Alicia Percival's words, the 'foundation and growth of a system which aimed at putting a good secondary education within the reach of any girl whose father was willing and able to pay about £16 a year for it'. To a governess in 1850, however, the possibility of widespread public education for girls would still have seemed very remote. Far more worrying to her was the thought that she might now be expected to possess *qualifications*. It was all very well for these bright young girls to attend lectures and collect their diplomas, but what of the older governess already in employment? She was used to thinking that her job had been adequately done if her pupil learned to write a fair hand and not to drop her aitches, possessed a modicum of general knowledge and a few words of French, and could sketch or sing or perform tolerably on the piano. Now, if she hoped to compete with the younger generation, she was expected to offer systematic instruction in a whole range of academic subjects. There would still be employers to echo the sentiments of the character in *Wives and Daughters*, who remarks of a former governess: 'She's not very wise, certainly, but she's so useful and agreeable, I should have thought anyone who wasn't particular about education would have been charmed to keep her as a governess'; but not every employer was going to be so undemanding.

By 1864, to judge from the speech made by John Ruskin at the Manchester Town Hall, there had been little improvement in the overall plight of the governess. Ruskin was no less eloquent on her behalf than Dickens had been twenty years previously, and was even more scathing about the kind of treatment governesses received from their employers:

But what teachers do you give your girls, and what reverence do you choose to show the teachers you have chosen? Is a girl likely to think her own account or her own intellect of much importance, when you trust the entire formation of her character, moral and intellectual, to a person whom you let your servants treat with less respect than they do your housekeeper (as if the soul of your child were a less charge than jams, jellies and groceries) and on whom you yourself think you confer an honour by letting her sometimes sit in the drawing-room in the evening?

Given the overcrowded state of her profession, its poor financial rewards, the low regard in which she was held by her employers and by Victorian society generally, and the new competitive situation brought about by the advances in female education, it is not surprising that the eyes of the English governess turned further afield.

During the half-century from the 1860's to the Bolshevik Revolution, she was to become a familiar figure in upper-class Russian society. In a French guide to St Petersburg, compiled by J. Bastin and published in 1867, we read that the congregation of the English Church consists principally of business men, but also contains 'a good number of tutors and governesses, whose lives are devoted to teaching in the best families of Russia, where German, French and English are generally spoken, the last-named becoming more and more fashionable'. Whereas German was thought of as the language of commerce, French had always been the traditional language of the Russian aristocracy—the language of salon and ball-room—and remained so. The girl who was unable to answer a question put to her in French by her partner at a ball would have felt like dropping through the floor with shame. But the speaking of French had filtered down through Russian society, with the spread of education there too, to such an extent that it was no longer a distinguishing mark of an aristocrat. On the contrary, as spoken by Natasha in Chekhov's play, *Three Sisters* (1901), it has become a vulgar bourgeois affectation. English, being less widely spoken, was in a good position to take over as the fashionable, exclusive language.

Of course, going to Russia can never have been an easy step for an English governess to take. There must have been many who continued to feel that it was 'the equivalent of taking the veil or a ladylike form of suicide', and that life among the Russian bears, both real and figurative, was quite unthinkable. Yet the very steady flow of volunteers suggests that there were also considerable attractions about being an English governess in Russia.

To begin with, there was the question of qualifications. In England good qualifications were becoming more and more important to a governess. In Russia no qualification at all was needed, beyond the ability to speak her native tongue correctly. Other governesses and tutors would instruct her pupil in all those subjects that her counterpart in England was struggling to cope with single-handed, and this meant that she had considerably more time to herself.

Then it was almost always the case that she found herself working in a very well-to-do, often a noble, family. In Russia the nobility was a much larger class than in England, because a title conferred on one person automatically passed to all his descendants; and to be able to say that she had 'taught in a noble family' was bound to be a feather in her cap later on, if she decided to return to England. With these families she enjoyed a much higher standard of living than she was likely to have experienced before. Russian parents did not follow the English practice of keeping their children shut off at the top of the house away from everyone else. As soon as the children were old enough to sit at table, they had most of their meals with their parents, and their governess always accompanied them. Even on festive occasions, or when visitors were present, governess and children were never excluded from the sumptuous meals.

On top of all these advantages the English governess in Russia was also more handsomely rewarded than her counterpart at home, since the fierce competition for jobs was bound to keep salaries down in England. In St Petersburg, Moscow and other big cities she seems often to have been at liberty to augment her salary by giving private English lessons in her free time—something that could never have happened in England because of the long working hours. Gifts from the family, and even legacies, might be on a lavish scale; she was able to save money towards a comfortable retirement in England or the South of France; and though it was not part of her contract, and depended on the whim and generosity of her employer, there was a good chance that if she had given faithful service to one family, she would at the end of her working life either be invited to stay on with the family gratis, or else be granted a handsome pension. How commonly were pensions granted in England? Not very often, to judge from the fact that the provision of pension schemes was one of the first priorities of the G.B.I. And indeed it is a strange comment on Victorian England that a governess there was liable to find herself homeless and destitute at the end of her working life (for only a lucky few received help from the G.B.I.), whereas an English governess in Russia had much better prospects for her old age.

But these are all material considerations—and there was more to it than that. The English governess, so despised in Victorian England, found herself in quite a different position when she went to Russia. There could be no question of regarding her as 'a person whom you let your servants treat with less respect than they do your housekeeper'; 'silver forks for the children, steel ones for the governess' never applied in Russia. At its best her position was that of an equal and member of the family, something that had not happened in England since the eighteenth century; and we shall hear of English governesses attending important social functions on terms of complete equality with the other guests. Even at its worst her position was still clearly differentiated from the upper servants. Her nationality may have helped. Although England was regarded by Russians with suspicion and often hostility during the nineteenth century, her personal representatives were always treated with respect and even deference. Russians never entirely forgot that the English governess was a representative of one of the older European cultures and of a nation whose star was shining very brightly in the half-century up to 1917.

Such then were some of the attractions of being an English governess in Russia. But clearly the relations between Russian employer and English governess can only have worked well—and by and large they do seem to have worked remarkably well—if the governess had something valuable to offer in return for the advantages she enjoyed. Of course, there must have been bad governesses as well as good ones, just as there were good and bad employers; but we may hazard a generalisation and say that the English governess in Russia was well treated because she did provide an excellent service, thereby acquiring a high professional reputation and coming to be keenly sought after.

What were the qualities that she brought to her job? Bea Howe writes that 'the honesty, deep piety, and, above all, unswerving devotion to duty of our genteel ladies dedicated to their profession wherever it took them, soon became a byword throughout the civilised world'. Perhaps reliability is the word that sums it up most neatly: no matter in what country or in what circumstances she found herself, the English governess could be relied upon to do her best by the children entrusted to her care.

Especially remarkable about the English governess in Russia is her degree of physical and mental toughness. She needed to be physically tough to cope with the rigours of the Russian climate (is that why our governesses are so long-lived: because they were hardened by their youthful experiences in Russia?), and mentally tough to cope with children who were not renowned for their quiet dispositions or high standards of behaviour. At the first rebuff she did not dissolve into tears, throw a fit of hysterics, or hand in her notice. On the contrary, she was valued for the quiet yet determined way in which she introduced some order and system into the other-wise haphazard Russian approach to bringing up children. Because she was clear about her own values, she behaved consistently towards the children, and did not hesitate to follow her own lights. If, like Hannah Tracey, she found that the old Russian nanny from whom she was taking over still wanted the child to be pampered as before, she promptly introduced new methods of her own. If the children themselves were spoilt or badly behaved, she could be relied upon to deal with them firmly and fairly, without recourse to corporal punishment. It is easy to see how the calm presence of an English governess might become a secure point of reference in the life of a Russian child, especially one whose parents were erratic in the attention and affection they gave him—perhaps neglecting him for long periods, and then showering him with effusive love and expensive presents.

Our English governess may have been valued too because she was a reliable and good-humoured person to have about the house generally, and would not lose her head in a crisis. She did not become involved in family or household intrigues, and in contrast to the French and Swiss governesses, was unlikely to cause the kind of marital discord which is described at the start of *Anna Karenina*, after Dolly has discovered that her husband, Oblonsky, has been having an affair with the former French governess, Mlle Rolland.

The latter, one notices with a touch of national self-righteousness, has now been replaced by an English governess.

So far we have spoken of the relations between governess and employer as a business arrangement: professional services were provided, and received their just reward. No doubt many governesses preferred that it should remain that way, moving from family to family and leaving Russia after a certain length of time. But with others—and here we come to perhaps the most fascinating aspect of the English governess in Russia—with others it was not like that. They 'stuck' in Russia, coming to rest with a particular family, sometimes their one and only family. In letters I have received from Russian émigrés, and in memoirs, I have almost come to expect to read of some 'dear old English governess who was with us for many years and whom we all loved very much'. These were governesses of the pre-Revolutionary generation, who fled from Russia in 1917 with their Russian families. A few of them survive in person; memories of them are comparatively fresh. But what of their predecessors? We have no record of those earlier English governesses who chose to stay on with their Russian families, who died and were buried there, and whose deaths may not even have been notified to their families, if they had any, or to the British authorities. J. G. Kohl had referred in the 1830's to those 'after-growths of superannuated English nurses, Frenchwomen, and Germans, who have adhered to the family till they are considered regular parts of it, and enjoy all the privileges of adoption accordingly'. There seems little doubt that in the second half of the nineteenth century many an English governess enjoyed these same privileges. Her Russian family had become *her* family, and she stayed on automatically.

This phenomenon of the English governess rooting herself in her adopted country was not however peculiar to the English governess in Russia. Bea Howe has also commented on the interesting way in which 'the English Miss, a creature of such routine and habit, church-loving and moral, rooted herself in the establishment where she was employed. . . . One finds the German Fräulein and the French Mam'selle returning to die in their native lands, but how rarely our lean Miss Bensons and Miss Cholmondeleys.'

In the case of Russia, is part of the explanation that only those who had few ties of family and friendship in their native land would have thought of going to such an out-of-the-way country in the first place? The young girl who had gone out as governess to small children might well, if she liked the job and was liked in return, be asked to stay on: perhaps as a companion to the mother, or if her pupil was a girl, as companion and chaperone until such time as her former pupil married. Then the whole cycle might be repeated with the next generation. It is not hard to see how the Englishwoman, having relinquished the possibility of a family of her own, might concentrate all her loyalty and affection on the family in which she worked, and that this loyalty and affection would be returned. By the time her working life was over it was unthinkable that the family could part with her. Apart from limited contacts with others like herself, she would have had little life *outside* her Russian family. Even if the ties of loyalty and affection were not strong, there is force of habit to be reckoned with. However attractive the dream of that English country cottage, was it really so easy to imagine herself returning to a country she might not have seen, and certainly not lived in, for thirty or forty years? Could she even be sure that she would still be able to speak the language without a foreign accent?

And perhaps at the root of the mutual devotion between Russian family and English governess there is another element, an element of psychological fusion that is not so easy to write about. Our lean Miss Benson, I suspect, with her stiff English ways, thawed and melted in the company of her warm-hearted Russian family, just as the members of that family were more than a little affected by that cool common sense of hers, so lacking in their own culture.

6

Miss Emmie in Moscow

A week after the famous interview with the two young Russian ladies, Emma Dashwood was put on the night train from St Petersburg by Annie and Amy Kerby, and arrived in Moscow early next morning. As she alighted, she noticed a smartly dressed footman anxiously scanning the passengers, so she remembered her instructions and identified herself by flourishing a newspaper. There was scarcely time to collect her thoughts before the sledge stopped in front of an impressive house in the centre of the city. Here a hall porter helped her in to the lift and she stepped out on the first floor opposite the flat that was to be her new winter home. Breakfast had already been prepared in her room, and she was given plenty of time to enjoy it and to relax after her long journey before receiving a hearty welcome from her new pupil and his parents.

Emmie came to know her employers by the strange combination of Mr and Mme Rahl. Mr Rahl, or Boris Vasilyevitch, had no objection to being called Mr Rahl, but his wife, Vera Vladimirovna, absolutely refused to be referred to as Mrs Rahl. At some stage in their history Mr Rahl's ancestors must have been of German origin, though there was nothing Germanic about the appearance of his father, the late General Vasily Rahl, whose heavily bearded features became familiar to Emmie from the photographic portrait of him at the Rahls' country estate. Unlike his father, Mr Rahl had a moustache but no beard. He was in his mid-thirties, dark and dapper, and some ten years older than his wife, whom Emmie at once recognised as one of the ladies at the interview. Later Emmie learned that Mme Rahl had been married while still in her teens, that she and her husband had barely known one another before their marriage and were engaged only for a few weeks, and that everything had been arranged for them by their families. The marriage seemed nonetheless to be a very happy one.

Mme Rahl's maiden name was Tolmachóff. 'The Tolmachoffs,' she joked to Emmie, 'must have had English blood in their veins', for she was beautiful in an English kind of way: petite, with a very fair complexion, lovely skin and pretty auburn hair. Her two sisters were both much taller and became known to Emmie as Auntie Shoora, short for Alexandra—she had been the other lady at the interview—and Auntie Milochka (Lyudmilla). Because of their fine ruby-coloured lips none of the sisters ever needed to use lipstick. Their father had been a General, and he and his three brothers had all been cadets in the élite *Corps de Pages*, close to the Emperor. Only one of the four, an uncle of Mme Rahl's, was still alive.

Of the Rahls' two children, Vladimir Borisovitch (son of Boris), otherwise known as Volodya, was Emmie's pupil. He was six, dark like his father, but with the full red Tolmachoff lips, 'as if he'd been biting them all the time'. His younger sister, Irina Borisovna (daughter of Boris), was only three and still in the nursery with her Russian Nanny. To her pupil and his family Emmie was to be known henceforth as 'Miss Emmie'. The servants addressed her as *baryshnya* ('Miss'), an exception being made in the case of old Nanny, who was so used to the French governesses of the past that she continued to call her 'Mamsel', or more accurately, 'Mazélle'.

What a difference there was between life with the Rahls in Moscow and the modest routine Emmie had become used to with Edith Kovalsky in the country! She was soon aware of having moved on to a much higher level of Russian society. Had her stay with the Kovalskys come after the Rahls, it would certainly have seemed an anti-climax; yet had she gone straight to the Rahls without any previous experience, she would have been all at sea and unable to cope. As it was, the training she had received from Edith gave her enough confidence to adjust to this grander way of life. Not only did she not panic at being asked to officiate at the samovar, she was only too happy to volunteer for the task: 'you see, I had practised it beautifully by then'.

The Rahls had rented the furnished flat for the winter. It was in Tverskaya Square—Tverskaya Street, or the Tverskaya, being Moscow's most famous thoroughfare—close to the Skobelev Monument and the official residence of the Governor of Moscow. So numerous were its rooms that the staff quarters and nursery remained *terra incognita* to Emmie throughout her time there. She had her own bedroom next door to the Rahls, for Volodya still slept in the nursery with his sister. At first the central heating was a problem. She had been used at the Kovalskys to sharing a large airy bedroom with Tolya, heated by an old-fashioned stove. Now the atmosphere in her room was so stifling that she felt unable to breathe, and longed for some fresh air. One night she decided to leave open the *fortochka*, the small hinged window-pane in the top corner of her double window. When this became known in the household, there was general consternation, and Nanny decided that the strange young English Mazélle must want the heating in her room turned off altogether. Nothing Emmie said could make them understand that it was only a little 'English fresh air' she needed.

As for the meals, they made her feel that she was living in some rather grand hotel. The staff included a chef and kitchen-maid, who, like all the other servants, had been brought to Moscow by the Rahls from their estate. Every morning the chef would appear in his starched white cap and receive instructions for the day from Mme Rahl. He specialised in preparing French dishes. Instead of the maid who served at the Kovalskys, a butler and under-butler, both wearing white gloves, waited at table. Emmie's chair was always pushed in for her by the under-butler, Vasya—a dwarf with a broad grin who used to jump up on to a chair or table whenever he had to take off or put on the visitors' coats.

The first Sunday that she spent in Moscow still stands out vividly in Emma Dashwood's memory. Aunt Annie Kerby's English friend in Moscow proved to be a Mrs Fahrig, whose husband was not English though he spoke the language perfectly. The prestige of the English governess in the Rahl household was considerably enhanced when Mrs Fahrig gave Vasya a one-rouble tip. It was arranged that on Sunday morning Mrs Fahrig's daughter would be waiting for Emmie at the entrance to the English Church, within easy walking distance of Tverskaya Square. This young lady scorned such an unromantic means of identification as a newspaper: she had a red rose attached to her muff. After the simplicity of the British & American Chapel in St Petersburg, St Andrew's Church in Moscow, over which the Rev. Frank North presided, reminded Emmie more of a large English parish church, with its choir-stalls high up at the back. It seemed more formal than the Chapel, but equally important as a meeting place for friends.

There was a shock in store for Emmie that morning. Coming away from the church, she suddenly realised that she had left her jacket behind on the pew. It was the navy and white striped one given her by Ariadne Kovalsky. They hurried back to the church, but the main doors had already been locked. Fortunately a small door at the back was open, and they found themselves inside a very hot boiler-room; and there, much to Emmie's surprise and delight, was the missing jacket, neatly folded over one of the hot pipes.

Emmie was to spend all her following Sundays in Moscow with the Fahrigs at their comfortable house on Povarsky Street. They gave her lunch (Russian cabbage pie followed by an English roast) and tea, and in the evenings hired a sledge and carefully made a note of its number before seeing her off home.

On that first Sunday, however, she returned home for lunch with the Rahls. Volodya's English lessons had scarcely begun, so only Russian was spoken at table. Emmie knew the word *izvozchik*, meaning a horse-drawn sledge, and she gathered from the conversation that she was being invited by Mr Rahl to accompany them to their local church, because they kept on talking about going to the *tsirk*. The afternoon was bright and sunny, the snow crisp and clean, and Emmie settled back to enjoy the drive. But it was all rather puzzling. . . . They passed one church after another, each with its brightly coloured domes gleaming in the sunshine, and she could not understand why they needed to attend a church so far from home. Eventually they stopped—in front of a strange-looking build-ing in a back street. The weirdest noises were coming from inside. Emmie had begun to feel quite nervous, but Volodya was obviously beside himself with excitement. The four of them were taken up a wide staircase and shown into a small dark room. . . .

And the first thing Emmie saw, when she became used to the light and looked down, was—elephants. 'Oh, a circus!' she could not help exclaiming with astonishment. The others looked at her oddly: what had she been expecting then? So the story came out—of how she had confused *tsirk* with *tserkoff*, meaning 'church'; and, of course, 'we all got *tremendous* fun out of it!' The thought suddenly crossed her mind that this was the first time in her life that she had ever been to a place of amusement on the Sabbath, but it was too late to do anything about *that*. Afterwards she learned with relief that the Russian Sabbath included Saturday evening and Sunday morning, but not Sunday afternoon.

Emmie was receiving a much larger salary from the Rahls than she had from the Kovalskys, but right at the start there was a major expense, the biggest single expense she ever had in Russia, which used up all her previous savings. Edith's *shooba* might have been passable in the countryside, but here in Moscow—it would have to go. Mme Rahl's maid, Zina, accompanied Emmie to what seemed like a huge warehouse packed with fur coats of every description. The experienced Zina soon picked one out in black plush with a large fur collar, padded throughout and lined with lovely heavy silk. Emmie felt sure it would be too expensive, but it was just within her range. She never regretted the purchase. Carefully put away each spring, the coat was to be a good friend throughout her time in Russia.

In describing Miss Emmie's first winter in Moscow, it is hard to tell where play ends and work begins. One is tempted to conclude that it was all play. Nothing was laid down about her time off, but if she wanted to spend Sunday with the Fahrigs, it was enough to tell the Rahls that she was going out, and no objections were ever raised. Her duties too were very generally prescribed: to talk English with Volodya and to keep him usefully occupied for most of the day. This was not a difficult assignment. Volodya was an amenable child and quick to learn. Soon he delighted in using the new language and chattering away with his English-speaking relatives. Since Emmie had always been fond of walking, they usually went out twice a day—that English 'fresh air and exercise' again!—exploring the streets and boulevards of Moscow. At first Nanny accompanied them on these walks but was only too happy to desist when it became clear that Mazelle was quite capable of looking after Volodya and finding the way home. They took frequent drives as well, and in this way Emmie became familiar not only with all the sights of Moscow, but also with the habits of the Moscow cabbies, who invariably asked you for a much higher fare than they expected to get. These same cabbies always raised their turbans devoutly whenever they passed under the Kremlin Archway, for there was a church and shrine at the entrance.

Not long after Miss Emmie's arrival a German doctor was called

in to examine Volodya's larynx. Emmie remembers the occasion
well, as she had to receive him.

'How do you do? I speak English,' he announced.

'*Do* you?' she replied, much relieved.

'Yes. How do you do? I love you. Beefsteak.'

There was a long pause.

'Is that *all*?'

'*Da, vsyo*' ('Yes, that's all'), the doctor replied cheerfully in
Russian.

He recommended that Volodya's larynx should be painted regu-
larly with a mixture of iodine and glycerine. Both Mme Rahl and
Nanny jibbed at undertaking this delicate task and it was left to
Miss Emmie to come to the rescue.

'Come along, Volodya,' she said brightly, taking him off to one of
the many unused rooms in the apartment. 'Pretend I'm an English
doctor. *Aaaah!*'

Emmie found both Mr and Mme Rahl considerate, self-effacing
people, who seemed to her more interested in a quiet family routine
than in the life of Moscow high society. They seem to have been in
complete contrast to the stereotyped picture that we have of Russian
aristocrats: throwing riotous parties, drinking heavily, alternating
between sudden fits of elation and depression, and living in one
another's pockets. They were quiet, abstemious, even-tempered ('I
never once saw either of them at all cross') and had very few visitors
to the house. Every night just before bedtime Emmie would join
them in the dining-room, where they enjoyed a pleasant chat
together over the samovar before wishing one another 'a peaceful
night' (*spokoinoi nochi*).

But they were very anxious that *she* should have a good time in
Moscow. She was given free use of a box at the Bolshoi Cinema, to
which she could take the Fahrigs and any other English friends.
The cinema was on the Tverskaya and formed part of Tolmachoff
House, a large building which belonged to the Tolmachoff family
and also contained shops and apartments. Here they saw a newsreel
film about the *Titanic* disaster of 1912. And it was a great thrill
when the Rahls took her for the first time to the ballet. Emmie had
never been to the ballet before in her life. It was fortunate that she
and Mme Rahl were the same size, as the latter was able to pass on
to her a long blue dress suitable for the occasion. Mme Rahl's

French hairdresser came to the flat and after he had finished Madame's hair he went on to do Emmie's.

'How much would you give for those?' Mr Rahl asked the hairdresser, pointing to Miss Emmie's long heavy plaits. This was at the time when artificial curls were all the rage.

'Three hundred roubles,' he replied: about £30.

'Well, he's not having them,' said Emmie promptly.

So heavy were the plaits that it was impossible for her to coil them on top of her head. Edith Kovalsky had suggested having her hair right down, but she wouldn't have dared: it would have been thought too childish. The Frenchman showed her a special way of twisting in the plaits at the back of her head and keeping them in place with lots of strong hairpins; and this was the style Emmie used all through her time in Russia.

The three of them had the best seats in the stalls, and Emmie was thrilled by every moment of Tchaikovsky's *Sleeping Beauty*. It is the kind of treatment one might imagine being given to an inexperienced young niece from the country spending a winter in Moscow, rather than to a foreign governess. Volodya, of course, was too young for these evening outings, which gave Emmie splendid material for English conversation the next morning.

During the winter a letter arrived from Edith Kovalsky in Vladivostok. She was still anxious for Emmie to join them. The journey was long, she wrote, but it was really quite straightforward, and the practical Edith went on to give a detailed list of travelling instructions.

Mr Rahl would not hear of the idea. 'Miss Emmie's with *us* now,' he declared firmly.

But she would not have wanted to go to Vladivostok in any case. She felt absolutely at home with the Rahls and was far too busy having 'a right royal time' in Moscow. It was a terrific thrill, for example, just to go with Mme Rahl to Yeliseyeff's to help choose a *ryabchik* (a small game bird) for Volodya's lunch, as Yeliseyeff's was a large provision store full of the most wonderful and exotic foods. To a young girl who had led a simple life in England, all these experiences were quite new and very exciting. She never tried to conceal this excitement and pleasure. On the contrary, that she was someone to whom it was easy to give pleasure and who was so obviously enthusiastic about everything, must have appealed to Mr and Mme Rahl: this spontaneous enthusiasm was refreshing and could only be beneficial to their son.

Once the winter was over, the Rahls would be returning to their country estate and taking Miss Emmie with them, so there were still plenty of new experiences to look forward to.

7

The Younger Generation

The spread of public education for girls in Britain during the later part of the nineteenth century had meant that not only were fewer governesses needed, but that the governess ranks were open to any middle-class girl who had completed a secondary school education. This must have been the background of the governess who on August 25th, 1887, almost a quarter of a century before Gertie and Emmie set off for Russia, inserted the following advertisement in *The Lady*:

Resident Governess or Useful Companion (thirty) seeks re-engagement. English, German, fluent French. Eleven years abroad. Music. Salary £20. Excellent references.—Address 'X', 46 Oval Road, East Croydon. No agents.

Poor 'X' of East Croydon: one is tempted to whisper 'Russia' in her ear! Unlike another advertiser, she was obviously not 'a lady by birth, who has taught in several noble families', nor could she hope to compete with the snob appeal of advertisements like the following:

The Countess of Suffolk wishes highly to recommend a young lady as English Governess, about whom she will be very happy to give any particulars. Charlton Park, Malmesbury.

Nothing so vulgar here as the mention of a salary! Nor could her qualifications match those of Miss Louch, of Avington, Winchester, who is likewise too conscious of her own worth to name a figure:

An Associate of Queen's College, Harley Street (Cambridge Higher First Class Honours) wishes engagement. Age twenty-seven. Thorough English, Latin, French, German, also music and drawing; experienced in teaching.

Yet 'X' need not finally despair, for she does have one obvious advantage: her cheapness. The governess market in 1887 is so depressed that she is actually asking for less than those pale, despondent governesses of the 1840's. Her French might be 'fluent', rather than 'Parisian', suggesting that her last job had been in the French provinces; but did that matter greatly when her terms were so moderate? And it said something for her good sense and respectability that she did not want to be involved at all with agents. These governess agencies had sprung up in great numbers because of the desperate demand for work. According to an article entitled 'Robbing Governesses', which appeared in *The Lady* on February 20th, 1890, many of them were thoroughly dishonest: governesses 'find to their bitter cost that of a dozen agents to whom they apply ten at least are harpies, eager to prey upon their helplessness and inexperience, pocketing their hardly-earned fees, encouraging them in a vain hope, but never putting an hour's work in their way'.

Thus the incentive for a governess to look for work outside England seems even stronger in 1890 than ever before. At the same time the young girls coming forward to be governesses were drawn from a much wider variety of social backgrounds. It is noticeable that from about 1890 onwards a more varied type of English governess seems also to have been attracted to Russia. She tends to be younger, more adventurous, not necessarily so dedicated to her profession. There *were* more openings for women by this time, the label of governess was losing its Victorian stigma, and a girl was unlikely to feel that in taking a job as a governess she was sealing her future for the next thirty or forty years and renouncing the possibility of marriage. It is during this last quarter of her Russian century that we hear more commonly of the English governess marrying in Russia and often, as in the case of Edith Sinclair's marriage to Dmitri Kovalsky, marrying very well. Few of our twentieth-century governesses would have followed the example of Miss Winkworth, a governess in Russia some time before 1900, who, according to my correspondent, 'received a proposal of marriage from a titled Russian gentleman, but on being told that though married to him she would not be received at court, refused the proposal, feeling that an English gentlewoman was perfectly fit to appear at a Russian court'. Our twentieth-century governess, I feel sure, would have sacrificed the court rather than the titled gentleman! When last heard of, Miss Winkworth was believed to have retired to Switzerland and to be living 'in at least comparatively straitened circumstances'.

A more varied type of governess, and on occasion, it would seem, a more eccentric one too. What, for example, is one to make of the English governess described by Stanislavsky, the famous co-founder of the Moscow Art Theatre? In the summer of 1902, when Chekhov was preparing to write *The Cherry Orchard*, he and his wife were living in a cottage on the estate of Stanislavsky's mother at Lyubimovka, about forty minutes by train from Moscow. Stanislavsky recalls:

. . . Nearby, in our neighbours' family, there lived an Englishwoman, a governess, a small, thin creature with two long girl's pigtails and wearing a man's suit. Because of this combination it was difficult at first to be sure of her sex, where she came from and how old she was. She was on hail-fellow-well-met terms with Anton Pavlovitch, much to the writer's delight. They would meet every day and tell one another the most outrageous nonsense. For example, Chekhov would assure the Englishwoman that in his youth he had been a Turk, that he had his own harem, that he would be returning shortly to his native country to become a pasha, and would then summon her to join him. As if to show her gratitude, the agile English gymnast would then jump on to his shoulders, and settling herself there would greet all the passers-by on Anton Pavlovitch's behalf, i.e. she would take his hat off his head and doff it, adding in clownishly comical broken Russian:

'Gut mornink! Gut mornink!' (*zdlas'te! zdlas'te! zdlas'te!*)

Then she would give Chekhov's head a jerk as a sign of greeting.

Anyone who has seen *The Cherry Orchard* will recognize in this original figure the prototype of Charlotte.

When I read the play through, I realized this straight away and wrote a highly enthusiastic letter to Chekhov. How worked up he became! With what energy he assured me that Charlotte must definitely be German, and definitely not small—someone like the actress Muratova, who bore no resemblance at all to the Englishwoman from whom Charlotte had been copied.

Chekhov had portrayed an English governess once before, in the short story *A Daughter of Albion*, published in 1883, when he was still a penniless medical student not in the habit of frequenting families who employed English governesses. Tall and thin, the Daughter of Albion has protruding eyes like a lobster's and a large hooked nose. Her scraggy yellow shoulders can be clearly seen through her white muslin dress. 'There's a kind of rotten smell about her,' claims her employer, Gryaboff. Though she has been in Russia for ten years, she has not learned a word of the language. To do so, suggests Gryaboff, would be beneath her dignity: 'she doesn't regard any of us as human beings'. The climax of the story comes when Gryaboff, who has to admit that the governess is, after all, 'a lady', realises to his acute embarrassment that in order to free the hook on the end of his fishing line, he must strip naked in her presence and dive into the river where they have been fishing together (for several hours, and in total silence). Far from being embarrassed by his behaviour, the Daughter of Albion responds with 'a haughty, contemptuous smile which spread across her yellow face'.

Though it is an obvious caricature, Chekhov's portrait does vividly conjure up the unattractive image of the English governess in Russia: that of the middle-aged spinster, professionally competent— 'I only keep her because of the children,' says Gryaboff—but frigid, aloof and infuriatingly superior.

No one, however, could be less aloof than Charlotte's prototype, that agile English gymnast who enjoyed jumping on Chekhov's shoulders in the summer of 1902. 'If only you could play the part of the governess,' Chekhov wrote to his wife. 'It's the best part. I don't like any of the rest of them.' There seems little doubt that Stanislavsky was right in his supposition, for the eccentricities that Chekhov ascribes to Charlotte do seem very English. She likes to go out shooting on her own (just as the Daughter of Albion enjoyed long spells of fishing), she has a rifle slung over her shoulder and is wearing a man's peaked cap, and from her pocket she pulls out a long green cucumber which she unconcernedly starts to munch.

I wish I had more material to present on the *eccentric* English governess in Russia. Chekhov's neighbour cannot have been unique. I have been told of one English teacher whose lessons consisted of 'just a bit of small talk and telling the girl's fortune on cards', and of a governess, believed to be a Miss Cox, who was 'known to be addicted to automatic writing'. There is always Miss Agnessa Pocket, 'a person of the female sex but of male appearance', who was a heavy drinker and passionate steeple-chaser, and did not know any fear: but she unfortunately belongs to the realm of fiction—a novel of 1853 by a Russian lady novelist.

Who was the English prototype for Chekhov's Charlotte? When I began work on this book, it did not seem an altogether forlorn hope that I might succeed in identifying her. Though it was hard to conceive that she was still alive, she might well, given the notorious longevity of the English governess, have survived until the 1950's. So far, however, she has remained disappointingly anonymous.

Whoever she was, she was certainly not Miss Eagar. Miss Eagar has written about her Russian experiences in *Six Years at the Russian Court*, published in 1906, and has also been written about: Bea Howe claims her as a governess in *A Galaxy of Governesses* and Jonathan Gathorne-Hardy as a nanny in *The Rise and Fall of the British Nanny*. She seems in fact to have been a nanny, nursery governess and schoolroom governess all rolled into one. Her charges were the daughters of Tsar Nicholas of Russia, the four Grand Duchesses: Grand Duchess Olga, who was three when Miss Eagar took up residence in February 1899, Tatyana (one and a half), Marie, born in May 1899, and Anastasia, born in June 1901.

Like many governesses, Miss Eagar came from Ireland. It is tempting to call her the most prestigious English governess in Russia of all time, but for the fact that 'prestigious' properly means 'double-dealing', and on the face of it no one could have been more straight-forward than Miss Eagar. Her straightforwardness—does she not say in her preface that she will tell only the 'plain, unvarnished Truth'?—seems to shine forth from such sadly ironical reflections as the following on the Grand Duchesses:

. . . I often wonder what use they will make of all the talents God has entrusted them with, and feel assured that as the apple never falls very far from the tree, so with such good parents my dear little charges will never go astray.

This sentence also gives some idea of the bland and unrevealing style of Miss Eagar's narrative. 'The land of the Czar', one feels, remained an almost entirely closed book to her. She never learned the language properly, and because of her position enjoyed very little personal freedom: according to Bea Howe, who heard it from Miss Phair, a governess in St Petersburg at the same time as Miss Eagar, she was not even allowed to take tea on Sundays at the English Governesses' Club Room attached to the English Church.

There are very occasional moments in her book when Miss Eagar forgets that she is the 'royal governess' and becomes almost life-like. She tells the story of how in Yalta she sent one of the under-nurses to buy a bathing-dress for her. The shopkeeper turned scornfully on the girl and said: 'Bathing-dress, indeed! French fashions! Tell her to go and bathe in her skin as her grandmother did before her.' Then there is Miss Eagar's singing. 'I do not suppose,' she writes,

that the world holds anyone more unmusical than I am. My singing might, without in any way violating the second commandment, be worshipped, for it is like nothing in the heavens above, nor in the earth beneath, nor in the waters under the earth. . . . I have just a faint idea of two tunes. One of them is 'Rock of Ages'; the other, 'Villikins and his Dinah'. . . .

On one occasion when the Grand Duchess Tatyana was lying ill in bed, Miss Eagar sang 'Rock of Ages' to her until eventually 'the poor little sufferer rebelled, and flatly refused to listen to it any more, so I fell back upon "Villikins" '. No wonder that the Grand Duchess Olga thought Miss Eagar 'a marvel of education, and confided in her music master that no one in the world knew so much as I did; she thought I knew everything, except music and Russian'.

Miss Eagar might easily have come down to us on her own terms: as the faceless paragon, the discreet presence, whose loyalty and responsibility are never openly proclaimed but can be sensed between every line she writes. Fortunately, however, we have another glimpse of Miss Eagar. It is provided by the recollections of an aunt of the four young Grand Duchesses, the Tsar's younger sister, Grand Duchess Olga Alexandrovna. According to her Miss Eagar was fascinated by politics and talked incessantly about the Dreyfus case. Fascinated by politics! Not even the most intuitive reader could have guessed that from *Six Years at the Russian Court*. 'Once,' recalled the Grand Duchess, 'she even forgot that Marie was in her bath and started discussing the case with a friend. Marie, naked and dripping, scrambled out of the bath and started running up and down the palace corridor. Fortunately, I arrived just at that moment, picked her up and carried her back to Miss Eagar, who was still talking about Dreyfus.' Grand Duchess Marie *forgotten in her bath*! At once the blandly persuasive image of the 'devoted royal governess' is shattered, and Miss Eagar acquires a face at last for posterity.

Even 'Villikins' cannot quite stand up to this revelation, and begins to look like an artfully contrived 'human touch'.

On August 12th, 1904, a son, Alexis, was born to join the four young royal sisters, and shortly afterwards Miss Eagar left Russia 'owing to private and personal reasons'. Too many voices, one assumes (though probably not those of the Tsar and the Empress, herself a product of the English governess system), had been raised against the idea of the long-awaited heir to the throne being entrusted to the care of a foreigner. Yet Miss Eagar's five and a half years of irreproachable service—not quite six but it made a better title—must have done much to enhance the prestige of the English governess in Russia.

✻   ✻   ✻

Had the Tsarevich been born three years later, Miss Eagar might perhaps have been asked to stay on. For 1907 was the year of the Anglo-Russian convention, which ushered in a period of unusually cordial relations between the countries. Democratic Britain's traditional hostility to the Russian autocracy was forgotten in the interests of the alliance against Germany. To an English governess travelling to Russia in 1911 how solid the world must still have looked when she read in the *Russian Year Book* for that year of the shares in Anglo-Russian companies that were due to mature in 1945, or of the rail journey by North Express from London to St Petersburg: 'depart Charing Cross 9 A.M., fare £15. 18s. 3d., duration of journey 51¼ hours'. As in our own time, 'cultural exchanges' quickly followed in the wake of the improved political situation. In 1910 Pavlova danced for the first time in London and soon became a household name, while England, for her part, exported to Russia—still more nannies and governesses. It seems safe to assume that during the last ten or fifteen years of her century in Russia, the number of English governesses reached its peak. Professor Elizabeth Hill recalls that her Russian mother, 'who was a warmhearted and generous person full of good deeds, became Anglican because of my Anglo-Scots father and attended the English Church in St Petersburg. The result was that every Sunday we would have shoals of English governesses invited to our Sunday lunch. We children thought them a bore and called them the Limpets!'

During these years there was a growing demand for the English governess not only from her traditional employers, the nobility and well-to-do merchants, but also from the rising class of professional people, like doctors, lawyers, professors, civil servants and those engaged in the arts. To have a resident English governess for one's children had become an obvious status symbol. From these new employers the English governess could no longer be sure of receiving such preferential treatment as she had been used to in the past. One recalls the unpleasant *nouveau riche* family where Katie Sinclair had to sleep on a camp bed in the hall when visitors arrived, and the rats, so she claimed, used to scamper across her face during the night. Another governess did not stay long with a Moscow family because they were so mean about food, while one highly qualified English girl was so disgusted by the Asiatic eating habits of the family in Baku to which she was engaged that she handed in her notice within a week.

But the most striking and amusing experiences of this kind are those of Marie Russell Brown. Miss Brown was later to become quite a successful writer of stories and serials for women's magazines, and in the early 1930's she wrote a lively account, which was never published, of her two jobs as a governess in Russia before 1914.

Scottish-born Miss Brown was under twenty when she went out in September 1902 to her first job with a Doctor's family in St Petersburg. He was a Doctor at the Emperor's Court and had the official rank of General. The family had previously had a French Mademoiselle for four years and still had a German Fräulein, but they had never had an English governess before and no one spoke a word of English.

Miss Mary, as she came to be known, was engaged as governess to Manya, aged five, and Ira, aged three. Governess—or glorified nursemaid? 'The orthodox English governess,' she ruefully admits, 'would have been sadly disillusioned if she had found herself in my position.' Three-year-old Ira was 'a problem child if ever there was one': highly-strung, with a capacity for devilment that was equalled only by her capacity for spontaneous affection. It was Ira who, after Miss Mary had been in residence for two months 'with a great wall of silence around me', suddenly began 'chattering in English as freely as any normal English child, and became my inseparable companion', acting as an interpreter for her governess with the rest of the family and servants. But Miss Mary had to be on duty from eight in the morning till eight at night, and not for one moment could she afford to turn her back on Ira:

. . . In the midst of apparent peace Ira, a perfect little spitfire, would squabble with Manya over some trifle, and seizing whatever was nearest would attack poor Manya who was timid in spite of being almost half as big again as her little sister. One day the nearest weapon happened to be Nana's scissors which she had left lying on the table, and in a moment Manya was flying along the corridor with Ira close behind brandishing the scissors, while I followed at full speed to prevent bloodshed. Before I could reach the combatants however Ira succeeded in giving Manya a vicious cut on the head, and a howl of pain went up.

The cut was bandaged and peace restored, and in time Miss Mary might have managed to establish a more peaceful routine, had it not been for the four older children, whose ages varied from nine to thirteen (there was also a one-year-old baby). The older children had little intention of learning English seriously, but they 'collected all the uncomplimentary nouns and adjectives they could find in our English lesson book, and used them on suitable or unsuitable occasions alike'.

Life was just tolerable when the older children were at school all day; but six healthy children, in 'a country where children were disobedient and undisciplined', shut up on holiday in a St Petersburg flat during the winter, were bound to find some outlet for their overflowing energy. One day Miss Mary had just begun a letter when she heard a terrific noise:

. . . I ran towards the door, feeling sure that the little ones were in the clutches of their brothers or sisters, and hoping to save them before much damage to clothes or feelings was done. Before I could reach it however, a violent push from Natasha who was entering sent me flying back. In a moment she had locked all three doors, and then she spared a moment for explanation.

'Fima and Volodya are chasing me,' she announced, turning a laughing face towards her astonished governess.

'But I must go to Manya and Ira,' I protested. Natasha pulled me back just in time, for a stream of water flowed under the door.

'My goodness what is that?' I exclaimed, watching with horror a small river running over my beautifully polished floor. A laugh from the corridor answered me, and presently Natasha seized my water jug and began to return the stream. Efforts on my part were useless. I could only get up on a chair and watch with dismay the water pouring in under the doors. Fima and Volodya went from one door to another adding to the flood, and Natasha whose supply was soon exhausted, danced about in glee among the few dry spots left on the floor.

'The Sea of England,' she shouted. 'Poor Miss Mary you will be drowned. Don't you like your English Sea?'

. . . At last the children tired of their game; a servant with a mop and pail was called, and when the father and mother came in from paying visits all was dry, although the polish was off the floors. The lady from down below came up to complain that the water had been pouring into her room, but she was pacified at last, and the Doctor merely laughed. 'Children, children,' he exclaimed, 'What terrible children I have.'

At Christmas Miss Mary agreed to help the children decorate the tree. 'Come to me when you want your wounds bound up,' Fräulein observed mockingly. 'I have plenty of rags here.' But in spite of Fräulein's gloomy forebodings proceedings were 'comparatively peaceful':

Fima knocked Mischa off the steps, and Fräulein's rags were called into requisition to bind up his head, but with this trifling exception everything was done in an orderly manner. Mischa was a good-natured boy, and he contented himself with dropping candle grease on Fima's neck as she bent down to arrange some ornaments on the lower branches. She gave a violent start, and flung a small hammer at him, but admitted that she deserved some punishment, and thereafter the two worked harmoniously together.

It was fortunate that Miss Mary had never thought of herself as a quiet refined person, for she soon realised that if she could not beat them (and none of the older children took the slightest notice of her), she would have to join them: 'I could never have existed in that wild family if I had held back from anything it was humanly possible to do'. So it was that this 'young, shy, almost ignorant maiden of Edwardian vintage', who had never ridden a horse in her life, allowed herself one summer afternoon on the Doctor's estate near the Finnish border to be talked by the children into mounting a tall, awkward looking animal which had been described to her as 'very quiet':

Presently I found myself tearing along at full speed on the road, through ditches, and brushing through gaps in hedges. I held on with all my strength as the horse raced on, but found time to wonder what energetic horses were like if this was a quiet one, and to picture myself falling off and having my collar-bone broken like Mademoiselle.

'Come on,' shouted Fima from the front. I could not reply. My horse seemed to have tired of following the others, and had started off on a way of its own. I pulled at the reins to induce it to turn, and succeeded in swinging it round a little, but by now I seemed to be all by myself.

Some trees came into view, and the horse, evidently being tired of its incapable rider decided it would be a good idea to rub against a tree. With a mental picture of Absalom's end I bent low and gave my whole attention to saving myself from being hauled off by my hair. Every hair-pin was gone by this time, and I presented a very different picture from my usual one as my horse scraped past every tree. Feeling that this must come to an end I gave an extra strong pull, and the horse consented to be turned away.

Just as I had managed to slow it down a little, and to reflect upon the appearance I must present with my hair streaming behind I saw the Doctor, Madame and Ivan Ivanovitch walking down the road. They laughed and waved hats and hands when they saw me, and I, feeling hotter than ever, was thankful to perceive that I was on the road leading to the house.

I managed to get the horse round the corner of the wood, but once there it decided it would rather go to its village home than turn towards the stables, and it had gone several yards before I succeeded in turning it again. Then it was a circus performance for some time. The horse would turn so far, and I would pull it back again, so that we went round and round in the middle of the road.

Fräulein and the little ones who had been out for a walk, stood and watched with interest, Fräulein in the midst of her laughter, shrieking suggestions. The other children who had arrived home came out to see the fun, and presently the others came into sight.

Ivan Ivanovitch attempted to catch the horse in order to lead it, but I motioned him away. Entirely oblivious now of the spectacle I must present to the onlooker I continued to be moved round in a circle. The Doctor laughed and cheered on the rider, while Madame, an amused smile on her face, motioned to Mischa to catch the horse. But just at that moment the horse, reflecting that this performance was apparently going on for ever, decided that it might as well give in, and consented to be turned towards the stables.

'Bravo England,' exclaimed the Doctor as he helped me down.

'Never beaten,' added Ivan Ivanovitch.

With a sudden realisation of my appearance I put my hands to my head, and flew towards the house without making any reply, while the shout of laughter that followed me reached right up into my room. . . .

But if there is now an increasing amount of social variety and unpredictability among the English governesses' employers, the same is true of the governesses themselves. The Kerbys' friend from Ireland, Miss Ash, whose contacts had enabled Emma Dashwood to obtain her job, belongs to the traditional kind of governess. Like many others in the past, she had become a governess because of sudden family impoverishment. Her widowed mother was persuaded to take out an endowment policy, but within a month she too died and the capital was all lost. Miss Ash's sister decided to go into nursing, Miss Ash to become a governess in Russia. Since she came from a good Irish family, was well educated and popular ('always a live wire', apparently, at picnics arranged by the English community), she had no difficulty in finding good jobs. But while she was in Russia, several girls came out as governesses from her part of Ireland, who at home, she confided to the Kerbys, 'would only have been received in our kitchen'. Social differences of this kind, so critical then in Britain, obviously meant far less to Russians, for whom an English speaker still remained an English speaker—and to be prized as such—even if she did have a strong Irish brogue.

Another story is told of one uneducated English nanny who spoke English with her Russian charges. If asked the meaning of a word she didn't know, she would reply calmly: 'Go and look it up in the dictionary, my dear, and that way you won't forget it.' But then came the time when one of her pupils began to go out for proper English lessons. 'Nanny,' she said, returning home once from a lesson, 'why is it you always say *voilets*?' 'Well, my dear, it's like this,' replied Nanny, unabashed, 'there's some that says *voilets* and some that says *violets*.'

One cannot help wondering how a girl like Emma Dashwood was able to obtain such a good job in Russia with so little difficulty. Only twenty-two years old when engaged by the Rahls in 1912, and in her own words, 'still quite a child', she had no qualifications as a teacher and very limited experience as a governess. A likely explanation is that by this time something of a 'closed shop' had come into operation. Very exceptional is the case of the elder Miss Judge (Mrs van Doren) who, with her sister, formed the subject of a B.B.C. broadcast in 1959. Miss Judge, a true Cockney sparrow (being less than five feet tall once saved her life in Russia when a soldier about to take aim lowered his rifle, thinking she must be a child), presented herself at a domestic agency in Kensington some time about 1905 and said she was prepared to go anywhere in the world to teach or look after children. The agency referred her to a Russian general who was passing through London at the time and looking for a governess.

But this was just a happy chance, and I cannot think that many governesses were recruited in such a way. Recruitment seems to have depended more on a closed system of contacts and recommendations. Thus, Marie Russell Brown was the third generation in her family to be a governess in Russia. It was through her aunt, Lizzie Arthur, that she was recommended to the Doctor. Apparently they were the only family available at the time, and her aunt knew almost nothing about them; and very shocked she was too when she returned with her own Russian family from the South of France and heard about all the goings-on in the Doctor's household. For well over twenty years, until 1917, Lizzie Arthur was a nanny, governess and later housekeeper in the Obolensky family; and in his memoirs, *One Man in his Time*, Serge Obolensky describes her as an extremely outspoken, stout little Scots woman, born in Glasgow, who was devoted to Obolensky and his brother, and whose 'little acts of affection that are funny and unexpected, that make a child's dream-world day' helped to protect them from the immediate unhappiness of their parents' divorce. But Lizzie Arthur had in turn been recommended to the Obolenskys by *her* aunt, Mimi Brown, a governess and later companion with the Narishkins (Princess Obolensky was a Narishkin), who can be seen, looking very Scottish and matronly, in a family photo of 1894 included in *One Man in his Time*.

It was a closed system in that a good governess might be carefully handed on from one branch of a family to another, or from family to family, while the governesses themselves likewise kept their ears to the ground in the hope of hearing of some more attractive post. Individuals like Edith Kovalsky and Annie Kerby, who had many contacts on both the English and Russian sides, were obviously important as unofficial employment agencies helping to make the system run smoothly, while many a useful piece of information might be picked up at such focal points of English life in Russia as the church or chapel.

In that decade before the First World War the English governess in Russia was sitting pretty. True, she might have to take the rough with the smooth, but she was sought after and well paid: better paid now than even the French governesses, and much better paid than the German ones. Young engaged girls like May and Katie Sinclair went out to Russia not because they intended to be professional governesses, but because they saw in Russia an excellent opportunity for having a novel experience and saving money before they settled down to married life. The middle-aged governess must have viewed these young girls with some apprehension and wondered about her own prospects, but there was always the alternative of giving private English *lessons*, for which the demand seems to have been inexhaustible. As for the older governesses, they might be looking forward to a quiet life of semi-retirement with a Russian family, *their* Russian family, or perhaps they had saved enough to be able to retire to England or the South of France.

But wherever they were, whether on some rambling country estate in the middle of nowhere, in a comfortable apartment on a smart street in Moscow or St Petersburg, or just staying between jobs at the English Governesses' Hostel in Moscow, they none of them had the least idea of how soon their world was going to change, or of the demands that would be made upon their stamina and loyalty.

8

Scottie

It can be cold in Russia, very cold; and few are the visitors who cannot give you their own particular variation on the 'lost in a snow-storm' or 'attacked by frostbite' story.

Marguerite Bennet was out skating one day on the lake near the estate where she worked as a governess. Some posts had recently been removed and a thin coating of ice had formed over the holes where they had stood. Marguerite had forgotten all about these holes and suddenly found herself slipping through the thin ice. Somehow or other she managed to support herself by the elbows until her companions came and hauled her out. She raced uphill to the house, her frozen skirt clanging like a chain. They rubbed her all over with vodka, afraid that she might catch rheumatic fever. But she suffered no ill effects from this adventure. Born in 1882 in the ancient Scottish town of Arbroath, just opposite the Bell Rock Lighthouse, Marguerite Bennet, later Mrs Thomson, was still able in her nineties to tell her Russian winter's tale.

Though she was only twenty-eight when she went out to Russia, Marguerite Bennet, unlike Emma Dashwood, had already had some experience of the world. She was descended from a Scottish Huguenot family: hence the name Marguerite. The one Bennet son was followed by a long string of girls, and when this son died at school, the girls' father, a lawyer in Arbroath, decided that his daughters should be brought up as boys and taught how to earn their own living. Marguerite first started work in her father's office, where she passed the preliminary law exams. and learned all about book-keeping. An advertisement in *The Gentlewoman* for an educational bureau (or was it one of the infamous governess agencies?) attracted her to London, but the promised openings there did not materialise. She then enrolled at one of the first secretarial schools in the City and became secretary to a stockbroker. But the stockbroker failed, and her next job was as general administrative secretary at Studley Horticultural College, which had been founded by Edward VII's friend, the Countess of Warwick. After Studley there came two years as a governess at Düren, near Cologne, at which point in her life she decided that the time had come to fit in a university degree.

At Edinburgh she read French and History, and also contrived to work at the Oceanographical Laboratory with Dr Bruce, the Scottish Antarctic explorer. But before completing her course, she received a letter from Miss Faithful, headmistress of Cheltenham Ladies' College (successor to the pioneering Miss Beale, who had died in harness at the age of seventy-four), asking if she would like to go out to Russia as governess to two young girls. Russia! Marguerite had dreamed of going there ever since friends in Germany had told her all about it. She went to see her Edinburgh teachers, Professor Lodge (History), brother of Sir Oliver Lodge, the famous spiritualist, and Dr Sarolea (French), who had been on a pilgrimage to the Holy Land with Tolstoy. They were both very enthusiastic and agreed to let her continue her studies when she came back from Russia. Little did they guess how far off that day would be!

In May 1911, six months before the departure of Gertie Kirby and Emma Dashwood, she sailed by cargo boat from Tilbury to St Petersburg, where she was met by Marc, an elder brother of her two future pupils, and shown some of the sights. From St Petersburg she took the night train to Moscow, and there her pupils' elder sister, Galina, was waiting with a large Mercedes car. It was a perfect spring morning. They drove into Red Square and through the Kremlin, over the Moscow River to the Sparrow Hills, and on for some twenty miles through undulating country until they came to a cart road across a stream; then past a lake (the one from which she would later be hauled out) and up a hill, through big iron gates with an old church on the right, and so to the beautiful house of Voskresenskoye, recently restored to its original eighteenth-century splendour. All the family was at the door to greet the new governess. They were struck at once by her remarkably clear blue eyes with hazel spots, and her fresh complexion. It was not long before they nicknamed her 'Scottie'.

Scottie's new employer, Nikolai Karlovich von Meck, was in his late forties. He was a tall man of imposing appearance, and one is not surprised to learn that when he visited England, he was constantly being saluted by policemen. In her recently published autobiography, *As I Remember Them*, Galina von Meck writes that the earliest recorded von Meck was a Teutonic Knight Templar of the fourteenth century. Nikolai Karlovich's father, Karl Otto Georg von Meck, a professional engineer, was the first member of the family to settle permanently in Russia, marrying a Russian girl, Nadezhda Fralovsky, and making the name of von Meck famous in Russia through his activities as a builder of railways. Though he was not a trained engineer, Nikolai Karlovich had more than inherited his father's remarkable flair as a railway entrepreneur and had also acquired a considerable reputation as an enlightened employer.

Nikolai Karlovich's wife, Anna, came from the Davydov family. The name is well known in Russian history: Denis Davydov was the young officer, portrayed as Denisov in *War and Peace*, whose guerilla tactics helped to undermine Napoleon, while his cousin, Vasily, was a leading member of the Decembrists, the group of young noblemen who tried unsuccessfully in 1825 to replace the autocracy by a constitutional monarchy. Between the Davydov and von Meck families there was a most unusual link. Anna's uncle on her mother's side was the composer, Tchaikovsky: Uncle Peter, as he was known to the Davydov children; while Nikolai Karlovich's mother was that same Madame von Meck, *née* Fralovsky, whose strange friendship with Tchaikovsky has attracted so much attention: though they never met, she helped him financially and they corresponded on intimate terms for fourteen years, only for the friendship to come to a sad and enigmatic end.

By the time of Scottie's arrival, Tchaikovsky and Mme von Meck had both been dead for many years. There was, however, still one member of that generation living at Voskresenskoye. This was Baboushka (Grannie) Anna Petrovna, Annette in Tchaikovsky's letters: his first cousin and childhood friend. Baboushka was a universal favourite. Her stories of society life were endlessly fascinating to the young governess. But they were not to continue for long. Only a few months after Scottie's arrival, Baboushka died, and a magnificent funeral service was held for her at Voskresenskoye. For several days previously the body remained lying in the bedroom where she had died, just off the dining-room, as Nikolai Karlovich was unavoidably detained on business. 'You can imagine,' recalled Mrs Thomson, 'what kind of an atmosphere there was at mealtimes' the smell of food mingling with that of incense, and the clatter of plates with the endless chanting of the priests next door.

Baboushka's old bedroom on the ground floor was offered to Scottie. She had liked the room near her pupils in the tower at the top of the house, but had been a martyr to bedbugs. In their extensive modernisation not even the von Mecks had found the answer to this ancient problem, but then one must remember that the bug is a natural aristocrat, who much prefers the home of the rich man. Baboushka's room was sumptuously furnished. The maids, who never wore shoes or stockings, padded silently across its deep carpets. Scottie moved in—only to discover that the bugs were just as bad there too! Very concerned, the von Mecks got hold of some powerful preparation that was supposed to kill the bugs right off, but, said Mrs Thomson, 'it almost killed *me* off instead!'

Of course, English governesses were no novelty in the von Meck and Davydov families. By chance, one of Scottie's most recent predecessors had also been a Miss Bennet, no relation, who came from England and was nicknamed 'Missie'. A particularly memorable former governess was Miss Eastwood, who had been with the Davydov family and 'for a time gave English lessons to Peter Tchaikovsky'. Miss Eastwood, writes Galina von Meck,

was a great character, became a real member of the Davydov family and very often bossed them all, looking upon them as her own. As she grew older, however, poor dear, she became fantastically ugly. I remember her very well because she came once to stay with us in the country when I was about ten.

She spoke very good English and taught the children perfect English. At the end of her life, she fell in love—at the age of eighty. The man was one of the sub-managers on the estate, a young Ukrainian fellow by the name of Chuchupaka. Her favourite pastime was to go off for drives with this young man, sitting next to him in the little two wheeled carriage with her head on his shoulder gazing with admiration at the silly fellow. Actually not so very silly because he knew very well how to take advantage of her. All her little savings and all her little trinkets passed into his pocket. When my uncle Dimitri or his wife tried to stop her from being so foolish she used to get very angry indeed. In the end, of course, my uncle dismissed the young fellow, and poor Miss Eastwood was left sorrowing.

What delightfully un-English behaviour!

Nor was Scottie the only teacher in the von Meck household. A German tutor, a French tutor and a French governess were also in permanent residence, while in the summer a music teacher was engaged from the Moscow Conservatoire. Scottie was responsible for the two youngest girls: Lolya (short for Elena), an adopted daughter of the von Mecks, aged fourteen, and Lucy, aged twelve. Since both girls already spoke English well, they were in no danger, regrettably perhaps, of being infected by their new teacher's warm Scottish accent, which she retained until the end of her life. There was no fixed timetable. They talked together in English, read English books and learned English poetry. Scottie accompanied Lucy to her classes in speech therapy, and took both girls to their weekly dancing lessons at the Bolshoi Ballet.

Soon Scottie became popular with all the household. Mme von Meck had told her on arrival that she would never understand the Russians unless she learned to speak the language, and this she did, speaking Russian with everyone she came across; the Scots have always been less inhibited as linguists than the English. Dorothy Cooke (Mrs Russell), whose father had been an English tutor in Russia for some years, was only seven when Miss Bennet first came to their house. She too remembers her remarkable blue eyes and clear complexion, and how eager she was to hear all about other people's doings. To Dorothy and her sister, Miss Bennet, alias Scottie, became known by another nickname: 'Aunt Really'. Whenever she was told anything of interest, she would always reply, with a mixture of surprise and curiosity in her lilting Scottish voice: '*Really?*'

As an enlightened employer, Nikolai Karlovich did not neglect the young Scots girl within his own household. One is immediately impressed by his thoughtfulness in arranging for a member of the family to meet the new arrival at each stage of her journey to the estate. Scottie could look back and say of the von Mecks that they were 'just kindness itself'. She was always treated as a member of the family and taken to every social function. One particularly glamorous occasion was the Court Ball at the Nobles' Club in Moscow. She had been looking forward to this for weeks, but on the day itself

Mme von Meck was unwell. 'No, no,' decided Nikolai Karlovich, 'Scottie's not to be cheated of her ball. I shall take her myself.' On the huge dance floor at the Nobles' Club, the dance was led off by the Tsar's uncle, Grand Duke Nicholas, commander-in-chief of the Russian Army and son of that Grand Duke Nicholas to whom another Scotswoman, Helen Pinkerton, had been governess in the 1840's.

Not surprisingly, music played an important part in the life of the von Mecks. At their town house in Moscow there was a magnificent music room with three grand pianos, and beautiful gilt and white French chairs ranged round the walls. Everyone in Moscow's musical world knew of the 'Wednesday evenings' which took place at the von Mecks once a fortnight, while in summer performers regularly travelled the twenty miles from Moscow to play at Voskresenskoye. To this rich musical life Scottie once made a distinctive contribution of her own. On Mme von Meck's saint's day a huge party was held at Voskresenskoye, and the champagne flowed until the early hours. During the evening the guests were entertained by a cabaret. Scottie had had a kilt specially made for the occasion, and danced the sword dance and the Irish washerwoman: not without some skill, obviously, for the guests concluded that she must be a real professional dancer.

There were the von Meck railways, there was the von Meck music—and there were the von Meck cars. The first motor car in Russia, writes Galina, was delivered to her father in 1898. In the autumn of 1911 Nikolai Karlovich organised the first international 'reliability trial motor race' for the Imperial Automobile Club, of which he was commodore. Passengers were supposed to be strictly forbidden, but an exception was finally made in the case of Scottie. The route took the cars more or less due south from Moscow, through Tula, Kursk, Kharkov (after which the roads became little better than dust tracks) and Dnepropetrovsk, and finishing up in the south of the Crimean Peninsula, at Sevastopol. At night the drivers slept in a special train which followed the rally, while their cars were closely guarded by detachments of soldiers. Magnificent luncheons were given in honour of the drivers at the different stopping points on the way south—with what effect, one wonders, on their driving performance?—but it was at Sevastopol that the rally reached its climax. The Tsar, Tsaritsa and their five children were

staying on board the Imperial yacht, *Standart*, at anchor in Sevastopol harbour. They all came ashore to attend the reception at which
the Tsar presented prizes for the rally. Afterwards, members of the
Imperial party mingled with the guests, and the Tsar, recalled
Scottie, 'was as close to me as I am to you now'.

On that occasion there was nothing to suggest that the Tsarevich
was anything but a perfectly normal, healthy seven-year-old. When
Scottie next saw him, it was a different story. The year 1913 was the
tercentenary of the Romanov dynasty. Celebrations were held
throughout Russia, aimed at revitalising the traditional loyalty of the
Russian people to its Tsar. When the first Romanov came to the
throne in 1613, the Imperial capital of St Petersburg did not exist,
and although a number of ceremonies were held there in the early
part of 1913, it was not until June that the most solemn celebration
of the tercentenary took place in Moscow. From her special seat in
the courtyard of the Kremlin, obtained for her by the von Mecks'
cousin, Vladimir, secretary to the Grand Duchess Elizabeth, Scottie
watched as the Imperial procession, followed by all the members of
the Court in full ceremonial dress, came down the long flight of steps
known as the Red Staircase and crossed over on its way to one of the
Kremlin cathedrals. Behind the Tsar and Tsaritsa walked their four
daughters, the Grand Duchesses, but when Scottie looked for the
Tsarevich, she did not at first see him. In the previous autumn,
Alexis had bruised his thigh slightly while out rowing. Though
painful at first, the bruise appeared to clear up satisfactorily, but a
few days later the boy suffered a severe haemorrhage in the thigh and
groin. His death seemed imminent. After eleven days of exquisite
pain, Alexis surmounted the crisis, though his recovery was slow and
over a year passed before the limp in his left leg disappeared
completely. Those vast crowds who, like Scottie, were watching the
solemn celebration of the Romanov tercentenary in Moscow, did
not know that the heir to the Romanov throne was a victim of
haemophilia. All they saw was a small boy, still not well enough to
walk by himself, who needed to be carried in the arms of a burly
Cossack member of the Imperial bodyguard.

Few English governesses can have had a more colourful time in
Russia than did Scottie with the von Mecks. Little wonder that her
memories of Voskresenskoye are full of nostalgia: 'I loved my life
there in the beautiful countryside,' she recalled later, 'with lots of

67

roses in the garden and masses of wild flowers and the wonderful birch trees. It was marvellous in the warm summer weather, and glorious in the winter flying about the lanes in sledges.' In that land of extreme contrasts, there may have been families wealthier than the von Mecks—for Galina does not class her family among the *very* rich; while other governesses, from Miss Eagar downwards, might point to the blue blood of their employers compared to that of Nikolai Karlovich, whose family, though ancient, had been in Russia for less than a century. But Nikolai Karlovich clearly occupied an exceptional position in the Tsarist social hierarchy. Being that rare phenomenon in Russian history—a successful and respected man of action—he was able to maintain a position of independence. Though he was happy to let the Tsar garage some of his cars with him on the latter's visits to Moscow, he always refused court or civic titles. This democratic outlook explains why the von Mecks had no difficulty in treating their English governesses as equals. At the same time the family's spirit of enterprise and adventure made life very exciting for an English governess; how dull, by comparison, life must often have been for Miss Eagar and her like!

It was the kind of job that other governesses would have given their right arm for—but Scottie threw it all up. The reason? As she put it: 'I got tired of my easy seat.' The hard-working, independent Scotswoman reasserted herself. Nikolai Karlovich did his best to dissuade her from leaving. He had been particularly impressed by the business-like way in which Scottie had taken over the household accounts and paid all the staff during the temporary absence of the housekeeper; though, as she could have told him, it was 'child's play' for her after the work she had done at Studley Horticultural College.

No, it was time to move on. In any case, the girls were too old to need a governess. She found herself a secretarial job in the Moscow office of a London-based firm that mined copper in Siberia. Her new home was St Andrew's House, the hostel for English governesses and teachers working in Moscow, which will have an important part to play much later in this story.

9
The Reluctant Chaperone

It all sounds more like Paris than St Petersburg: on the stage—a line of chorus girls with tambourines ... the cancan ... popular music hall songs; in the parterre—young men in evening dress, wining and dining, waiting for the artistes to come out from behind the stage and start mingling with the customers.... This was the *Aquarium*, a *café chantant* in the Kamenno-Ostrovsky, one of St Petersburg's best known streets; and I think we can reasonably assume that though the *Aquarium* was always packed out, the English governess was not among its most frequent visitors.

Louisette Andrews, however, was not a governess. Nor had she the least intention of becoming one. In fact, she had never had a job in her life. When she went out to Russia in 1912, after several years spent nursing her mother at their home in Wimbledon, it was with the intention of spending a long holiday with her younger brother, Emile, who had been in Russia for some time as an engineer with the Westinghouse company. She had also brought out with her some family furniture, since Emile intended to make Russia his permanent home. The attractive, sociable Louisette was in her early thirties. With her dark wavy hair, she looked more Spanish or Italian than English; her mother was in fact French. Emile had promised that she would have a really good time in Russia, and judging by the zest for life that Miss Andrews now shows in her early nineties, I have no doubt that she did so.

She went first to stay with friends of her brother's, the Tamplins. This family came from Brighton: the name is still well known in the south of England because of Tamplin's Breweries. They had a large paint and enamel factory outside St Petersburg, a big house and a 'gentleman's farm': Mr Tamplin was always winning prizes with his beautiful tandem of bay horses. One of his wife's sisters had married into the Thorntons, a family from the north of England who were among the biggest mill-owners in Russia, while another sister had married into the Swedish family of Nobel—Alfred Nobel being the Swedish chemist who invented dynamite in 1862, amassed a huge fortune from explosives and the exploitation of Russia's Baku oil-fields, and bequeathed his fortune for the establishment of the Nobel prizes.

All these families belonged to the foreign commercial aristocracy of St Petersburg. The Tamplins were always welcome at the British Embassy, supported the English Church and the English Club, and ordered from England whatever they could not obtain from the English Shop on the Nevsky Prospect. Louisette was often taken by the young Tamplin sons to Krestovsky Island (one of several islands in the delta of the River Neva, all linked to the mainland by bridges and forming part of the city), where the English community had organised their own facilities for tennis, golf and yachting, and in winter, skating and toboganning.

After her stay with the Tamplins, Louisette went to her brother's flat on the Kamenno-Ostrovsky. 'Of course,' she now explains, 'having a *brother* made all the difference,' for it meant that she was able to visit places that no Englishwoman on her own, and certainly no English governess, would have dreamed of going to. She was warned at the outset that being an unmarried woman she must never use paint or lipstick, as otherwise she would be taken for a prostitute. A night out in winter with her brother would not begin before ten, and would go on until four or five: in his book on St Petersburg, published in 1910, George Dobson, for many years correspondent of *The Times*, wrote that during the winter 'night is turned into day and 'the streets are quite lively at three or four o'clock in the morning, for nowhere else are such late hours so generally indulged in'. Usually in evening dress and wrapped up well, they would hire an *izvozchik*—the best ones were always plentifully supplied with furs of their own—and drive to the home of one of Emile's English friends, or to a restaurant or *café chantant*. Emile would not let his sister sit in the parterre at the *Aquarium*, so they hired a box and ordered champagne and caviar. As a change from the *Aquarium*, they sometimes visited the smaller and more select *Villa Rodé*. Once in the summer they were returning by car with friends after golf at Krestovsky Island when their Russian driver, who had been drinking, swerved off the road and nearly plunged them into the river.

Since cars were still a rarity in those days, they had to stand by the roadside and wait until a haycart came along and offered them a lift back to the centre of town. By the end of this laborious journey it was so late that there was no time to change before they were due at the *Villa Rodé*. They decided to take a chance and turn up as they were. Agreeing to let them in, the manager quickly conducted them to a *cabinet particulier*—with whispered instructions that on *no* account were they to let themselves be seen by the other visitors.

Apart from members of her brother's circle, Louisette did not meet many English people in St Petersburg, though on one occasion she and a friend organised a dance at the English Badminton Club— yes, they had badminton as well as all their other sports! The English churches were invaluable meeting places, but Louisette, as a Catholic, attended only the Catholic Church in St Petersburg. Her holiday, originally planned to last for about six months, must already have been going on for more than a year—so obviously she was enjoying herself—when her brother was recalled to London on business. She was expecting him back soon, but it turned out that the Admiralty, foreseeing the European crisis, was anxious not to part with him. This put Louisette in a quandary. For several months she lived with the Tamplins but could not go on accepting their hospitality indefinitely; yet neither could she return to her brother's flat, since it would then have been regarded as highly improper for a young unmarried woman to be living in a flat on her own.

'I was absolutely *terrified*,' recalls Miss Andrews, 'at the thought of having to take a job, but there was nothing else for it . . . it was one of those things that just fell on me.' She was recommended to a family in St Petersburg called Gagarin, who had a large estate at Oberpahlen, near Riga. The daughter, Kira, was sixteen and needed a companion-chaperone, since no Russian girl of noble family was supposed to go anywhere on her own before the age of twenty-one.

And so the long holiday came to an end. With much trepidation Louisette Andrews took up her first job. As it turned out, her fears were quite unjustified. The Gagarins were a quiet family and there was little of the formal social etiquette that Louisette had been dreading. Kira was an outdoor girl who enjoyed tennis and walking. 'No tennis court but lots of balls,' I have written cryptically in my notes; but this only means that Kira also enjoyed going to dances. Since French and English were the languages used in the family,

71

Louisette, who was bi-lingual and had been to school in France, did not have to bother to learn Russian. As for teaching, 'we might have read an English book out loud together but that was about all'; it was fortunate that Kira's English was already so good, since, as Miss Andrews declares with conviction, 'teaching would *never* have suited me!'

Once she had recovered from the first shock of being employed, Louisette soon realised that her new job was not really at all demanding. There were many servants in the house to cope with every little difficulty. Having to accompany Kira to the ballet or opera could certainly not be called a hardship. Afternoon tea parties were sometimes tedious, for on these occasions the young girls would all go off to a room on their own, while the chaperones, varying in age and of every European nationality except Russian, would have to take tea together in a large reception room.

Kira, indeed, found it pleasanter to be with the sociable, easy-going Miss Andrews, who liked tennis and fashionable clothes and had a charming smile, than with her own mother, who was a strict disciplinarian. A chaperone was not given much free time in the Gagarin household. Louisette usually spent it with the Tamplin boys. She was coming back with them one winter evening when the car went down in a ditch in very deep snow. It was well past eleven by the time she reached home. Princess Gagarin was waiting up for her.

'Whatever do you mean,' she asked, 'by coming in at this hour of night? Don't you realise that it's most improper for you to be out after ten o'clock?'

And to think that not long ago with her brother, the night was only just beginning at ten!

10

Miss Emmie in the Country

Pervitino—the stress is on the beginning, as in *pervyi*, meaning 'first'—was the name of the Rahls' country house and estate near Staritsa, a medium-sized town on the Volga, more than a hundred miles north-west of Moscow. Emmie arrived there in the spring of 1913, and judging from a photo of the entrance and a rather muzzy postcard of the back of the house (all her other mementoes having been lost during the Second World War), what a fine house it must have been! Should we speak of it in the past tense? Perhaps it still survives as some kind of school or hospital.

There was very little traffic on the road from Staritsa. Twice a week the post was delivered to the estate post office, and whenever she heard the faint bell of the posthorses jingling in the distance, Emmie at once began to think of letters from home. The house stands over there, to the right of the road. You can see it through the tall wrought-iron gates at the entrance, beyond a circular gravel drive running round a large flower bed, where in summer the date is changed in pot plants every day: a white building of three storeys, very grand and solid, with tall, stately windows ranged along its first floor. In the middle of the first floor you step out of French windows on to a wide and lofty terrace that stands forward. The six columns rising from this terrace are Corinthian columns, elaborately carved at the top; the wide band across the top of the columns, with the scollop motifs on either side, is the entablature; and the flat triangle above that—could it be a coat of arms in the middle or is it just another elaborate decoration?—that is the pediment, the crowning glory of this very classical, very eighteenth-century building.

I asked Miss Dashwood to tell me what the different rooms were like inside, and she did so, but she was clearly not undertaking the task with quite her usual relish. Later the reason emerged. She felt all those questions were 'stuffy': why was it necessary to go into so much detail? 'I never thought of that place as a collection of different rooms. To me it was a *home* and I was happy there'—a remark which calls to mind what another young Englishwoman, Helen Clarke (of whom more later), wrote about the Russian estate where she lived for a number of years:

in that home with its large, cool rooms, with its wide corridors and comfortable nooks, you would feel yourself no stranger; for your welcome would be so sure that in less than no time you would be wondering if by any chance you had been there before.

The character of a Russian home, whether big or small, is enshrined in its inhabitants, not in bricks and mortar. Unlike the stately home in England, it was not over-furnished and contained few memorials to the past. The rooms of that grand house at Pervitino were there to be lived in; governess and children were given the complete run of the house.

On the ground floor were the servants' quarters, where the kitchen staff, the carpenter and the boilerman, lived and worked. A visitor to the house would be shown up a wide staircase—when the family was in residence, a red carpet was put down and pot plants placed on either side of the stairs—and asked to wait in an ante-room. The best rooms were on the first floor at the back of the house: the ball-room, drawing-room and dining-room. They all had parquet floors, lofty ceilings and very tall windows, with pelmets, curtains and upholstery to match in each room: lime-green and gold in the ball-room, gold and navy blue in the drawing-room. Elegant chairs were ranged right round the walls in the ball-room, except for the huge double doors at either end and the corner in which the grand piano stood. In the drawing-room there was a gramophone. Nanny was always being egged on by the children to ask Miss Emmie to play a record for them. Sporting Miss Emmie usually agreed: in England she was only used to the phonograph, whereas this was the very latest machine with a needle that didn't have to be changed. Then the door on to the balcony at the back of the house would be opened, and fat old Nanny would gyrate comfortably while Volodya and Irina, the two children, spun wildly round her. There was one other room of importance on the first floor: the 'English Room', which had previously been unused and which Miss Emmie now designated as a room where only English was to be spoken.

On the top floor were the bedrooms, including a number of spare rooms for guests. Miss Emmie and Zina, Mme Rahl's personal maid, both had big rooms of their own, but the biggest room by far was the nursery, where Nanny and the two children slept. A smaller room next to it, not used before, was turned by Emmie into 'Volodya's workshop'. Then there was a kind of staff sitting-room, where Nanny, Zina and Sasha, the nursemaid who came in daily, spent their free time—'and there always seemed to be plenty of time off in that household!' Nanny liked 'going to the kitchen', both figuratively and literally. Figuratively meant drinking her tea in the kitchen style by pouring some out on to a saucer, breaking off a lump of sugar with the clippers and putting it in her mouth, and sucking the tea in through the sugar with a very loud slurping sound. Literally meant sneaking off to the kitchen on the ground floor and dipping into the communal bowl in the middle of the table with all the downstairs servants.

Fat old Nanny sounds almost too plausible!—just like one of the numerous nannies and grannies, the *nyanushki* and *babushki*, so often described in Russian literature. She was a peasant girl, with the peasant name of Tatyana: Tanya for short. She had looked after three generations in the Tolmachoff family. As a young girl she had been in Moscow with Mme Rahl's mother, the *generalsha* (General's wife), and had helped to look after her during her final illness. She had been wet-nurse to Mme Rahl herself, who still referred to her as *kormilitsa*, and now she was looking after Mme Rahl's children. Like all Russian nannies she had grown big and stout and comfortable, and was always in demand to provide extra ballast for the triangular wooden snow plough, drawn by an equally heavyweight horse, which the family used for making paths through the snow all round the house. Her hair was combed straight back with a little bun. Occasionally Nanny might be persuaded to perform on her concertina, but mostly you saw her knitting, managing somehow to manipulate five steel needles instead of the usual four; and always she was knitting the same thing—large brown speckled man-sized socks.

Fortunately perhaps for credibility, however, Nanny was not quite a saint. Emmie liked to sit unobserved in a corner of the huge nursery when Nanny, impatient to join the others down in the kitchen, was trying her hardest to persuade Irina to go to sleep. Did you know that if you count sheep, it is watching the sheep *jump* that sends you off? Perhaps not. But after Irina had said her prayers, Nanny would start crooning a dreary lullaby, and every so often there would be a strange little upward lilt in her voice: 'By-you . . . by-you . . . by-you . . . *by!*' The crooning gradually became softer and less frequent until it died away altogether, and then Nanny would tiptoe silently over to the nursery door and turn the handle. . . .

'Again, Nanny! Again!' piped up Irina, and back Nanny would go, with little clucks and moans of frustration, and muttering fiercely to herself under her breath: '*Proklyataya devchonka!* Wretched little brat!'

The excellent English habit of daily walks with Volodya, already well established in Moscow, was enthusiastically transferred by Miss Emmie to the country. They always took with them, or more accurately were escorted by, Bandit (stress on the second syllable in Russian, Band*eet*), a St Bernard dog of massive weight and placid temperament. There was so much to see and do on the estate. For a small boy it made a wonderful natural playground at all times of the year; for a young English governess, used only to town life, it was a treasure trove of unexpected discoveries.

Immediately opposite the wrought-iron entrance gates, facing the house, stood a small white church with a cupola. To the left the road led to Staritsa; to the right, to the forest, though they never went that far on foot. By a stream on the forest road was the distillery, where vodka was made from the large quantities of pink potatoes grown specially for that purpose on the estate. On the same road was the granary, and when Mr Rahl accompanied them on their walk one day, he insisted that Miss Emmie should be weighed on the large scales by the granary entrance. Returning by this road, they passed on their left the post office and the estate shop or *lavka*, both only a short distance from the house.

Behind the small church was a churchyard, and a number of buildings were grouped roughly round the churchyard to form a square. On the right side of the square stood the priest's and deacon's houses, very plain wooden buildings with wooden steps and double windows, and next to them a hut which Emmie visited quite often, as the old woman who lived there was a wonderful seamstress and made her many useful garments. Her upstairs room was clean and tidy, but Emmie was startled on one occasion by a loud noise on the stairs, for she had not realised that the hens were kept in the room below all through the winter and had come up unbidden at their regular time to be fed. On the far side of the square, opposite the church, was a fairly large wooden chalet-style building occupied by the steward of the estate and his wife. A road running past the steward's chalet, away from the big house, led to the workers' hostel and a more distant peasant village. Emmie never saw the hostel: it must have been a large barracks, since whole families lived there, and she understood that as many as two hundred workers were employed on the estate.

On the left of the square stood all the farm buildings. Volodya loved animals, and no walk was complete without a visit to that part of the estate. An outstanding attraction was the Swiss dairy—in winter especially, as it was always so warm in there. Towards the end of their walk the same little ritual would be observed. 'Oh, Miss Emmie,' said Volodya, 'let's go and see the cows,' and Miss Emmie, after studying her watch carefully and giving the matter serious consideration, would reply: 'Yes, I think we've just got time.' Built on the Swiss model, the dairy was very up-to-date and always spick and span. Much of the milk went into a huge shiny copper cheese-maker and was turned into Gruyère cheese for market. Once when they were going round and the dairy seemed quite empty, they heard a great amount of mooing and lowing coming from one of the stalls. They could see a calf inside its mother's skin waiting to be released. 'Quick, Volodya,' shouted Emmie, 'we must fetch someone,' and she would have found it hard to say whether governess or pupil was more excited after the calf had been safely delivered.

Almost equal in attraction to the dairy were the stables. The 'red' or working stable housed horses that were used for work on the estate, while the 'white' stable contained about a dozen of the best horses, used only for driving. In the white stable they fed sugar to a venerable white mare called Generalsha: another General's 'wife', this horse being the one ridden by Mme Rahl's uncle, General Tolmachoff, throughout the Russo-Japanese war of 1904–5. Nikolai, the young under-coachman, was always pleased to see them. He had been given instructions to take them for a drive whenever they wanted, and they soon got to know their own two horses, Nabát ('bell' or 'tocsin') and Petúkh ('cock', 'rooster'). In summer the horses grazed in a paddock with a high wooden fence round it, and to give them sugar meant climbing to the second rung. Picture Miss Emmie, one hot sunny day, wearing a shady black crinoline straw hat from Bonds of Norwich, trimmed with foliage round the crown in a good imitation of real rose leaves. She reaches out to give one of the horses its sugar but as she does so, another horse sidles up and snatches the leaves from her hat, evidently thinking they are edible. Luckily Nikolai is at hand with coaxing words to persuade the horse to yield up its trophy.

After the stables and the paddock, they often returned to the house through the orchard, kitchen garden and greenhouses. Because of the rapid change from cold to hot weather, gardeners were unable to grow many flowers out of doors, so the greenhouses were always well stocked with pot plants, which could be put out in the summer or used to decorate the house. Near the greenhouses they were likely to find one of the estate's best known characters. According to the Russian custom with people who are very old or very respected, she was always referred to by her patronymic only, as Nikolayevna. Nikolayevna was reputed to be almost a hundred and would always be sitting on the same bench, wearing the same mauve dress and a small kerchief. They only ever saw her in summer; in winter she hibernated.

The Rahls did not return to Moscow for the winter of 1913–14 but divided their time between Pervitino and their much smaller town house at Staritsa, so that frequent journeys had to be made between the two homes, which were twenty-one versts (about fourteen miles) apart. It was on one of these journeys by sledge to Staritsa that Emma Dashwood had *her* frostbite experience. The temperature of − 21 °C. was not unusually low by Russian standards, but low for that part of Russia. They were all well wrapped up in leggings, turbans and *shoobas*, and in addition Emmie had a big driving cloak covering the whole of her. When they were settled, bearskin rugs were fastened over them and tucked in by the head coachman, himself padded like a great fat bear. As they sped along, Emmie's collar became white from her breathing and reminded her of an old man's beard. But somehow a draught managed to penetrate all those layers of warmth, for when they arrived at Staritsa, she immediately noticed a funny stiff feeling in the lower part of her left leg. At once Mr Rahl took charge of her. He hurried her into the garden and told the cook to massage the leg vigorously with snow. 'Now go indoors

and run up and down stairs,' he instructed her. 'Stampede about!
Bang your feet! And we'll get Volodya to chase round with you.'
Emmie knew when the circulation was coming back all right: the pain
was so excruciating. That most celebrated of Victorian writers on
Russia, Mackenzie Wallace, who spent six years in Russia in the
1870's, likewise suffered no serious injury from his frostbite experience: 'for some days,' he writes, 'my right hand remained stiff,
and during about a fortnight I had to conceal my nose from public
view'; and Emmie would have appreciated his characteristic comment that 'if this little incident justifies me in drawing a general
conclusion, I should say that exposure to extreme cold is an almost
painless form of death, but that the process of being resuscitated is
very painful indeed . . .'.

Emmie had two Christmases that year. Her English Christmas
was spent in St Petersburg with the Kerby Aunts, to whom she
presented a large Gruyère cheese from the estate, and they also gave
a party to celebrate Emmie's birthday on December 24th (she was
twenty-four) and that of Gertie Kirby (twenty-five) on the 26th. By
the time of the Russian Christmas on January 6th, Emmie was
back at Pervitino, not at all sorry to exchange the damp rawness of
St Petersburg for the dry cold, powdery snow and pure air of the
countryside. Decorating the tree was the most important part of the
Christmas festivity. A fir was carefully measured in the forest to fit
exactly into the space between the ball-room floor and ceiling. Six
enormous crackers, each about a yard long, were used to decorate the
top part of the tree. Down below there were paper lanterns with
candles inside them, so that when the candles were lit someone had
to be on watch all the time with a long pole which had wet cotton
wool on the end. On the lower branches, as well as tinsel and
drapery, there were all kinds of decorative things to eat. A large box
of apples, almost tasteless but very beautiful to look at, was ordered
specially from Yeliseyeff's in Moscow. Then there were dates, figs,
chocolates, *pryaniki* (little cakes made with treacle or honey),
baranki (ring-shaped biscuits) and the sweet fruit jellies which are
known in Russian as *marmelad*: pink or white with a hardish outside
and a centre rather like a marshmallow. Oh yes, and walnuts too. . . .
Miss Dashwood was never to forget the vast quantity of walnuts
that she and Volodya decorated for the tree at Pervitino—'goodness,
that job did keep us busy'. First you sharpened the end of a match-

stick and stuck it into the thinner end of the walnut to make a 'stem'. Then you took a packet of very fine gold and silver leaf paper and some egg white to act as glue. After dipping the walnut into the egg white, you carefully pressed your piece of gold or silver paper round it, so that it moulded itself to the exact contours of the walnut. Not only the gold and silver walnuts but all the other small objects then had to be tied with cotton and looped, and suspended from the tree by Miss Emmie and Volodya, since Vasya, the dwarf under-butler, could not do the reaching.

Emmie had told the children about the English Christmas, and how Santa Claus came down the nursery chimney and filled the children's stockings. This led to speculation about whether he might visit Russia. But there was a snag. The nursery had no chimney. There was only one in the whole house, and that was in the dining-room. 'I expect he'll realise this isn't England and he'll come just the same,' said Miss Emmie. She filled a couple of stockings and hung them down from the chimney-piece, and in the grate she left an old galosh with a lot of snow packed round it. 'Didn't the snow melt?' I asked, zealous for truth and thinking perhaps of those legendary Russian soldiers who entered Paris with snow on their boots; but she dismissed this feeble remark by saying they could still tell at a glance that he'd *been*.

Not Christmas, of course, but Easter was the important church festival in Russia, and for visitors from England the Easter service, with its intensely emotional atmosphere and richness of sound and colour, could be an unforgettable experience. Helen Clarke recalls Easter at St Isaac's Cathedral in St Petersburg. They went by carriage, but as they approached the cathedral, there was such a vast throng of people pressing against the carriage on either side that it began to sway and tilt ominously. 'Hold on for your life,' shouted her escort, scrambling up on to the box and taking the reins while the coachman jumped down to steady the frightened horses. Eventually they could go no further. 'Keep very calm,' Helen was instructed, 'put your arms round my waist and we'll force our way through.' In the cathedral everyone was standing. From time to time you felt a tap on your shoulder and someone would pass forward a candle, which you passed on to the person in front. At midnight, after the solemn announcement by the priest in his loudest voice that 'Christ is Risen', a great flare was lit on the top of St Isaac's Cathedral in

St Petersburg, while at the same time in Moscow the Kremlin cannons were being fired in a triumphal salute.

But for Scottie with the von Mecks it was the intimate atmosphere of Easter in the village church at Voskresenskoye that appealed even more than standing among the vast crowd in the Moscow Kremlin. 'It was a dream,' she wrote,

> to go to our little church on Easter Eve where the peasants had spread all their eggs and cakes round the church for the priest to bless, and then to go into the dark church and listen to the service. At midnight everyone came out of the church and walked round it three times, and on the stroke of midnight the priest knocked at the door, and when it was opened he called out 'Christ is Risen' and the congregation replied 'Indeed he is Risen'. The bells rang out and all the candles were lit inside and outside the church all round the cupolas, till it shone in the dark night like a wonderful jewel.

At Pervitino too, though the Rahls were not regular churchgoers, they would never have dreamed of missing the Easter service in the small white church with the cupola that stood opposite their gates. Easter preparations had begun in the house some time before: sprigs of pussy willow had been gathered and put in water so that the cat-kins should be at their best by Easter Day, lots of eggs had been coloured, the tall Easter cakes had been made, and the special sweet cheese pyramid prepared by the family.

The tiny church was packed, lit only by the candles held by each member of the standing congregation. When they came out after midnight, they saw all the tall windows of the house streaming with light. It was the first time Emmie had seen the gorgeous candelabra lit up in the ball-room. Here the Easter feast had been laid out on a very long table. Mr and Mme Rahl presented Miss Emmie with a bracelet as an Easter gift. Each kissed her three times, saying 'Christ is Risen,' and she replied 'Indeed he is Risen,' handing to each a coloured egg taken from the table.

But time was running out for Miss Emmie. In June 1914 she was due to return to England, having been away for two and a half years instead of the one year intended. The Aunts were booking her passage and had arranged for her to spend a few days with them before leaving. Emmie said goodbye to her pupil and his parents, who urged her to come back to them in the autumn; but she would not make any promises.

In St Petersburg the White Nights had arrived, when the sky remains light until morning. On such nights Louisette Andrews liked to be out enjoying herself with friends on the river, while Edith Kerby once sat up by her window all night reading *War and Peace*. Emmie shared a bedroom as usual with Aunt Annie, who nailed a large plaid rug across the window to help them to sleep.

There was one last surprise in store for Emmie. The city was teeming with British sailors: Admiral Beatty was then on a goodwill visit to Russia. After an official reception had been given for them by the Russians at the People's Palace (*Narodnyi dom*) just off Kronverksky Prospect the sailors came out and were met in the gardens by members of the British community, including, of course, the Kerby Aunts. Emmie revelled in the cheerful atmosphere. As souvenirs, the sailors gave her and Gertie black and gold hatbands with the name of their ship. It might almost, thought Emmie, all have been planned as a wonderful climax to her long stay in Russia.

PART TWO

II

'Der Tag'

In May 1914, when Emma Dashwood had already begun to relish the agreeable prospect of returning to her native city, the thoughts of another English girl, also from Norwich but a stranger to Emmie, were turned in just the opposite direction . . . and *her* thoughts were nothing like so cheerful. Standing by the rail of the familiar-sounding 'small cargo boat' that was taking her to St Petersburg, Rosamond Dowse watched her father's figure become tinier and tinier on the quayside at London Docks. She felt dreadfully alone, as well she might—for it was the first time in her life that she had been abroad, and she was only two weeks past her eighteenth birthday.

There seems, however, to have been a tradition of independent travel and responsibility in the Dowse family. Her elder brother, Tom, had once travelled on his own to stay with the Dreyfus family in Paris. The Dreyfus sisters—three very dark good-looking Jewish girls, daughters of Captain Dreyfus of the notorious *affaire*—were all pupils at Thorpe House, the private school in Norwich owned and run by Rosamond's parents. At the time of his solo visit Tom was just nine years old. Those were the days, of course, when passports were not required for any foreign countries except Russia and Turkey, with the result that several friends asked specially to have a look at Rosamond's before she set off.

It was thanks to brother Tom that she was going out to Russia. For nine years their Aunt Margaret (Mrs Goodier) had been a governess in St Petersburg to the younger daughter of the des Carrières family, and was now a teacher at the Smolny Institute, that very superior young ladies' seminary where her pupil had gone to 'finish'. On hearing of an aristocratic family in Simbirsk, now Ulyanovsk, who needed an English tutor for the summer of 1913, she thought of her nephew Tom, who was then twenty, had just taken his degree and was going on to study law before entering the Indian Civil

Service at the age of twenty-five. Tom enjoyed his Russian summer so much that he wrote home asking for permission to spend the winter there too, and found a job in Samara, now Kuybyshev, as tutor to Alexander, elder son of the Naumoff family. And when Mme Naumoff asked Tom if he knew of an English girl who would join the family in the summer of 1914 to teach English to the three older sisters, Tom at once thought of Rosamond, who was quick and efficient beyond her years and had already had some experience of teaching in her father's school. Rosamond was hoping to make music her career. She had accepted an offer from Miss Smythe, the dancing mistress at Thorpe House School, to be her accompanist at a dancing school which she had bought in Germany. The timing, it seemed, could not have been better, for the job in Germany was not due to start until October 1914.

The cargo boat was English, the first of the season, as the ice in the Gulf of Finland had only just broken up. At the entrance to the Kiel Canal, the German officials were rude and kept them waiting; already they were referring to 'der Tag', meaning the day war was to start. It was bitterly cold as they entered the Baltic, and when in her recent memoir, Rosamond Dawe (*née* Dowse) writes of how she put on every warm garment she had, yet still the wind seemed to blow through everything, one realises that there was no exaggeration in J. G. Kohl's description of governesses arriving in the 1830's, 'pierced through and through by the chill breath of a St Petersburg May'. The Customs officials paid no more attention to Rosamond's bunch of asparagus from the garden for Auntie than they had done to Emmie's rhubarb plants, but books—that was a very different matter! Auntie's husband, Herbert Goodier, was assistant to Dr Keynes at the St Petersburg depot of the British and Foreign Bible Society, and Rosamond had brought out a case of Bibles for him. Only after a fellow passenger had explained in Russian what the case contained did the officials agree, with some reluctance, to let her through.

Rosamond spent five days sightseeing with her aunt in St Petersburg. She kept on being scared by the large number of drunken peasants who lurched along the pavements day and night or tried to board the trams, where the conductor pushed them firmly along the gangway and off again. Then came a three-day journey by rail to Samara, via Moscow and Simbirsk—and wasn't she relieved when at ten o'clock on the evening of the third day she arrived at Samara and saw her brother running along the platform to meet her. As Naumoff House was full, she and Tom would be staying temporarily in a hotel—and great was her admiration as she listened to the fluent Russian with which he instructed the cabbies to collect all her luggage and drive them both there!

Next morning Tom took her down Samara's main street to Naumoff House to meet the family. M. Naumoff was Governor of the Province and Hunting Master to the Emperor at Court. His wife was the daughter of a very rich tea merchant. The three girls, aged thirteen, fourteen and fifteen, all had their hair up and looked very adult, and perhaps it was then that Rosamond decided she would have to insist on being addressed as Miss Dowse. They already had one governess. Mme Duburguet, a widow of about sixty, was a French Swiss and also, in defiance of all ethnic rules, 'a bit of a Tartar'. She had been with the family for nine years, and her nose had undoubtedly been put out of joint by the arrival of this very young English girl, whose salary of 100 roubles a month was almost certainly higher than her own.

Unlike the girls, who spoke no English, the twelve-year-old Alexander (Sasha) already spoke English well. His tutor before Tom Dowse had been another young man from Norwich, Harris Middleton, son of the vicar of one of Norwich's innumerable churches. The girls, Rosamond learned later, never took to Harris. Like Bazarov, the nihilist hero of Turgenev's *Fathers and Sons*, there was nothing he enjoyed more—and the girls less—than dissecting frogs on a bench in the garden. At dinner he was in the habit of kicking off his shoes, and the girls used to encourage their youngest brother to crawl under the table, pinch the shoes and hide them somewhere. Poor Harris would start groping round with his feet, not daring to stand up because his socks were always so full of holes.

After a few days Tom left Samara, as he had to return to England for his Intermediate law exam. (Rosamond was not to know that she would never see him again.) Once more she felt dreadfully alone and homesick, but there was no time to start moping, as Tom's departure was immediately followed by the Naumoffs' annual two-day migration by paddle steamer from Samara up the Volga to their summer estate. The significance of this event in the life of the provincial capital (population in 1914: 146,000) can be judged from the fact that the Police Commissioner came to see them off—with a click of his heels and a deferential salute, one imagines; and its magnitude, from the information that they took with them twenty-two servants, including grooms and coachmen, three horses, two cows, an unquantifiable amount of luggage, and to cap it all, a new piano for the girls, carried on board in a special case across the broad backs of two Volga stevedores, who were singing—yes—the Volga boat song to help them in their work! For the last part of the journey, when they had to leave the Volga and go along a small tributary, they transferred to the family's steam yacht, as the land was still flooded from the melted snow and they could steam right up below the house and garden.

In the hot dry summer of 1914 there was little to disturb the gentle rhythm of life on a remote Russian country estate. Frogs croaked by the river, nightingales sang in lilac bushes in the garden, and clouds of mosquitoes hung motionless in the air. Occasionally there would be a heavy thunderstorm, but otherwise there was no rain and cracks began to appear in the parched ground. Life for the young people followed a fixed routine. In the morning and early afternoon there would be French and English lessons with the two governesses, and—for the girls—painting and piano practice. At tea the various troikas and carriages would be ordered, and it was quite a large and colourful cavalcade that drove out later towards the forest along open tracks, leaving a great cloud of dust in its wake. The evenings might be devoted to tennis, or Rosamond would teach the girls to ride their bicycles, or else go fishing in the river with Sasha. After lunch on Sundays, if Monsieur and Madame were at home, they would take a picnic and cruise down their little river towards the Volga, while the girls took photographs or sang to their own balalaika accompaniments.

Visitors to the remote country estate were rare, but there was one important visit, of a kind that will be very familiar to readers of the nineteenth-century Russian classics and which gives us a fitting last glimpse of aristocratic country life in pre-War Russia. 'Once that summer,' recalls Rosamond,

a cavalry battalion on distant manœuvres passed our way and stayed over the weekend, so on Sunday evening the officers called on Grand-mother and asked if their band might play in the garden for the daughters and officers to dance, which was quite an event—I even got one dance, a Mazurka, with an English speaking officer which was fun, but he couldn't give me another as, being the Colonel, he had to chat with the old Grandma.

How peaceful it all sounds—the distant summer manœuvres, the regimental band playing on the lawn in front of the tall windows, young officers dancing and flirting mildly with the still younger daughters of the house, the English speaking colonel who might have stepped straight out of a Chekhov play or story, even the disappointed English wallflower—and how quickly it was all to vanish. By the end of July Russia and Germany were at war. On August 4th England declared war on Germany. Within a week or two that same battalion may well have been engaged in bloody battle on Russia's western front.

So 'the day' had come at last; and among the many millions whose lives were to be disrupted, how was the army of English governesses in Russia affected by the outbreak of war? Few of them, so far as I can make out, attempted to return to England during the early war years, though the North Sea route remained open—if dangerous, as witness the sinking by German submarines of the *Hampshire* on which Lord Kitchener was travelling to Russia in 1916. Why bother, they must have thought, to leave a good job and rush back to England when, as everyone said, the war was bound to be over within three months? And when the three months passed and the war was not over, it became clear that the life they were used to seemed to be continuing much as before; and on the distant estates you would scarcely have known that there was a war on at all. Better to stay put; though it was aggravating that news and letters from England were so heavily censored and long delayed.

Rosamond Dowse was advised by her father to stay on in Samara if the Naumoffs would have her, and since the Swiss tutor from Berne who had been engaged for Sasha was no longer able to travel, Madame was happy for Rosamond to take his place, while Mme Duburguet worked more with the girls. Like many English governesses, Rosamond was soon busy with voluntary war work. On the summer estate they seem to have started knitting socks and sewing shirts almost as soon as the first communiqués began to arrive. This was the kind of work that the briskly efficient Rosamond found very much to her liking, and she soon set up a record of completing a whole shirt in one day. Back in Samara Madame became Directrice of the local Red Cross. The Naumoff children used to put on play-lets for the wounded soldiers in hospital. The appearance of Rosa-mond, given a walk-on part as the maid or the nanny, was always the occasion for wolf whistles, which made the shy young English girl blush to the roots of her hair.

There were at least two English governesses whose contribution to the relief of suffering went far beyond either this kind of work, or the various forms of relief work organised in St Petersburg and Moscow by the British Embassy and the British community.

Prudence Browne, from Tipperary, had joined the Bobrinsky family as a governess in 1910. The three children, one of whom is my informant, 'loved the gay and very young Miss Browne right from the beginning and she was very much a member of the family'. In 1914 she joined a Red Cross detachment which was formed by the children's aunt, Countess Sophie Bobrinsky, and stayed with her in front line Red Cross work until 1917. She *nearly* married a Russian officer but in the end returned to Tipperary and died there quite recently.

Florence Farmborough, from Buckinghamshire, was twenty-one when she went out to Russia in 1908 as a governess, first in Kiev and after 1910 in Moscow, where she taught English to the daughters of a famous heart surgeon. Through him she was accepted as a Voluntary Aid at a hospital in Moscow, gained promotion to the rank of qualified Red Cross nurse and in January 1915 achieved her ambition when she was enrolled in a Front Line Surgical Unit. But of Florence Farmborough I need say no more, as she has given a unique account of her experiences in the recently published *Nurse at the Russian Front*—not the least remarkable aspect of which is that it was compiled, on the basis of original diaries, when Miss Farm-borough was already eighty-four. What is it about these governesses that makes them so extraordinarily robust?

When 'the day' arrived,˙Scottie having given up her job with the von Mecks, whom she continued, however, to visit frequently, was working for the Siberian copper company and living at St Andrew's House, the governesses' hostel in Moscow; Louisette Andrews, in her position as companion-chaperone to Kira Gagarin, was staying on the family's summer estate at Oberpahlen, near Riga; while Edith

Kerby, now twenty-two, was not far away in Pernau, a holiday resort on the Baltic. No one had a moment's doubt that the first priority of the German fleet would be to sail straight up the Baltic and raze unoffending Pernau to the ground, and there was a mad scramble to catch the last train back to St Petersburg. Edith was pushed through a window into the corridor and sat, wedged in on top of two 7 lb. pots of jam, unable to move a foot and nursing a small child on her lap, all the way back to St Petersburg. Her brother Harry had an even narrower escape. He had been to Germany for a throat operation, and only managed to catch the last steamer for Copenhagen by jumping aboard after it had already started. On the trip from Copenhagen to St Petersburg he noticed a man smoking a pipe who looked very English, so in his usual hail-fellow-well-met fashion he went up to him, slapped him on the back and asked where he was going. The man introduced himself as Mr Wilcox, former Berlin correspondent of the *Daily Telegraph*. He had been instructed to transfer himself to St Petersburg: a splendid scheme, but for the fact that he had no idea where he was going to live, and did not speak a word of Russian. Why not stay with me, suggested Harry, while you look for somewhere? And when in St Petersburg he introduced his younger sister, Edith, to Mr Wilcox, Harry turned to her and said: 'Flurry, you must know Russian as well as English, why don't you try your hand at translating for Mr Wilcox?'

Mr Wilcox looked a little doubtful. His attitude changed considerably, however, when he heard that she already knew shorthand, though she did not tell him just *how* she had come to learn it. He suggested a three weeks' trial. They took in half-a-dozen Russian daily papers and Edith had to learn up some military and naval terms, but translating itself was very simple and at the end of three weeks she found herself engaged as translator-interpreter to the official *Daily Telegraph* correspondent in St Petersburg. It was a vital step towards the fulfilment of that ambition of living permanently in England: an ambition which had become more like an obsession ever since an unforgettable summer holiday spent in England with her mother and sisters.

And what of Emma Dashwood? By rights she should have stayed safely at home in Norwich and become engaged to the young man from the Norwich Union to whom she had been 'unofficially engaged' for some time. But fate, as the saying goes, decreed otherwise; or rather, not fate so much as Emmie herself. When the war started, her young man volunteered immediately and left to join his regiment. Nothing was said between them about an official engagement; the times were too serious to think of personal matters like that. And much as she had enjoyed returning to the family and meeting all her old friends, Emmie was aware that life at home did not feel quite the same any more: two and a half years was a long time to be away and her sisters were all grown up now. She felt at rather a loose end. With her old friend and teacher, Mrs Nash, she went to Red Cross classes, and took notes, and bandaged a Boy Scout's head correctly, but somehow nursing didn't seem to be quite her line. Mme Rahl wrote to her frequently, urging her to return. It *was* a good job, she did want to go on teaching, Pervitino was her home too and the Rahls her second family. Gertie Kirby had been on holiday in England the previous summer and was now back in St Petersburg again. And Emmie kept on thinking of what Mr Stephens had said to her on the boat coming home from Russia. 'Oh, you'll be back all right,' he had replied, when she explained that she was probably returning to England for good. 'They all come back to Russia. They always do.'

And the danger? 'Well, I knew the Kiel Canal was out, of course, but I thought—how lovely to go by this *different* route hundreds of miles away from Germany and see all those wonderful new countries like Sweden and Norway. . . .' If she did have any last minute fears, they were quite forgotten in the great scare about her passport. Since Katie Sinclair was now married and living in Norwich, she had sold Emmie her trunk, and this trunk, already packed, was standing open in Emmie's room with her passport lying in the tray on top. Emmie returned home one afternoon from paying farewell visits to find that all her luggage had been collected for dispatch to the docks at Newcastle.

'Did you take out the passport?' she asked her mother.

'Oh no, I didn't know anything had to be taken out.'

An urgent letter was sent off to the docks: on no account was her trunk to be loaded into the hold! And what a relief when she arrived at Newcastle Docks, and the first thing she saw was her trunk, lying in solitary state on the quayside.

Emmie was travelling first class. Her uncle had insisted on this, since she was travelling on her own, and the Rahls had agreed to pay her fare of about 200 roubles. She thought of herself now as quite a seasoned traveller but had not been in her cabin long when an official knocked and wanted to know where she was travelling to. She told him. He looked at her.

'If you were a daughter of mine,' he announced gravely, 'if you were a daughter of mine, you'd go straight home—at once!'

'Oh, but it's perfectly all right. I *have* been there before and I know exactly where I'm going.'

The grave official looked at her again. He still didn't seem *convinced*.

12

Governess as Teacher

It was a surprise for the Kerby Aunts when there was a ring at the bell of their flat in Kronverksky Prospect one Sunday afternoon, and they found Emma Dashwood standing on the doorstep. Because of wartime delays, the letter she had sent off three weeks earlier to warn them of her arrival did not turn up until the following day. All five Aunts were at home and made her very welcome, but Aunt Annie was alarmed when she heard that Emmie intended to isolate herself in the countryside during the uncertain conditions of war and tried to persuade her to look for a job nearer them. But Emmie had set her heart on returning to Pervitino; and to Pervitino she went.

There were no obvious signs of war activity either in Petrograd—the new name for St Petersburg, which sounded too offensively German—or in Moscow, or on the estate. During the winter they spent most of their time at Staritsa, since the smaller town house was so much more economical, and it was only in Staritsa that the war began to seem real to Emmie. Soldiers in training were to be seen marching through the narrow streets of the town, singing their familiar wartime marching songs; the army mobile kitchen was another common sight, being pushed along by a small group of soldiers; and when the Volga became ice-bound, you could see soldiers fetching buckets of water from the ice-holes which had been specially cut out of the frozen river.

It must have been in Staritsa that winter, turning to less serious matters, that Emmie did not receive a proposal of marriage. The local doctor asked Mme Rahl whether it would be in order for him to make Miss Emmie a formal proposal. 'Certainly not,' was the prompt reply, 'she is engaged already.' And from that time on Emmie was always attended by a woman doctor.

Once the muddy roads had become passable again after the spring thaw, they returned to Pervitino, and there life went on more or less as usual. They saw very little of Mr Rahl, who had taken charge of a Red Cross train based at Kiev as soon as the war began. Many of the estate workers must have been serving in the army, but Emmie was aware of this only indirectly, because of the larger number of women working in the dairy and stables. Regularly each week Nanny and Sasha the nursemaid went off as usual to the estate bath-house, there to beat one another with birch twigs. Old Nikolayevna had come out of hibernation and was sitting on her seat, pleased to see them back again. One spring morning Volodya and Miss Emmie took up their position on a mound of logs, and watched the cows being let out for the first time after winter. It was an extraordinary sight. Emmie had never seen cows leap and gallop before—and what a noise they made, ringing their bells and lowing with ecstasy. Soon the family was able to take meals on the balcony at the back of the house, while on summer evenings, sitting on the terrace at the front, Emmie listened to the folk songs, accompanied by concertina or balalaika, which the peasant women sang as they strolled off together to the circular clearings in the woods where they held their traditional singing and dancing. Many of them had lovely voices which travelled a great distance, and Emmie sat on and on, waiting for the voices to rise and swell as their owners made their way slowly back.

On her return to Russia Emmie had resumed her English lessons with Volodya, who was now eight; and this is a suitable moment at which to comment more generally on what was after all the main purpose of the English governesses in Russia: to teach her charges English.

The Russian upper classes had long been proficient and adaptable linguists. Their own language was of no use to them beyond the borders of Russia. They could all make themselves understood in French as well as Russian, and it was not unusual for a nobleman to be fluent in English and German as well. What seems more surprising is that very often the *first* language learned by an upper-class Russian child was not Russian but French or sometimes English. Russian was felt to be of inferior status; it was the language of the kitchen, to be picked up in passing from nannies and servants; it was felt Russia had no culture of its own, but had borrowed its culture from Western Europe, especially France. True, there had been a strong reaction against this during the nineteenth century, when Russia developed its own cultural traditions and itself began to influence European culture. But we should not be surprised to hear of an English governess being asked by her six-year-old Russian pupil the names of quite simple objects in *Russian*; or to learn that in the 1920's Dorothy Cooke, who had been brought up bi-lingually in Russia, was engaged as a governess in the south of France to that young Prince Obolensky who was to achieve sporting immortality in 1936 when he scored the winning try for England against the All Blacks at Twickenham: a strange case of an Englishwoman engaged to teach a Russian Russian!

An upper-class Russian child might well therefore be highly proficient in French or English by a very tender age. This is made clear by Russian-born Mrs Anna Collingwood in a letter recalling her English governess around the turn of the century:

Her name was Louisa Sanders, she came from Folkestone. We lived at that time next door to the English church in St. Petersburg. I believe my mother made her comfortable & she must have had as good a life as possible in the circumstances. In return she performed her duties very conscientiously, she stayed with us 2 or 3 years and in that time taught me and my sister to talk English fluently and also to read & write, anyway she left when I was 6 years old and I was able to read on my own such books as *Little Lord Fauntleroy* and *Little Women* by L. Alcott. She used to show us pictures in the *Illustrated London News* to which my father subscribed and left us with vivid impressions of fighting in the Boer War and of Queen Victoria & her family. We were taught to remember the names of Queen Victoria's children and were duly impressed by the might and size of the British Empire.

But a price had to be paid for the ability to read *Little Women* by the age of six, and I do not only mean having to memorise the names of Queen Victoria's children. Mrs Collingwood continues:

Miss Sanders was not popular with my sister & myself, she did not inspire affection, I don't remember her ever being gay or mixing with our friends & relations. Her method of correction was to isolate the culprit on a chair perched on the nursery table and there was always at hand a piece of paper gummed on one side for the purpose of sealing my lips if I became too noisy. This, however, was only a threat and never applied but left a bad impression and we were not sorry when she left. Her reign in the nursery was peaceful if dull. Her age at the time was about 30, her hair black, her complexion sallow. To me she seemed an old woman and I resented her touching me.

Here we have it: the real-life counterpart to Chekhov's Daughter of Albion! Even their complexions are similar. But with due respect to my favourite author, it must be said that Miss Sanders is by far the more convincing character. The *Illustrated London News* and Queen Victoria's children carry more weight than lobster eyes and white muslin dresses. The landowner in Chekhov's story comments that the governess is always 'dreaming of a husband', and one might well see a connection between the strict regime imposed by Miss Sanders on two ebullient little Russian girls, and her own feelings of frustrated spinsterhood. It is in keeping with these Daughters of Albion, stern professionals that they were, that 'after she left we never heard of her again'.

Two other governesses known to Mrs Collingwood later, were members of the British community in St Petersburg and lived with their families:

They were quite different in character, much more gay and better mixers. But their accent was not so good, neither their teaching. One was called Miss Amy Carr and she used to come twice a week to keep up our English conversationally. Sometimes we were made to read Dickens or Walter Scott, but the rest of the time it was fun & games. She used to stay with us in the summer for long periods in the country—this was some years after Miss Sanders. The other lady was the governess of my cousins— her name was Miss Nina Smith. Both these girls eventually married in Russia and became our family friends.

Let us go back to Mrs Collingwood's earlier comment that Miss Sanders 'taught me and my sister to talk English fluently and also to read and write'. This order of importance—to talk . . . and also to read and write—seems to have applied generally. Being able to *talk* English was by far the most important requirement. It was a social rather than an academic accomplishment. Parents could take pride in listening to their offspring chattering away confidently in English to friends and relatives. To have read the classics of English literature was a desirable cultural asset, but socially not essential. Mrs Minorsky, whose father was a Russian diplomat, is scathing about her schoolmates who 'were mainly girls of well-to-do families (three generals' daughters!) but there was only one who borrowed some volumes of Dickens from me'. The writing of English seems to have been of least importance. We hear of governesses giving their pupils dictations, but translating passages of Russian into English or writing free compositions do not appear to have formed part of the governess curriculum.

In teaching their pupils to speak English our governesses relied on the direct method, whereby the child picks up a language much as he would his own: by hearing it spoken, imitation, and learning from practice and experience. Grammar plays no part, since the very concept of grammar is meaningless to a small child. Sometimes imitation could have strange consequences. Serge Obolensky's governess, Lizzie Arthur, spoke Russian with a rolling Scots burr, and her English accent 'could hardly have been surpassed by Robert Burns himself. The result was that I learned to speak English like some Russian branch of a Highland clan, which highly amused my English friends later on at Oxford.'

Miss Dashwood was appalled to hear of Miss Sanders and the sticky paper—and isn't it a condemnation of such methods that even after seventy or more years the resentment had still not been forgotten?—since she saw it as her main task to encourage Volodya to talk as freely as he liked. 'It all seemed to come quite naturally,' she recalls, 'with little effort noticeable on either side.' While Volodya was getting to know the English alphabet from English nursery bricks, Miss Emmie was busy studying his Russian bricks so that she could look things up in the dictionary. (But what was that strange word *topolok* which Irina kept using? Emmie couldn't find it anywhere. At last the penny dropped: it was Irina's childish distortion of *potolok*, meaning 'ceiling'.) They played games together in English: their own versions of snap and lotto, and all kinds of word and letter games; they got permission from Nanny to go and unlock the store-room so as to weigh things; and they visited the estate shop where they discussed the various goods in English before Volodya asked for something in Russian. But mostly Volodya picked up his English because he and Miss Emmie did things together, like going for long walks, not so much on a teacher-pupil basis, but more as English-speaking companions.

For their reading material they had some of the 'good old children's annuals', like *Chatterbox* and *Children's Friend*, chosen and bought by Mme Rahl from the English Shop on the Nevsky Prospect in St Petersburg. These annuals were quite expensive and hard to obtain in wartime, so each one had to go a long way. Beatrix

Potter was another favourite with English governesses. Sometimes the choice of reading material was even less adventurous. Mrs Minorsky recalls her elderly English teacher, Miss Turner, sister of Charles Turner, who had been Lector of the English language at the Imperial University in St Petersburg since 1864. 'She was a small, neat, retiring person whose lessons were limited to dictation, reading aloud from the *Royal Reader*' (widely used then in English elementary schools) 'and making us learn by heart pieces of poetry for our parents' namesdays and birthdays'—a frequent governess ploy, reminding one of Victorian girls having to learn their party songs or recitations. Under protest she agreed to a request from Mrs Minorsky's father that the children be allowed to read from Mark Twain's *Adam's Diary*: 'it shocked her Victorian sensibilities'.

Emmie was given an entirely free hand in arranging Volodya's timetable, but by the time of her return in 1914, Volodya had already begun other lessons at home in general subjects. His teacher was the estimable Marya Mikhailovna, niece of the old woman with the chickens who was such a wonderful seamstress. Marya Mikhailovna and her sister ran a school for village children on the outskirts of the estate. Emmie went there once with Mr Rahl. It struck her as old-fashioned and Dickensian: many of the pupils were wearing overcoats, there was chalk dust everywhere, and what particularly caught her eye was the hare's foot used for cleaning the blackboard. Always neatly dressed, Marya Mikhailovna arrived at the estate every morning to give Volodya his lessons in Russian at the desk which Emmie had set aside for them in her own room on the top floor.

It was important therefore, Emmie felt, that for a certain part of each day she should keep Volodya right away from any possibility of hearing Russian. Her chosen spots were either the English Room on the first floor, or in fine weather a rustic seat in the park. This seat was a decent distance from the house, it had the narrow river on one side and a pond on the other, and there was a lovely old overhanging tree to provide the necessary shade; in short, as Miss Dashwood now points out, with a lifetime's experience of teaching small boys behind her, 'it was an ideal spot for a child to concentrate without realising that he was actually working'. One hot afternoon they made their way to the seat as usual—but let Miss Dashwood go on with the story:

There we were having this lesson when a storm came on quite suddenly, we hadn't noticed it coming because we were under the tree. Of course, we both had light summer clothes on.

'Volodya,' I said, 'come along, we must run!'

We could both run jolly well, we ran like hares back to the house . . . just tearing along—we always did keep together. Then who should come *tearing* across to the house but the steward of the estate.

'Volodya, Miss Emmie: are they here? are they in the park?'

And the relief when he knew we were both safely indoors. He kept an eye on *everything* that happened on that estate. He knew where we always had our afternoon lessons—and the tree by our seat had just been struck by lightning.

The year is 1915. The sun is still shining for the Russian aristocracy; but a storm is moving up, the lightning will strike, and not everyone will succeed in finding a safe shelter.

13
My Little Englishman

Talking, reading, writing English; but is that quite all? Wasn't a Russian child, a boy especially, also expected to acquire from his governess certain English tastes and manners?

In the closing years of Tsarist Russia there was a fashion among the aristocracy to show a preference for what the novelist, Vladimir Nabokov, describes in his autobiography, *Speak, Memory*, as 'the comfortable products of Anglo-Saxon civilisation':

Pears' Soap, tar-black when dry, topaz-like when held to the light between wet fingers, took care of one's morning bath. Pleasant was the decreasing weight of the English collapsible tub when it was made to protrude a rubber underlip and disgorge its frothy contents into the slop pail. 'We could not improve the cream, so we improved the tube,' said the English toothpaste. At breakfast, Golden Syrup imported from London would entwist with its glowing coils the revolving spoon from which enough of it had slithered onto a piece of Russian bread and butter. All sorts of snug, mellow things came in a steady procession from the English Shop on Nevski Avenue: fruitcakes, smelling salts, playing cards, picture puzzles, striped blazers, talcum-white tennis balls.

Nabokov was one of those who learned to read English before he could read Russian, though on hearing of this, his patriotic father immediately called in the Russian village schoolmaster to put matters right. From his birth in 1899 until 1906, he was in the charge of 'a bewildering sequence of English nurses and governesses', to be superseded by a French Swiss Mademoiselle, who, 'as soon as she came, had taken me completely aback by patting my cheek in sign of spontaneous affection': something that his English governesses were obviously not given to. Miss Lavington and Miss Greenwood were the only English governesses who appear to have lasted for any length of time in the Nabokov household, but they were responsible for the—more tractable?—younger girls during the years leading up to 1914.

Tempting to speculate for a moment here on whether, among that bewildering sequence, there was one who implanted the seed that bore fruit many years later in Nabokov's dazzling English prose. We can rule out straight away poor myopic little Violet Hunt. Her brief stay with the family in Wiesbaden came to an end one day when 'my brother and I, aged four and five respectively, managed to evade her nervous vigilance by boarding a steamer that took us quite a way down the Rhine before recapture'. But what of the pseudonymous Misses Clayton, Robinson and Norcott? Miss Clayton encouraged her pupil to breed caterpillars (the experiment was unsuccessful) and 'when I slumped in my chair, would poke me in the middle vertebrae and then smilingly throw back her own shoulders to show what she wanted of me'. She cannot have disliked the job too much as she returned for a second spell, but does she really sound like a great lover of the English language, capable of firing her pupil with the same enthusiasm? Pink-nosed Miss Robinson was resourceful in the devising of sledging games in the garden, but soon went back 'to that ambassador's family, about which we had heard from her as much as they would about us'. Which only leaves Miss Norcott, 'lovely, black-haired, aquamarine-eyed Miss Norcott' (can she have been *English*?), 'who lost a white kid glove at Nice or Beaulieu' and 'was asked to leave at once, one night at Abbazia. She embraced me in the morning twilight of the nursery, pale-mackintoshed and weeping like a Babylonian willow, and that day I remained inconsolable. . . .'

Miss Norcott sounds more promising; for it was at Abbazia, trailing along in her wake, that Nabokov has the following recollection of himself:

As I crawl over those rocks, I keep repeating, in a kind of zestful, copious, and deeply gratifying incantation, the English word 'childhood', which sounds mysterious and new, and becomes stranger and stranger as it gets mixed up in my small, overstocked, hectic mind, with Robin Hood and Little Red Riding Hood, and the brown hoods of old hunchbacked fairies.

More prosaically, Miss Norcott subscribed to an English illustrated weekly (the *Illustrated London News* again?) but even she is not at all a strong candidate, no more so than Nabokov's own mother, who, before he went to bed, would often read to him in English in the drawing-room of their country house.

Alas for the honour of the English governess in Russia, no startling literary claims can be made on her behalf; and had I been less intent on wandering down Nabokov's beguiling by-ways, while at the same time embracing a few more—albeit mainly pseudonymous—governesses, I should have said at the outset that his dazzling prose seems to me to have the sharp, freshly minted quality precisely of one who has *not* had the edge taken off his language by the dulling demands of everyday usage early in life.

But to return to those 'comfortable products' of Victorian and Edwardian England. There was, as Nabokov writes, a 'snug, mellow' quality to those collapsible tubs, striped blazers and talcum-white tennis balls; they were solid and lasting, they spoke not so much of the might and size of the British Empire, as of a social stability and continuity that were quite absent from the Russia of 1905, convulsed by strikes, riots and peasant risings.

Yet in spite of the links between the Russian and English royal families—Tsar Nicholas was a nephew of Edward VII and cousin of George V, whom he closely resembled in appearance—the fashion for things English was not universal among the Russian upper classes. England and English ways appealed to the more liberal, free-thinking, forward-looking members of the aristocracy, not to the conservatives. Had it not been for the English constitution, I suspect that Tolstoy would never have taken on Hannah Tracey in the 1860's. Nabokov's father had been imprisoned for three months for his part in the protest against the Tsar's unconstitutional dissolution of the newly formed Duma, or Parliament, in July 1906. (He spent the time in comparative comfort and was even allowed to have his collapsible English bathtub with him.) The Liberal government of the day in England made no secret of the fact that its sympathies lay with the Duma rather than the Tsar. It was a sign of their liberalism that the Nabokovs read *The Times* and took a very English interest in such activities as cycling, archery, fencing, boxing, football and tennis: Nabokov and his father followed Wimbledon closely in the London press.

Whether Mr Rahl was a liberal or a conservative was the kind of question that Emma Dashwood would never have dreamed of asking herself. Clearly he had broken with tradition in not following his father into the army, even rejecting the conservative Russian beard in favour of a European-style moustache. That he was a man of progressive outlook is also suggested by the up-to-date conditions on the estate. Be that as it may, neither he nor his wife had any hesitation about giving Miss Emmie carte blanche to bring up their son in the English manner.

One of the first steps in this process was to make the Russian boy *look* English. Whereas upper-class Russian women traditionally bought all their clothes in Paris, fashion-conscious Russian males were catered for by the English outfitters in St Petersburg; and when Miss Emmie remarked that she thought Volodya would look nice in an English suit, Mme Rahl was not slow to take the hint. From her next visit to the capital she returned with a lovely suit of grey tweed, consisting of a Norfolk jacket—an appropriate choice, thought Norfolk-born Emmie—and knickerbockers, together with a tie and a quantity of Eton collars. These stiff collars did not worry Volodya in the least; on the contrary, it was he who always insisted on putting one on when he changed into his suit for lunch.

To create the atmosphere of an English childhood for her Russian pupil was a task that Emma Dashwood could throw herself into with real enthusiasm: 'after all, I was still quite a child myself then'. She discovered that the children had been given all kinds of expensive toys which now lay unused and neglected in different parts of the house.

'We must have a proper English Toy Cupboard,' she said to Mr Rahl, who readily agreed.

'How big do you want it? Would the stables be suitable?'

'No,' replied Emmie, 'it needn't be *quite* as big as that. I can have it in my room if you like, right along one wall.'

Shelves were built by the estate carpenter, with glass sliding doors, and everyone hunted high and low in search of all the toys and dolls they could lay hands on. Emmie knew exactly how she wanted it to look: like the window of Galpin's Toy Shop in the Royal Arcade in Norwich. The English Toy Cupboard quickly became a showpiece and relatives who came to the house were allowed to see it only as a special privilege. Among the rescued toys was a very expensive model railway, with a steam engine that worked on real steam and could only be operated by an adult. As so often happens, it was not son but father who became the enthusiast and decided that the track must be extended and taken into other rooms.

Volodya's workshop next to the nursery was the equivalent of his father's study on the first floor. At Miss Emmie's suggestion Mr Rahl had a proper carpenter's bench installed and bought his son a marvellous set of tools. Not that Volodya's carpentering was ever a very serious business: Miss Emmie could not instruct him, though occasionally they would see if the estate carpenter had a nice bit of wood to spare and ask him how Volodya could best make use of it. But the workshop was an ideal place for Volodya to mess about in on his own. Let him mess about and get his hands dirty for a change, thought Emmie, it'll do him good; and she turned the other eye and was even quite pleased when he started collecting mud pies from the garden in his wooden Easter eggs and turning them out on the carpenter's bench.

'Mazelle! Mazelle!' croaked Nanny urgently, hurrying in once in the middle of the night from the nursery into Miss Emmie's bedroom. 'Whatever is it?'

'Whatever's what?'

'The noise, the noise in Volodya's workshop.'

Intrepid Miss Emmie put on her dressing-gown and went to the workshop door to investigate, while Nanny hovered anxiously behind. There certainly was a very strange noise coming from inside: like some kind of toy engine moving rapidly across the polished lino, which at Emmie's suggestion had been put down in several rooms on the top floor so that the children could play easily right through them. Miss Emmie opened the door—and a small rounded object went skedaddling past, which they barely had time to recognise as a hedgehog. Volodya must have taken to heart what Miss Emmie had said about being kind to animals—and *not* like the butler who had offered to show Volodya the squirrel he kept in a cage—and decided to do the hibernating hedgehog a good turn by bringing it into the warm.

Soon after the war began, Volodya had been given a khaki tunic and shorts by one of his aunts, and playing at soldiers soon became a favourite pastime. In one of the English annuals he came across a soldier on duty outside his sentry-box, and this very much took his fancy. Why couldn't he have a sentry-box of his own, he kept imploring, until eventually Miss Emmie said she would ask the estate carpenter if he could make him one. As one craftsman to another, Volodya was always at hand to offer helpful advice, and it did not take the carpenter long to knock a few pieces of wood together. They placed the sentry-box on the gravel drive in front of the house and Volodya marched up and down to his heart's content, carrying an improvised rifle. The eleven-year-old Tsarevich was behaving in just the same way at Russian Military Headquarters, to which he had been taken by his father in the autumn of 1915.

All might have been well had it not been for the visit of Uncle Vasya.

It is a pity that Uncle Vasya should make a somewhat unsympathetic entrance into the story, since he strikes me as one of its most attractive characters. He was Mr Rahl's half-brother, a man in his forties, not very tall but well built, and unlike Mr Rahl with his moustache, he had a fine black Imperial beard. When, several years and many events later, he told Miss Emmie that he had decided to hire himself out as a coachman, she could not be quite sure that he was joking: he would certainly have looked the part. Uncle Vasya was not a rich man. He held an administrative post in Staritsa and wore a chain of office, had a smallish house there, and—so Emmie understood—a family of his own.

During Mr Rahl's absence, Uncle Vasya was in the habit of visiting the estate from time to time to make sure that everything was in order. Hearing the sound of voices down below one morning, Miss Emmie went across to the window of the English Room and looked out. There was the circular gravel drive and the flower bed, the wrought-iron gates and the small white church with the cupola immediately opposite, and in the distance, uninterrupted woods stretching as far as the eye could see.

In the middle of the drive stood Uncle Vasya, talking to one of the old gardeners.

'What on earth,' Emmie heard him say, and his naturally quiet cultured voice was raised higher than usual, 'what on earth is that extraordinary object over there?'

Emmie's heart sank. She knew exactly what Uncle Vasya was referring to.

'Why, it looks like—like a—like some kind of public convenience!' he exclaimed. 'Remove it!'

Miss Emmie was hoping to keep the news from Volodya as long

as possible. But hearing the sound of his uncle's voice, he too rushed straight across to the window. The worst was revealed. Volodya, of course, was inconsolable and not even Miss Emmie's most ingenious efforts could turn his mind to other things.

There were times when Emmie felt that Volodya had spent too much of his sheltered life in adult company and had become more obedient and submissive than was good for him. He needed to become more adventurous, to learn how to stand on his own feet. The mud pies had been a start; but not until the incident with Irina's bow did she really feel that he had entered a new phase of growing up.

It was an important occasion. Mr Rahl was paying one of his rare wartime visits to the estate, and he and Mme Rahl were due to arrive that afternoon. In the nursery there was great activity as Nanny prepared the two children for the homecoming. Volodya was no problem. He had changed into his Norfolk jacket and knickerbockers, put on his tie and Eton collar, and was sitting quietly. But Irina . . . no one, not even her mother, could have described Irina as a pretty child. Nanny had been doing her best to make the ends of her straight hair curl with eau-de-Cologne, and had pinned a large white bow on the curl at the side of her head.

'Mazelle! Mazelle!' there came an anguished cry from the nursery. 'Mazelle! Come quickly!'

What now? Emmie hurried into the nursery, to be told that while Nanny was out of the room, Volodya had taken a pair of scissors and chopped off the white bow and the large corkscrew curl to which it was pinned. Neither bow nor curl was anywhere to be seen.

'Volodya,' said Miss Emmie, 'I want you to take me *straight* to that bow!'

('I wasn't usually stern,' comments Miss Dashwood in retrospect, 'but he could see I really meant it.')

Volodya walked out of the nursery and went straight across to the washstand in Emmie's bedroom. This washstand was a fixed basin in a square table with a narrow tank above that was filled daily, and a cupboard underneath with a pail for the used water. He opened the cupboard door and there, lying forlornly in the pail, were the curl and the bow. Fortunately the pail had recently been emptied and the bow had come to no harm. There was nothing else for it: Irina's hair had to be swiftly parted in the middle and the bow made to cover the shorn patch. That was all right for the moment, but what would happen when Mme Rahl came to kiss Irina goodnight? Emmie determined to speak to her in advance and ask her to make light of it; she was anxious that Volodya should not be punished for his mischievous prank.

But that was not the end of the story. It turned out later that it was not Volodya but Irina who was the real culprit. It was she who had asked Volodya to cut off the curl and the bow: why should she have to wear the beastly things when he didn't? Not wanting to give her away, Volodya had taken all the blame on himself: a piece of 'standing on one's own feet' English behaviour which gave Emmie the greatest satisfaction. It no longer struck her as odd that Mme Rahl, watching her son talking away in English in his English suit, should exclaim with pride: '*Akh, moi malenkii anglichanin!* Ah, my little Englishman!'

14
Old Russia

Before her return to Russia in 1914, Emma Dashwood had seen little of Volodya's younger sister, Irina, who was still in the nursery. Irina seemed a more intense child than the equable Volodya. She often prayed earnestly by herself, having been taught her prayers by Nanny, who regarded her with a mixture of affection and exasperation, and looked forward to the day when she would be able to hand her over finally to the care of a governess. But Irina was extremely attached to Nanny, to the exclusion even of both her parents, so that Emmie was very surprised to learn that Irina had been praying for her to return from England. Apparently it was the music and the dancing on the balcony that had done the trick: 'she could see I was a playful type'.

Each morning Volodya was in the habit of going to greet his mother.

'May I come in, *mamochka*?' he would say, knocking on her door.

'Yes, come in, darling.'

Now Irina had never done this. Miss Emmie resolved to take a firm line. When Irina next came to her room in the morning and asked her to play, she replied: 'No, first go and say good morning to your mother, *then* you can come and play with me.'

A very reluctant Irina walked slowly down the corridor and gave a timid knock on her mother's door.

'May I come in, *mamochka*?'

Mme Rahl could scarcely believe her ears.

'Come *in*, darling!'

Irina went in and immediately burst into loud sobs. Later a similar scene was enacted with her father, who concluded that Miss Emmie had left Katya behind in England—Katya was the grumpy girl in the children's stories—and brought back their own charming little Irusha.

Leaving the nursery was always likely to be a painful experience. Mrs Minorsky recalls an English governess who 'was with us in Cairo where my father was Russian vice-consul in 1897–1900. She was a delightful person who came to us when I was four and my brother five and soon made me forget the tragedy of losing my beloved *nyanya*.' There was no tragedy for Irina. She did not lose her beloved Nanny and did not even have to start lessons, but she had taken the first difficult steps into the wider world outside the nursery. And Irina is the heroine of a story in which for the last time in this narrative, the outwardly untroubled world of old Russia is conjured up before us.

It was the fruit season, when fruit was picked and pickled (white currants, pickled in white vinegar, were delicious with cold meat) or turned into jam. Each summer by the pond a brick stove was erected, where Nanny made her jam in huge copper preserving pans. Raspberry jam was a marvellous colour and the whole raspberries tasted just like fresh ones. Another favourite was strawberry, made with the tiny wild *zemlyanika*, which gave a bitter-flavoured jam, firm and brownish-red in colour.

'You can't make jam *and* look after children,' grumbled Nanny, sensing a chance to be free of Irina for a couple of hours, and suggested that Mme Rahl and Miss Emmie might take the children out to the woods to gather strawberries for jam-making.

The light trap or tarantass was brought round to the front entrance. It had four wheels and was much faster than the two-wheeled vehicle normally used by Miss Emmie and Volodya (and which Miss Dashwood, I regret to say, has likened to a governess cart). Between the shafts stood Nabat, the children's favourite horse, black with patches of white. Away they went, with Mamochka driving. Nabat clip-clopped over the gravel drive and soon they were travelling smartly along a narrow track through the forest. On either side stood tall pine trees and birches with slender white trunks.

They drove for some time until they reached a part of the forest where Mamochka was sure they would find plenty of strawberries. Nabat was tethered to a tree in a nice grassy spot, and they set out, each carrying a small jar.

It was exciting work. No sooner had one of them discovered a good patch of strawberries than someone else would shout: 'Come over here, there are *lots* more over here!'; and they would all move on to the new patch. In this way two or three hours must have passed in no time at all. On several occasions Mamochka said they must think about going home, but when they looked to see how many strawberries they had managed to collect in the communal basket, the children insisted that Nanny needed *far* more than that.

Suddenly it began to feel chilly in the forest. Mamochka was adamant that they must go back straight away as they were all wearing only light summer clothes. She claimed to know every track in the forest like the back of her hand. But now, as they were about to make their way towards Nabat and the trap, she hesitated. They had doubled back on themselves so often that afternoon, and the trees all looked so much alike, that it was difficult to keep one's bearings. They set off along one track, but after they had been walking for some time, the track became narrower and finally petered out altogether.

There was no doubt about it: they were lost! Meanwhile it had become much cooler and darker. Until that moment Mamochka had pretended she knew where they were, but now it was obvious even to the children that they were completely lost in the middle of the forest, where they could be exposed to many dangers and no one would know where to look for them.

They all stopped, wondering what to do next.

Then, to their considerable astonishment, Irina suddenly knelt down on the damp grass—Mamochka was about to stop her but something made her hold back—and began to pray. She started by repeating the words she had learned from Nanny: 'O my God, help us' (*Bozhe moi, pomogaite nam*), and when she had finished, she called out:

'Where are you, Nabat? Nabat, where are you?'

She held her finger up to her lips. They all remained perfectly still. Nothing happened.

'Where are you, Nabat, where are you?'

Once more they were silent. Mamochka was just about to speak when suddenly they heard a high-pitched neighing in the distance. The sound took them all so completely by surprise that they could not be sure from which direction it had come.

'Again, Nabat! Again!' said Irina.

Another long pause. Then the high-pitched neighing sounded a second time and on this occasion they had no doubt from which direction it was coming.

15
The Old Regime

The English governess was not a political animal. Miss Eagar may have talked incessantly about the Dreyfus case, but even she, I feel sure, valued her job too highly to start discussing internal Russian politics. There must have been many governesses, like Emma Dashwood, who were completely ignorant of the subject, as sheltered from the social realities of life in Russia as the children entrusted to their care. With one voice they would have declared that Russian politics was no business of theirs, and that they had a job of work to do: a very responsible job too during the war years, when normal family life was so disrupted. To have started prying into social conditions on the estate where she was employed would have seemed to the English governess like the height of disloyalty. But if it is not until the eleventh hour that she begins actively to glimpse the state of revolutionary ferment in Russia, we can still see through her eyes many of those features of the old regime that were going to help bring about its downfall.

When Marie Russell Brown had arrived in St Petersburg in 1902 to join the Doctor's wild tribe of children, she had been immediately struck by the way in which wealth and poverty seemed to jostle one another. It was a city, she wrote,

where one section had the finest shops in the world with English and French-speaking salesmen and women, and only a short distance away dark little bread, sausage or meat buildings which showed their consciousness of dealing with an illiterate population by gaily coloured representations at their doors of the wares they sold. It was startling to come suddenly on a picture of several varieties of sausage at a door of what might appear to be the entrance to a cellar, but hardly more surprising than finding that Prince So and So's Palace was entered by a door at the side of a chemist's shop.

In the countryside wealth and poverty did not jostle one another in this way, but the contrasts could be even more striking. When they were staying on the Doctor's estate, Miss Mary occasionally went with the children to buy things at the village shop, whose whole stock seemed to consist of 'a bag or two of the soft sweet biscuit peculiar to Russia, a few household articles, and some loaves of black bread'. The village itself was

a sordid collection of miserable little dwellings huddled together in any sort of order. . . . The road, winding unevenly along by the village, was a foot deep in slimy mud although there had been little rain for weeks, and the hot sun only served to bring out unpleasant odours without apparently taking away any moisture. . . . A small child dressed in a tiny shirt reaching to his waist, stood ankle deep in the slime, gazing up with an expressionless face. He deftly caught the biscuit thrown to him by Natasha as she came out, but not a sign of emotion showed.

As soon as the first wild strawberries appeared in the woods, the peasant children were encouraged to gather them and bring them to the Big House. Scales were fixed on a table at one end of the verandah, and here the strawberries were weighed and paid for at a stipulated price per pound. One morning a woman arrived whose appearance was wretched even for a peasant, while the two children with her were thin miserable looking little things, who clung to their mother's skirts and looked wonderingly around them. (These two children, incidentally, would just about have reached maturity, assuming that they survived until then, by the time of the Bolshevik Revolution.) Madame weighed the strawberries in a business-like way and paid the woman, who went off with many protestations of gratitude.

Later that day Miss Mary went to the village with Manya and Ira, who had been given twenty-five kopecks to spend by their grandmother. She was leaning against the counter in the dark little shop waiting for the children's purchases to be wrapped up when a woman standing alongside greeted her:

I returned her greeting absently. Presently I was astonished to find that she had seized my hand and was vigorously kissing it, weeping all the while.

'Oh barishnia,' she exclaimed, 'God be praised for your goodness to me. Until I got the money for the strawberries this morning we had nothing to buy food with, and now we can have a good meal.' I recognised her as the woman who had brought the strawberries in the morning, and in embarrassment tried to withdraw my hand.

'But I had nothing to do with it,' I said nervously, feeling at a loss in the midst of this emotion. 'It was Barina who gave you the money.'

'Ah, it was all of you at the Big House,' almost sobbed the woman. 'It is so hard to see the little ones starving, and to have nothing to give them, and when Barina gave us the money this morning it was a gift from Heaven. May Heaven bless all of you at the Big House. Here are the children. Come forward little ones, and say thank you to the barishnia from the Big House.' She pushed forward the children, who curtsied shyly and then withdrew behind their mother's skirts once more.

I felt my heart contract with a dreadful feeling of pity and shame, for the sum that had saved the woman and her two children from starvation, and over which she was so grateful, was the exact amount that Manya and Ira were spending on sweets and biscuits. Never had I realised that the small sum of sixpence could mean so much to anyone.

After her turbulent two years with the Doctor's wild tribe, another eight years were to pass before Marie Russell Brown ventured back to Russia. In the meantime she had been working in Canada, and her return to England coincided with a visit from Russia by Aunt Lizzie Arthur, who had heard that the Countess X. was looking for someone to take charge of her two small children.

'It won't be anything like your last experience,' Aunt Lizzie reassured her. 'There are only the two children, the salary is better than I have had all the years I have been in Russia, and you will have six weeks in France.'

Poor Miss Brown! This time, it seemed, she must surely have drawn a winning ticket in the governess lottery; and the thought of basking in the sun at Biarritz among pleasant companions (Aunt Lizzie had often said how much she enjoyed such visits with the Obolenskys) was enough in itself to make her accept the offer. When they were good, like the Rahls and the Obolenskys, the Russian aristocracy could be very very good, with a kind of instinctive flair for human relationships; and when they were bad . . . they were like the family of Miss Brown's second job in 1912–13. But her misfortune is our gain, since we see through her eyes some of those qualities which so alienated the aristocracy from the Russian people.

To begin with, she had been engaged under somewhat false pretences. Once more she found herself having to perform the duties of a nursemaid rather than a governess. Anda was three years old, her brother Nicky less than one. Aunt Lizzie, recalling with horror the ordeal her niece had been subjected to in the Doctor's family, had told her to insist firmly on her rights. 'Now remember,' she said, 'whatever you do, you must never push a pram. There is always a nurse or a boy to push it.' But when Miss Brown arrived at Tsarskoe Selo, the 'Royal Village' near St Petersburg, and heard from Miss Annie, an elderly subdued Englishwoman who had been governess to the Countess and was now companion to the Countess's mother, all about the various duties she was expected to perform, her rights appeared to have been totally ignored; and she never felt strong enough to stick up for them. Many a time she pushed a pram; she had to wash and dress the children, and give them their bath; and when the foster-mother was no longer needed, she had to prepare the food for Nicky and to feed him.

None of this would have mattered to her greatly, had the Count and Countess been considerate employers and appreciated what was being done for their children. But an incident that happened not long after Miss Brown took up her duties revealed only too clearly her employers' attitude to their staff.

The family by this time was on holiday at St Jean de Luz, near Biarritz; 'and I never did have a chance', Marie Russell Brown comments ruefully, 'to see Biarritz during the whole time we were there'. One hot day the Count and Countess came down on the sands to say they were going into the country and would probably be away all night.

I wondered what they were making the fuss about. It was nothing to me if they stayed away all night. By this time the children's routine was second nature to me, and as their parents never did anything but come and watch them being bathed, I wondered why they were so insistent, and repeated so often that I was just to go on as usual, and they would be back tomorrow.

We finished our day, and at six o'clock collected our belongings and went back to the hotel. I was bathing one of the children when the door burst open and in came the Count and Countess. I went on bathing the child and made no inquiries as to why they had come back.

'We came back after all,' said the Countess, looking I thought a little disappointed at my want of interest.

'Yes?' I answered politely, and went on with what I was doing.

'It was too hot to stay,' put in the Count, evidently feeling that his wife needed some help. This did not seem to require an answer so I made none.

Something was making an impression on my mind, but it seemed so stupid that I could hardly believe it. Was it possible that the Count and Countess had been trying to trap me? That they had insisted they were going to be away all night merely to find out if I would neglect my duties? What did they think I would do? Omit to bath the children, or leave them with the others and go off to town? Later on I asked Marya, the Countess's maid, very diffidently, if it was possible they had meant to come back all the time. It seemed such a senseless idiotic trick to play.

'Why yes, they do that with all the nurses,' said Marya. 'That is why Grafinushka (little Countess) has had so many. They never believe anybody can tell the truth, because they never tell it themselves perhaps.'

Miss Brown felt justifiably incensed: 'such a thing as trust in anyone they employed seemed foreign to their nature. I had come with good credentials; members of my family were well known to two generations of the Russian aristocracy, and there was never the slightest ground for supposing I would not do the best I could for the children.'

But if this strain of meanness and suspicion in the Count and Countess is not, as she points out, necessarily Russian, then their preoccupation with social status does seems a more obvious product of the Tsarist regime. On arrival at St Jean de Luz, Miss Brown discovered that 'we were terribly exclusive':

We mustn't mix with any of the people further along the shore although this was the 'Russian Season', and there were probably plenty of the Countess's acquaintances with their children among the groups in front of the row of tents, where the children played with each other, and their governesses exchanged gossip and crochet patterns.

So our tent was pitched on the sand just below the hotel, away from any other tent, and here we lived from eight in the morning till six at night. The children never even went inside for meals which were brought to them.

Just above the tent was the road, and people would come and lean on the railing and look down on us as if we were a show. We must have been a curious sight with three of us attending to two small children. We were not allowed to sit inside the tent, but only in the shade of it, so that we were always on view. But one becomes used to anything in time I suppose, even to ten hours daily on the sands in view of the multitude.

But at least it was a novel experience to be told by the head waiter that 'you and the Queen of Spain are the only Englishwomen in the hotel'. King Edward VII had also stayed there several times: 'a very nice gentleman'.

Later, on the journey back to Russia, Marie Russell Brown had another revealing insight into the status-conscious, role-playing nature of the old regime. She had previously been aware of the Count only as a rather diminutive figure who trailed in behind the tall young Countess to watch the children being bathed and seated himself on the chintz-covered divan, 'staring vaguely at the bath, at the children, at the walls, and occasionally addressing a remark to his small daughter'. But somewhere in the train between Warsaw and Kiev the count had changed into uniform:

He was now a Russian General, and his very demeanour seemed to have changed with his clothes. He was an important officer as could be gathered from the deep bows and respectful servility with which he was treated on the platforms of the stations. His voice was curt, and he issued orders in a tone that brooked no contradiction. It was evident he was on his own ground.

The journey from St Jean de Luz, near the Spanish border, via Paris, Vienna and Poland, was a long and trying one for Miss Brown, with two small children to look after; but she would never have dared say so out loud, for 'it was regarded almost as a sin for an employed person to be tired or ill, and one never knew who was listening'. The Countess had suddenly announced one morning that they were returning the same night, giving Miss Brown no time for advance packing. This lack of any time sense irritated her, but all the members of the family were quite unreasonable in this respect, none more so than the Countess's mother, to whose vast estate in the Ukraine they were now travelling before returning to Tsarskoe Selo. Marie Russell Brown had been carefully briefed by Miss Annie before her first meeting with this autocratic *grande dame*: 'I must stand when Madame appeared, and on no account was I to speak or even appear to see her unless she spoke to me. All very silly I thought, but interesting as a relic of a bygone day.' (Miss Brown, of course, was not long back from democratic Canada.) A single piercing glance was all that Madame bestowed on the new English governess at their first meeting.

In time Marie Russell Brown came to feel that there was something about Madame that drew from her 'an almost unwilling affection'. This slender dignified woman of sixty, capricious, chain-smoking and very much the holder of the family purse strings, was not without charm and humour, and could be kind and generous when it pleased her; but she was peremptory, unreasonable and overbearing, and very few days passed without trouble or tears for someone. 'Reasonable, reasonable, how you harp on that word,' Miss Annie snapped irritably one day. 'Nothing is reasonable in this house, and it never will be.' Miss Annie was liable to come into the nursery at any moment, for one of her duties was to spy on the other members of the staff and make sure they were obeying instructions implicitly. 'You think you have a trying life,' she said one evening when they were alone together in the nursery,

but you have a recognised position. When the children are in bed you are free to occupy yourself as you like, or you can go to bed. Last night I read aloud to Madame and Natalie while they played Patience till my throat was sore. Every time I stopped reading one or other would say 'What are you stopping for?' It was two o'clock before I went to bed. They can sleep till twelve, but Madame expects me to be up seeing that the servants are doing their work.

With characteristic suddenness Madame announced that they would all be leaving in three days' time, and on the appointed morning quite a crowd of servants and estate workers with their wives and children gathered in front of the house, 'for the departure of Madame like her arrival was an event in the lives of these people'. Opposite Miss Brown stood 'a group of the workers' children staring at Anda, while she stared back at them, like the inhabitants of two different worlds. . . . There was a stir in the crowd and all eyes turned towards the steps where the principals of the play were coming on to the stage.'

But before Miss Brown had time to observe Madame's Royal Progress, Miss Annie came hurrying up, in a fever of excitement as usual, and told her to go at once with Anda to Madame's carriage as they were to travel with her. An alarming prospect! But fortunately Madame was in one of her charming moods and kept them both entertained with her remarks. Presently they approached a village:

a ramshackle assortment of huts from which most of the inhabitants had emerged and were lining the roadside, waving, bowing and cheering as we passed. It was evident the villagers had been awaiting our arrival. The carriage slowed down.

'Now Anda,' exclaimed Madame. I put down the window, and Anda who had been told by her grandmother what to do, began to throw out sweets, with my help as her hands were too small to throw many at a time.

The same procedure was followed at the next two villages but at the fourth there was an interruption. The horses suddenly reared up in fright: a peasant woman had thrown herself in front of them. Madame was beside herself with fury at this affront to her good horses and angrily summoned the woman to her.

But she had not waited to be fetched. She was there, elbowing the footman out of the way, and clinging to the door with clawlike fingers, screeching at the top of her voice: 'My daughter lies with a newborn babe. No warm clothing has the child, no food the mother. Help us your Highness.'

Madame seemed quite unmoved by the old woman's pleading:

'Tell Josef to drive on,' she ordered the waiting footman. 'Do you imagine I pay stewards so that every whining *baba* who thinks she does not get enough attention should come to me with pitiful tales?' she inquired of the woman who stood silent and dejected. 'I should never be doing anything else but listen to them.'

With a sudden change of mood and tone she addressed the woman once more.

'Go up to the steward's house and tell him I order him to see that your daughter and her child have all they require. And here is some money for you. No, I won't have my hand kissed, and you can keep all these blessings for someone else.'

At Tsarskoe Selo life was less eventful, since Madame had returned to her own residence in St Petersburg. Every morning Miss Brown and Annushka, the nursemaid, took the children to the Catherine Park and more than once they saw the Tsar's young family out driving. The four girls were jolly and laughed among themselves, but the Tsarevich was a sedate little boy, and 'although he bowed and smiled politely in answer to salutations, was evidently of a serious disposition, and had a strong sense of dignity'. In the Catherine Park Miss Brown made a friend. Miss Jackson had been a governess in Russia for fifteen years and delighted in telling gossipy stories of high life among 'the nobles', sitting in the evenings over tea and biscuits in Miss Brown's upstairs room next to the children's bedroom.

Madame arrived to spend Christmas and gave everyone handsome presents, but it was a lifeless formal affair and no one seemed particularly interested, not even the children. Did Marie Russell Brown's mind perhaps go back to that first Christmas in the Doctor's family which, whatever else she might have said about it, could never have been described as lifeless and formal? Strange to reflect that she had after all stayed the course with her wild tribe, whereas now the idea of living this restricted life for any length of time was unthinkable, however cushioned in luxury it might be. She could see herself turning into a second Miss Annie. Even Miss Annie had said to her once: 'Go home before it is too late. There are openings now in England for women that were not there in my day.'

Some time before her departure the Count and Countess gave a party. The orchestra was expensive and there was a wonderful singer. Miss Brown was not invited. Sitting in her upstairs room listening to the faint strains of the orchestra, she found herself pondering on the difference in people's lives. Take the Countess and Annushka, the nursemaid. Why had Annushka lost her previous job as a lady's maid? Because she had dared to complain that her mistress's husband had been bothering her. They had warned the people they knew not to employ her, and she had only found her present job because nursemaids were more difficult to obtain than ladies' maids. Now, even though she was counted as an upper servant and ate at the Count's table, she was always served after the governess, the housekeeper and the lady's maid, and could not even be sure there would be anything left by the time the dishes reached her.

All the same, Marie Russell Brown concluded,

I would not willingly have changed places with the Countess in spite of her beauty, her opportunities or her money, though the immense gulf between the Russian people and those whom Miss Jackson called 'the nobles' could not be denied.

'What is there for us?' Annushka had asked me once, not expecting any definite answer. 'We might as well be dead.' Born in a poverty-stricken home, with scarcely any education and few chances of improving her lot, yet a clever intelligent girl, in another country she might have made her way through school and university with the aid of scholarships and risen to an important position. Here she would never be allowed to be anything but a servant. And the Countess? Born evidently to be waited on hand and foot she took this service as a divine right, was arrogant, unreasonable and often unjust. The world had been made for her and her kind, she might have said, and believed her words.

16

Worlds Apart

Reading Marie Russell Brown's account of her experiences in Russia, one stops and wonders: can this really be the twentieth century that she is describing? The images of children especially catch one's attention and seem to belong to a much earlier age: that primitive little boy, standing ankle deep in the slime of the village street, deftly catching the biscuit thrown to him but showing no sign of emotion; the stunted couple, clinging to their mother's skirts, for whom twenty-five kopecks meant the difference between eating and going hungry; Anda and the estate workers' children, staring at one another 'like inhabitants of two different worlds'; and those children scrambling in the dust for sweets thrown out from the grand carriage as it slowed down to pass through their village. Madame herself reminds us of some medieval autocrat, deciding her subjects' fates according to the whim of the moment: was it only, one wonders cynically, the presence of her granddaughter and Miss Brown that made her change her mind towards the peasant woman who had had the impertinence to throw herself in front of her wonderful horses?

Medieval autocrats could still survive in Russia, even in 1912, for the peasants came out to wave and bow and cheer, and may well have believed that life would be even worse without her; but how shaky Madame's position will look, once those feelings of fatalistic resignation begin to alter. As for the attitudes attributed by Marie Russell Brown to the Countess—her divine right to be waited on hand and foot—here we are confronted by the philosophy of reaction in its most undiluted form. When the Revolution came, those who upheld this philosophy would be among the first to flee the country or to lose their lives through the intervention of some slighted, revengeful Annushka.

But what of the more forward-looking, well-meaning representatives of the aristocracy?

It could not be said of the Rahls, for example, that they were unreasonable and overbearing, or inconsiderate towards their employees, or that they failed to place the most complete confidence in their English governess. Unlike Rosamond Dowse's employer who, when her young son began rolling gold five- and ten-rouble pieces along the floor, told her not to bother to retrieve them, they were not irresponsible about money, nor extravagant in their tastes; they did not flaunt their wealth; nor was there any trace in them of that wild, degenerate streak to be seen at that time in the upper-class preoccupation with spiritualism and the occult, in fashionable homosexuality, and in a high incidence of broken marriages, suicides and mental breakdowns.

Yet the Rahls too were exclusive; and it is hard to imagine how it could have been otherwise, given their basic acceptance of the Tsarist social system. As a Marshal of Nobility, Mr Rahl was second in importance only to the Governor of the Province, and so they had no social equals in the district. Only once can Emma Dashwood remember them paying a social visit: to a house in Staritsa for the traditional Shrove Tuesday pancake lunch. Nor did any visitors come to stay at Pervitino other than members of the family. One memorable visit was that of Mme Rahl's uncle, General Tolmachoff, and his son, which took place some time before May 1914 (we can be sure of this date, since he presented her with a purse, and in the summer of 1914 she had it stolen on an outing to Great Yarmouth). Apart from his niece and her husband, the General had also come to see his old white horse, Generalsha. Emmie found him most entertaining, but his arrival was the occasion of an unfortunate social gaffe on her part. Remembering the lesson that Edith Kovalsky had impressed upon her at the start of her stay in Russia—'watch other people and do as they do'—she noticed that Mme Rahl remained seated when the General came into the room, so she did the same. But Mme Rahl had only remained seated *as a married woman*; and in failing to rise Miss Emmie had been guilty of a breach of social etiquette that was quietly pointed out to her later.

Neither the steward of the estate, nor his wife, whose face Emmie could scarcely be sure of recognising, nor the village priest, nor even Marya Mikhailovna, though she came regularly to give Volodya his lessons, ever received any form of hospitality at the house. There was one occasion, however, when they did give a dinner party at

Pervitino. The guests were a dozen or so of the *zemskii nachalniks* from the district (*zemskii nachalnik* was the position which Mr Kovalsky had occupied, as head of a *zemstvo* or local rural council). Mme Rahl was away, so Miss Emmie had to act as hostess, wearing the same long blue dress that Mme Rahl had passed on to her in Moscow at the time of her first visit to the ballet. She had to welcome all the visitors in Russian and felt very important, sitting at one end of the long dining-room table, while Mr Rahl presided at the other end. There was black and red caviare, and an unusual vodka brought out specially for the occasion. But though Miss Emmie did her best to make conversation, it sounds a formal, dutiful affair, and none of the guests was asked to stay the night.

As for Volodya, he had no friends at all of his own age. This was why he attached himself so completely to his English governess: 'he seemed to feel that he belonged to me somehow . . .', comments Miss Dashwood, 'regardless of age we became good friends'. But she would be the first to agree that a small boy needs companions of his own age as well.

When Emmie first arrived at Pervitino with the Rahls in the summer of 1913, she had the feeling that 'we were almost like visitors coming to them'; and time was to strengthen the impression that 'we were living in a world *apart*'. The family was cut off from the downstairs servants, who ate in the kitchen and whose quarters she never saw; from the staff working in the gardens and green-houses, who, she felt, 'were shy and wouldn't have wanted to know me'; and even more from the permanent workers on the estate, and the hired hands taken on during the summer months only, when work on the estate was at its heaviest.

If there seemed to be no obvious friction between the family and those beneath them in the social hierarchy, this was because each kept itself to itself, recognising that 'we have our lives to lead and you have yours'. If we do our best by you—as Mr Rahl seems to have done by his employees, for working conditions on the estate sound very modern and Emmie never saw the slightest hint of poverty or ill-treatment—then we expect you to do your best by us. And here one sees the vital importance of the estate steward as a kind of insulator between employer and employees. Emmie was aware that the Rahls leaned very heavily on their steward, who is the one person who *must* interfere in other people's lives, telling them what to do and making sure they do it. It may have been for this reason that the best stewards were so often foreigners, uncommitted outsiders; the steward at Pervitino spoke Russian well but was not Russian by birth.

This agreement not to interfere too much in one another's lives worked very smoothly in the case of the household staff. Emmie was impressed by how independently they lived: each person seemed to know his own job and to go about it quietly, no orders needed to be given, there were no maids in uniform scuttling about because some-one in the house had rung a bell demanding attention; and yet every-thing seemed to run pleasantly and efficiently, and the staff were never short of time to themselves.

One small incident described by Miss Dashwood shows how trouble might arise if the different worlds were *not* kept strictly apart. Nikolai, the young under-coachman, had instructions to take Miss Emmie out driving whenever she wanted. Emmie counted him a good friend, for he seemed to enjoy the frequent drives in the country with her and Volodya as much as they did. One day she sent for him to drive her to a nearby village to see her dressmaker. But she had forgotten, or perhaps did not know, that it was one of those numerous Russian saints' days when no work was done. Nikolai was entertaining visitors. He was not at all pleased to be called away from his guests and Emmie felt that she had made a bad blunder.

The problem of the gulf between the aristocracy and the people, between the educated class and the uneducated, had exercised many famous minds in nineteenth-century Russia. But the attempts by well-meaning people to bridge this gap were liable to meet with an unexpected resistance, as Chekhov shows in several of his short stories. When Marie Russell Brown writes of Annushka that in another country she 'might have made her way through school and university with the aid of scholarships and risen to an important position', she is assuming that Annushka would have *wanted* to climb this kind of social ladder. This was not necessarily so. One summer at Pervitino, among the peasant women who went off every evening to the circular clearings in the woods to sing their tradi-tional songs, there was one girl whose voice was truly outstanding. She was a laundress, engaged for the summer only and probably from Moscow, as these laundresses were always short of work in the summer when the rich families left the big cities. Auntie Milochka,

Mme Rahl's sister, herself a good singer, was staying at Pervitino and offered to pay for the laundress to have a proper voice training in Moscow. But the girl refused: she had no wish to change her way of life, however limited its horizons.

And here one thinks too of old Nanny, who had been an upstairs servant for many years and would have been entitled to have meals served to her in her room, but whose great delight it was in life to sneak down to the kitchen and dip into the communal bowl.

What happened to Mme Rahl and her plans for a peasant crèche would have provided excellent material for a Chekhov short story. Mme Rahl had made it known that if her first-born child was a son, she would do something to help the children on the estate. After Volodya's birth she decided to build a crèche where the peasant babies and infants could be left and looked after during the day while their mothers were working. A solid wooden building was erected with small hammocks for the babies to sleep in, a full-time nurse was engaged, and the opening of the crèche was scheduled for May 1st, 1914. In the preceding weeks Mme Rahl and Miss Emmie spent hour after tedious hour embroidering the word *yasli* ('crèche') on a vast quantity of babies' nappies; the word imprinted itself on Miss Dashwood's memory for all time.

But when May Day arrived, there was an anti-climax. 'I don't think there was a row or anything like that,' recalls Miss Dashwood, 'but I do seem to remember a group of women coming to the estate . . . and anyway, the upshot of it all was that they didn't want anything to do with the new crèche. They preferred to go on just as they always had done.' Mme Rahl was very disappointed. 'We've done all this for them,' she grieved, 'we've gone to all this trouble, and now they don't want it.'

It is not hard to see those glaring defects that helped to undermine the old regime in Russia: the extremes of wealth and poverty, of culture and ignorance, the selfish abuse of wealth and privilege, the social exclusiveness and lack of contact between classes. But the old regime was also undermined in a more subtle way—by this popular resistance to all change and interference, however well-meaning, from above. It was the legacy of centuries of serfdom, and it was a formidable obstacle in the way of gradual non-violent social evolution.

Not until the summer of 1915 did Emma Dashwood first come

into direct contact with the revolutionary stirrings just beneath the outwardly calm surface of life in the Russian countryside.

With Mme Rahl and the two children she had been attending Sunday morning service at the small white church with the cupola. As they were coming away, Mme Rahl said: 'You've never seen them picking the potatoes, have you, Miss Emmie? Let's drive out with the children and go and watch them.'

The four of them took their seats in the trap, drawn as usual by the children's favourite horse, Nabat. The potatoes being harvested were the pink ones used for making vodka. It was very hot. The men were in shirt sleeves and the women in cotton dresses and bright kerchiefs, and they all moved in one long straight line across the fields, picking row by row.

The family were sitting quietly in the trap when without warning a man suddenly appeared from the direction of the fields and began trying with all his strength to overturn the trap with the four of them in it. Emmie could not catch exactly what he was saying, but its general message was very clear: how dare they come and watch the potato-picking, flaunting all their fine clothes and sitting back in luxury in their comfortable carriage! The man had obviously been drinking. Luckily the foreman in charge of the pickers saw what was happening and came racing across at top speed. He managed to restrain the man and calm him down; then he caught hold of Nabat, who had been badly frightened, and calmed him down as well. The horse seemed to know the foreman and responded quickly. They recognised him as one of the workers on the estate, who told them that the drunk was not an estate worker but one of the hired summer labourers.

Emmie never heard Mme Rahl allude to this incident again. Had Mr Rahl been told of it, he might have thought his wife had acted rashly in driving out unaccompanied to the fields in the first place.

When Emmie told the story to the Aunts on her Christmas visit of 1915, they were quite adamant. They would not dream of letting her go back to the estate. This time she took their advice.

17

Turn of the Year

There comes a single brief period when Edith, Scottie, Louisette, Rosamond and Emmie must all have been in the same city at the same time. The city is Petrograd; the time—the turn of the year 1916–17.

Since 1914 Edith Kerby had become more and more absorbed in her job as assistant to Mr Wilcox of the *Daily Telegraph*. She soon added typing to her shorthand accomplishment, and they both worked very hard in their small office in Singer House on the Nevsky Prospect, carefully studying the Russian press and following the course of the war on one-inch maps. But as the war continued, their attention was constantly being diverted towards the political situation inside Russia. They became regular attenders at the Duma, where Edith took down the members' speeches in shorthand. On one occasion there was a terrific scare inside the Duma building. Proceedings were suddenly interrupted by a loud crash of splintering glass. In the highly charged atmosphere of the times, the same thought passed through everyone's mind: 'This is meant for *him*!' No matter that the Tsar's hostility to the Duma was well known and his presence there most unlikely—everyone still jumped to the conclusion that for some reason he must be in the building and that an attempt had been made upon his life. But once the panic had subsided, it turned out to have been nothing more serious than a spectator leaning too heavily on a pane of glass.

During 1916 the speeches in the Duma, especially those of Kerensky, became increasingly inflammatory, but not a word of this was ever allowed to appear in the Russian press. When Mr Wilcox tried to send off his dispatch on the day's proceedings, the censor would let none of it through, and by the autumn of 1916 this problem had become so acute that Lord Burnham decided to recall Mr Wilcox to London, in order to find out at first hand just what was going on in Russia.

So Edith's job came to an end, but she had been well paid during those two years, and in sterling too. Her promised land of England was inaccessible because of the war, but true to the Kerby tradition of enterprise and self-reliance, she now conceived the adventurous idea of going off alone on a trip to China and Japan, and visiting her married sister in Shanghai. This was the sister who had outraged their father, Henry William Kerby, by insisting on travelling out unaccompanied to China after an engagement that had already lasted seven years. Times had changed to the extent that Edith's mother did not object to her travelling alone, but did insist on her travelling first-class. Then came anti-climax: Thomas Cook could not give her a booking until January 1917 and this was only November. Every day the food shortage in Petrograd was becoming more critical. 'We stood thirteen hours in a queue for our black bread, and even so, often came away without any, as it was all sold out. We never saw meat or butter. We lived on buckwheat porridge and cereals of different kinds.' But at last the long-awaited January day arrived. Contrary to all the known behaviour of Russian trains, and to the horror of Edith and her many relations, who had not finished saying their goodbyes or handing over their presents, the Trans-Siberian Express left right on time, pulling slowly out of Petrograd at the start of its not very express-like fortnight's trek to the Far East, while parcels were still being pushed and finally hurled through the window of one first-class compartment.

The versatile Scottie had been variously employed since the time when she decided to give up her 'easy seat' with the von Meck family, and had gone to work as a secretary in the office of the Siberian copper company in Moscow. This job must have come to an end soon after the outbreak of war. Later she became a companion to two Russian girls and had even stepped in at short notice as a replacement for one of the teachers at a Russian girls' school in Moscow. Then in 1916 she received a telegram from the firm of Vickers in Petrograd inviting her to apply for the job there of office manager. Vickers were supplying large quantities of arms to Russia. By chance her companion on the train from Moscow to Petrograd was a representative of Vickers' great rivals, the Westinghouse company, employers of Louisette Andrews' brother, Emile.

'Ask for £300,' he said to her, when they were discussing salaries. But did she have the nerve? She knew that she was not lacking in experience, she had no doubt of her ability to do the job, and she was now thirty-three; but with her clear blue eyes and schoolgirl complexion, she did not look her age. Moreover, in those days £300 was a very respectable salary for a man, let alone a woman; it was the salary R. H. Bruce Lockhart received when he arrived in Moscow at the beginning of 1912 as British Vice-Consul. At Studley Horticultural College she had been paid £30 a year.

'Of course, they nearly died on the spot when I asked for £300 but I got it all right—no Englishman in Russia then could have done the job at all.'

Louisette Andrews had also been on the move. No longer did she hanker after those late nights with her brother at the *Aquarium* and the *Villa Rodé*, for by now she had become quite reconciled to the working life. In 1915, after some eighteen months as a chaperone with the Gagarin family, she took a summer holiday job as English-speaking companion to the seventeen-year-old daughter of a General. His estate was in the Penza district, in the very heart of European Russia. A French girl and an English tutor had also been engaged, as there were two boys in the family, and after travelling by train to the town of Penza, the three of them had another full day's journey by troika in stifling heat to the estate itself. Here Louisette first became aware of the vastness of Russia: when you climbed to the top of the little village church and gazed towards the horizon, 'you'd think to yourself that the world never came to an end'. At night the villagers would sit on the church steps for an hour or so and sing their part-songs, which always sounded very sad and very beautiful.

It was a delightful summer. After the strict routine at the Gagarins, it made a change to find youngsters allowed plenty of freedom, even if the wretched boys would insist on keeping an owl as a pet, and they all did lots of silly things, especially the French girl, until she slid off the top of a haystack and strained her leg. There was plenty of riding, and every week dances were held on neighbouring estates within a radius of twenty or thirty miles. It is the kind of life that Edith Kerby and Aunt Annie must have enjoyed before the war, when they accepted similar summer jobs and travelled hundreds of miles into the Russian interior.

But this was 1915. In that spring and summer half the Russian army was destroyed. Almost a million and a half men were killed or wounded, another million taken prisoner. One day Louisette accompanied the General and his daughter to the village. A crowd of about a hundred village boys, all very young, had been assembled in a large open space. The General addressed them, explaining carefully that their country was at war, that Russia was being attacked by the Germans, and that it was their duty to go and fight these Germans and defend their country.

But what possible meaning could such words have in the peaceful, uneducated heart of central Russia, in a village where the world never seemed to come to an end and an invader had not been seen for centuries? What are the Germans, they asked, and why do we have to fight them? They did not understand; and, one reflects, if they *had* understood what lay ahead of them, they might never have been persuaded to leave the village. There was no complaining, only bewilderment followed by resignation. After a few weeks of rudimentary training, this latest batch of recruits was sent off to fill a tiny part of the gap left by the missing millions.

'. . . And my next job? Oh, that was the easiest one of the lot. If things had worked out differently, I'd be with them today.'

The Korniloffs, who engaged her as companion to their teenage son and two daughters, were a very rich merchant family living in Petrograd, who came originally from Tobolsk in Siberia and whose fortune was based on their Siberian boat company. Not being aristocrats, they were informal and immensely sociable. They knew everyone in Petrograd and were always giving terrific parties, even though it was wartime. They took an immediate liking to Louisette, with her dark wavy hair and attractive smile. She went about everywhere with the boy, Vsevolod, and his two sisters, and though she was twice their age, the four of them were nicknamed 'Paris and the Three Graces'. Life with the sociable, easygoing Korniloffs was very congenial to Louisette's temperament: how pleasant to be able to come and go whenever she pleased, without having to worry about being indoors by ten o'clock!

The summer of 1916 proved even more memorable than that of the previous year on the General's estate. The Korniloffs went cruising on one of their own company's fleet of pleasure boats in southern Siberia, down the river Ob, wandering in and out of the beautiful bright emerald Altai Mountains, seeing all kinds of exotic wild birds and fishes, and visiting Irkutsk and Lake Baikal. Again it was terribly hot, and at Tobolsk on their return journey the Siberian autumn was warm enough for them to have tea out of doors without coats or jackets. Tobolsk was full of Austrian prisoners-of-war, and many stars of the Vienna Opera were singing in the choir of the Catholic Church. The Korniloffs still owned a large house there, and when the Tsar and his family were exiled to Tobolsk in August 1917, it provided lodgings for most of the Imperial suite.

With many other well-bred Russian ladies and foreign governesses Louisette took part in voluntary war work: in winter at the Winter Palace in Petrograd, and in summer outside Petrograd at the 'Royal Village' of Tsarskoe Selo, in the huge Catherine Palace which had been converted by the Empress into a military hospital. Wearing white aprons and kerchiefs, and seated at long tables, they made bandages and dressings of every description: 'and don't think we didn't do the job properly, because we did'. (Miss Dunnett, however, another former governess, has a pleasant recollection of a Russian princess at a wartime sewing party, sewing on an arm where the leg should have been.) The Empress paid them frequent visits and everyone had to get up and curtsey whenever she passed through. But she was not popular and seemed 'awfully stiff', whereas the Grand Duchesses were 'nice girls and spoke jolly good English too'.

When Rosamond Dowse first arrived in the distant provincial capital of Samara in the spring of 1914, she did not guess that two whole years would have to pass before her departure. Though still barely twenty by the time she left, she was no longer the shy young English girl who blushed at the sound of a wolf-whistle or was scared by the sight of a drunken peasant in the street. Mastering the Russian language had given her more self-confidence. But her homesickness was still as strong as ever. There were no well-established British families in Samara who might have provided a reassuring presence in the background of her life; her only English-speaking friend was an Irish governess called Miss Masterman, who had been in Russia for a number of years and was quite out of touch with home.

In the spring of 1916 Rosamond accepted a post with the Tolstoy family at Tsarskoe Selo, where she would at least be likely to hear of any opportunities of returning to England from Petrograd. Monsieur was a Colonel in a crack cavalry regiment at the front, and the family was close to the Court: Madame was on good terms with Anna Vyrubova, the Empress's confidante, while the old grandmother was a close friend of the Dowager Empress Marie (the Tsar's mother and sister of Queen Alexandra), who spoke only French and was a frequent visitor. The Tolstoy children shared the same priest, music master and French teacher as the Imperial children, so the family always sent each of them greetings telegrams on their name's days and birthdays, and received acknowledgements by return. Like Volodya Rahl, the twelve-year-old son, Sergei, enjoyed dressing up in soldier's uniform, and once, when Rosamond was out walking with him in the park round the Old Palace, she was very taken aback when the guard at the entrance turned out to salute. They had mistaken him for the Tsarevich.

During that summer Rosamond attended weekly working parties at the Catherine Palace and may well have seen Louisette Andrews. It was the kind of useful, practical activity that always appealed to her. What stands out in her memory about these occasions is not, however, the Empress, whose public appearances had become rare by this time and whom Rosamond does not remember seeing at all, but the strong feeling of distaste and disapproval that she experienced at the sight of the obsequious Imperial lackeys and flunkeys, who tied on the ladies' aprons for them before they started work and waited on them afterwards at tea. It is a very British reaction, reminding us of the Kerby philosophy of self-help and self-reliance which differentiated the family so clearly from the Russian life around them, of Scottie deciding to give up her 'easy seat' with the von Mecks, and of Miss Emmie's concern that Volodya Rahl should learn how to stand on his own feet.

In September 1916 Rosamond heard that her brother Tom, whom she had last seen two years before in Samara, had died of wounds received at the Battle of the Somme. Her feelings of homesickness became even more acute, but there was no chance of returning to England. Shortly after, she left the Tolstoys and travelled south for three days to Kislovodsk, a health resort in the North Caucasus famous for its mineral waters. Here she took charge of six-year-old Nadya Miklashevsky, whose father, a Colonel in the Chevalier Guards, was also on active service at the front. As Nadya's baby brother was delicate, it was felt that mild and sunny Kislovodsk would be more beneficial to him than the damp rawness of a Petrograd autumn, but after Christmas they returned to the capital, by which time the cold there had become crisp and dry. England seemed as distant as ever. 'I dreamt I came home last night,'

Rosamond adds plaintively on the back of a photograph of herself, dated February 2nd, 1917, which she sent off to her parents in Norwich. She had now begun to attend the British & American Chapel in Petrograd, and it is here that she unknowingly overlaps with Emma Dashwood, who had been attending the Chapel regularly since the start of 1916 when she had been persuaded by the Kerby Aunts not to return to the Rahls at Pervitino.

Thanks to the Chapel grapevine Emmie had quickly found a job in Petrograd, as governess to the only son of the very tall and splendidly named Commander Dolovo-Dobrovolsky, of the Naval Staff. Lyovochka, her young pupil, had two celebrated great-uncles on his mother's side: Admiral Brusiloff, the explorer, and General Brusiloff, the most successful Russian general of the war, who was also the boy's godfather. These interesting connections only emerged later; what immediately pleased Emmie was to be within easy walking distance of the Aunts on Kronverksky Prospect. Emmie's original companion to Russia, Gertie Kirby, was with a doctor's family about the same distance from the Aunts but on the other side, so inevitably the flat on the Kronversky became a regular meeting-place on Sunday afternoons.

Lyovochka was soon introduced to the English walking habit: 'he gradually got accustomed to long walks', recalls Miss Dashwood, with the faintest hint at coercion. The most frequent of these was across the Troitsky Bridge and along the Kamenno-Ostrovsky Prospect. Gertie often took the same walk with her pupil. As Emmie was having lunch one day with the Dolovo-Dobrovolskys, the telephone rang in the sitting-room next door. It was Gertie. She had only just got in from her walk and had been unable to resist phoning straight away.

'Emmie, what do you think has happened?' she gasped, almost speechless with laughter. 'I've gone and lost my hat! A gust of wind caught it and it blew right over the Troitsky Bridge and went sliding *miles* down the ice. . . . Yes, yes, that pretty blue one I'd only just bought!'

The Dolovo-Dobrovolskys were intrigued by the shrieks of laughter coming from their sitting-room and asked Emmie what had happened. 'Why not ask your friend to tea?' they suggested, and in this way the vivacious Gertie soon became a popular visitor.

One evening towards the end of 1916 Emmie accompanied her pupil and his parents to a special dinner at the Admiralty, that graceful building with the narrow golden spire which is still one of the city's chief adornments. At the entrance they were joined by another Commander, his son and two ladies. The men were in very smart full-dress uniform and the boys in sailor suits. To Emmie's great surprise, the moment they entered the banquet hall, there was a loud clink of swords being drawn from scabbards, and all the officers—there were no other ladies present—sprang up smartly to attention and saluted. Everything was so grand and took her so much by surprise that for once Miss Dashwood has quite forgotten all the details of the menu.

The food was good though—of that she feels sure; yet this was the time, as Edith Kerby reports, when her family was queuing thirteen hours for black bread and living on porridge and cereals. Whereas the Kerbys had to take their chance along with the Russian man-in-the-street, the upper classes were still cushioned against the full impact of the food shortage. Certainly Emma Dashwood was not then aware of it. The Dolovo-Dobrovolskys decided nonetheless to live away from the capital. Like Rosamond, Emmie wanted to remain in Petrograd in case an opportunity arose of returning to England, so just before Christmas she left the Dolovo-Dobrovolskys and took a job with another naval family. This was even closer to the Aunts, for her new family lived in the fashionable Kamenno-Ostrovsky Prospect, and by using the back entrance of the flats and cutting off a large corner, she was able to come straight out into the not quite so fashionable Kronverksky.

The name of the new family was Rozhdestvensky. In Russian *Rozhdestvo* means 'Christmas'. A Christmas job with a Christmas family, was how Emmie thought of it.

But the turn of the year 1916–17 was significant in Russian history not only because of Emma Dashwood's new job with her Christmas family.

18

Collapse

Those glaring defects of the old regime that contributed to its downfall are like the ugly cracks in some ancient building, more noticeable to an uncommitted observer than to many of those living inside. But it is doubtful whether the cracks were enough in themselves to bring the whole edifice tumbling to the ground. For that to happen an extraordinary sequence of events and combination of personalities were also necessary. Among the personalities, the most extraordinary was that of the holy devil, the devout debauchee, Gregory Rasputin, whose power at Court was based on the simple fact that the Empress believed—not without cause, as Robert Massie has shown in *Nicholas and Alexandra*—that he alone had the power through his prayers to save the Tsarevich from suffering and an early death.

What possible connection can there have been between Rasputin and the English governess?

Little Cockney Miss Judge remembered him once coming to visit 'her' General. Like everyone else who saw him, she was struck by the hypnotic quality of his eyes. She also remembered him as very tall and dark, and wearing a long black robe. Dark Rasputin certainly was, but not tall. Even a man of average height may have seemed tall to Miss Judge, who was under five feet, but it is more likely that the sinister figure of Rasputin had grown taller in her memory over the years. Miss Dunnett was once asked by an American lady if she would like to meet him, but declined politely. And Emma Dashwood cannot remember ever having been told anything about him, but is quite sure that if she had been, she would have been 'terrifically shocked': Russians in her experience were not like that at all.

Louisette Andrews however did meet him. Rasputin's birthplace was a village in the Tobolsk Province of Western Siberia, and the Korniloffs, because of their connections with that part of the world, had known him from his early days. Louisette was among the company of twenty or so who sat down one evening to dinner with Rasputin at the Korniloffs' home in Petrograd. 'Was he the guest of honour?' I asked, to which she replied that he was 'not so much the guest of honour as an object of curiosity'. She had been warned to be on her guard when introduced to him, as he was said to have a special way of hanging on to your hand and peering at you intently with his hypnotic eyes. She managed to resist his lynx-like stare (one of the milder comparisons with various animals and reptiles that abound in the literature on Rasputin) and today can claim to be probably the last surviving Englishwoman to have met the holy devil in the flesh. Though he was decked out in all his gala clothes, he ate with his fingers, having no desire, as he put it, to ape the manners of the nobles. Miss Andrews, of course, cannot speak too badly of him, and there is one word in her comments which, though relatively mild, seems to me to sum up the kind of genteel revulsion that every English governess would have felt immediately and instinctively towards Rasputin. Rasputin, she says, was 'greasy'.

Whether the connections between Rasputin and the English governess ever went further than that formal handshake with Miss Andrews, whether any of them ever climbed the stairs to the modest and surprisingly bourgeois apartment that he occupied in Petrograd from 1914 to 1916—this can only be a matter for conjecture. I doubt it and am far too discreet to enquire.

Rasputin had made many enemies in his stormy career. At the Korniloffs' dinner party he said openly that he knew there were people who wanted to kill him. In the autumn of 1916, when Rosamond Dowse was in Kislovodsk with the Miklashevskys, they had a visit from Prince Yousoupoff, sole heir to the fabulous Yousoupoff fortune. Rosamond heard him ask if she understood Russian, and as she did, only very general topics were ever discussed in her hearing. Later she came to the conclusion that the purpose of the Prince's visit had been to find out whether Madame and her sisters would be willing to become involved in a plot to destroy Rasputin.

Like their mother, Countess Bobrinsky, all three sisters were great anglophiles. So too was Felix Yousoupoff. Before going to Oxford, he had been tutored by a young Englishman, Frank Cooke, who also became tutor to the Grand Duke Dmitri. Dmitri was actually a first cousin of the Tsar, though he always referred to him as 'Uncle Nicholas', being more than twenty years his junior. Frank Cooke gave up tutoring after his marriage and rented a large house at Nikolskoe, a village some forty miles from Moscow, where he and his wife gave English lessons. It was here that their seven-year-old daughter, Dorothy, first met Scottie and gave her the nickname of 'Aunt Really'. Another welcome visitor was Grand Duke Dmitri. On one occasion he and his former tutor went out shooting together. Mr Cooke was carrying his heavy old-fashioned rifle, the Grand Duke a very expensive new one bought specially for the occasion. But it was Mr Cooke whose shots kept finding their mark, while the Grand Duke missed just as regularly. From this Dmitri could draw only one conclusion: that his old tutor must have much the better rifle. He proposed an exchange which, needless to say, Frank Cooke was only too happy to agree to.

I am reminded of this story in a very different context. Together with Purishkevich, a middle-aged Right-wing member of the Duma, Prince Yousoupoff and Grand Duke Dmitri, then both in their late twenties, were the chief participants in the murder of Rasputin, which took place one night just before the end of 1916. Rasputin's death was perhaps the most macabre event even in his extraordinary life, for he withstood attempts to poison him, to shoot him and to club him to death, dying eventually from drowning after his body had been pushed through a hole in the frozen river. Later Purishkevich and Yousoupoff both published accounts of their part in the night's events, but Dmitri remained silent, even with his own sister. It is not in fact likely that the Grand Duke fired any shots at Rasputin; but even had he done so, it seems reasonable to guess that he would have missed.

Rasputin had always been given to prophecies. Near the end of his life they became increasingly dire. If I am killed, Louisette remembers him saying at the dinner party, it will mean the end of the Russian Empire.

*   *   *

In the flat on Kamenno-Ostrovsky Prospect, Emma Dashwood was sitting with her latest pupil, Oleg Rozhdestvensky—the jolliest, she now feels, of all her pupils in Russia:

It was one morning, and I was giving Oleg his usual English lesson. I think we must have been in the dining-room, because I seem to remember the light wood table—being a smallish flat we had to make use of the dining-room as our study—when suddenly, right in the middle of the lesson, we heard a terrific noise of gunfire.

'Oleg,' I said. 'Quick! Under the table!'

He thought it was all *great* fun. . . . No, I don't remember how long we stayed there, but no one came to see us. Then that evening we heard that our car had been commandeered.

I think the morning in question must have been that of March 12th, the so-called 'Red Monday' of what has come to be known, thanks to the backwardness of the Russian calendar, as the February Revolution. There had been disturbances and sporadic firing in the streets for several days previously, but Monday was to prove a turning-point. At about eleven that morning, the French Ambassador, venturing out into the street, suddenly heard the crack of machine-gun fire splitting the air: a group of regular soldiers had just taken up position near the Nevsky Prospect. It must have been this burst of machine-gun fire, which would have been clearly audible from the flat on the other side of the Troitsky Bridge, that sent Emma Dashwood and her pupil diving for cover.

On that same morning Scottie had an appointment with her dentist.

When she began her job as office manager with Vickers in Petrograd, Scottie had taken a room as paying guest with the elderly Misses Chamot, members of an Anglo-French family which traced its links with Russia as far back as 1819. They had a house on Vassilevsky Island, one of the islands in the delta of the River Neva linked by bridges to the main part of the city. Scottie's dentist also lived on the island, and after leaving him, she was faced with a long walk (all means of transport having ceased by this time because of the disturbances) across the bridge and up the Nevsky Prospect to the Vickers office. But before reaching the office, she recalls,

I met a company of Cossacks on horseback with a great crowd. Sometimes they were calling for bread, next moment the Cossacks and crowd were all singing together. Suddenly the Cossacks charged the crowd with their long whips. I had been warned that this might happen, so I dashed into a shop and the man shut the door and barred it, and the Cossacks clattered past.

She was wise to have taken this precaution, for a blow from one of those long whips, which had on the end two small pieces of leather about one inch in diameter, with a piece of lead in between, could maim a person for life. An English business man, Stinton Jones, who had lived in Russia for twelve years, was a close eye-witness of the February Revolution, and in his book, *Russia in Revolution*, he describes how in earlier riots, a Cossack's whip caught the shoulder of a student in front of him and 'in an instant his coat was cut through and soon the whole of that side was saturated with blood from the deep wound', while the whip of a second Cossack 'caught the face of a woman standing next to the student and gashed it open to the bone. The wound reached from eye to chin as if it had been cut with a butcher's knife.'

The Chamots also had lodging with them a member of the Duma, who came back that evening

in a great state of exhaustion. He was very lame but had managed to get a lift on a sledge. He said he had seen the Law Courts burning. He disappeared in the night back to his home in Finland. All that night there was firing, one regiment fighting against the other, and all against the police.

The British Embassy had warned everyone of the need to get in extra provisions, but the old ladies had paid no attention, with the result that there was very little food in the house. On Tuesday, when they went out in search of bread, 'the streets were thronged with people all bearing a red flag', while the cars, which must have included the one commandeered from Emma Dashwood's family, 'had machine-guns lying along their mudguards'. Not until Wednesday were the provision shops reopened. On that morning, recalls Scottie, 'soldiers came to search the house for arms. When they came to my bedroom door the old butler told them there was an English lady in there and she wasn't well. I really had a bad cold.' *Really?* Reassured by the old ladies, the soldiers soon went away empty-handed, but Scottie could not help being amused when not long after, the Misses Chamot discovered to their indescribable horror that the member of the Duma had left behind in his room a revolver and some ammunition.

By Thursday the serious fighting was practically at an end. On that day the Tsar abdicated, first in favour of his son, and then, changing his mind, in favour of his brother, Grand Duke Michael, who quickly informed the Provisional Government that he would only accept the throne if invited to do so by a constituent assembly.

So in less than a week, the long awaited Revolution, triggered off by disturbances in the bread queues, had come about. The defection of the soldiers, and still more of the Cossacks, had been critical factors. Yet no one was quite expecting this Revolution to happen, even though everyone had been saying for some time that revolution was imminent. Sir George Buchanan, the British Ambassador, was on holiday in Finland when it all began. The revolutionaries were as much taken by surprise as anyone. Quietly and without warning the ancient cracked building had chosen that particular moment to collapse.

During and immediately after the February Revolution, the people's most bitter and unequivocal hatred was directed against the Tsarist police and their agents, for there were many old scores to be settled. Every building connected with the administration of justice was an immediate target for the revolutionaries. They burst open prisons, releasing all the inmates and setting fire to the buildings; they set fire to the Law Courts, destroying the archives of centuries; and in all parts of the city they attacked police stations, killing the men in charge and setting fire to the buildings, which were soon, as Mrs Dawe (Rosamond Dowse) has written, turned into 'blackened shells with long icicles hanging from the eaves and gaping window frames and doorways'.

The police were among the last to hold out against the Revolution. Stationed with their machine-guns on the tops of buildings, sometimes in the belfries of churches, cut off from one another and ignorant of the turn that events had taken in the streets below, they fought on, encouraged by the belief that sooner or later loyal troops would be drafted into the capital from outside. Later they were ruthlessly hunted down throughout the city. 'When caught,' writes Stinton Jones, 'they were in some instances shot, but more often taken prisoner and escorted to places of detention.' One day Rosamond 'saw a mere lad with two swords, one on each shoulder, leading a miserable cowed policeman beside him in his charge. Someone in the crowd shouted "Off with his head", and I felt sick at the thought of seeing such an act, but luckily the boy just grinned.' Their only hope of escape lay in disguise. Hearing a commotion in the hall of their flats, Rosamond 'went to investigate and found a couple of soldiers undressing what I thought was a woman—but it was a policeman in lots of petticoats!' According to Stinton Jones, this was a favourite—and grotesquely humorous—disguise of these fugitive policemen. He himself noticed one walking along disguised as a woman:

He was a tall man, standing fully six feet, and broad-shouldered, and his general bearing and walk was certainly anything but feminine. He was wearing a thick veil at the time. He was soon noticed by people in the crowd, who stopped him and took off his hat, which came away with a long wig and the thick veil, leaving a very coarse-featured masculine face with a heavy moustache. He immediately fell on his knees and begged for mercy, but the crowd dispatched him without further ado.

Members of the officer class also went in fear of their lives at this time. It must have been on one of the days before Red Monday that Rosamond, instead of hearing the steady tramp of soldiers being drilled in the street outside their flat, 'heard shots and the loud murmur of discontented voices, and on looking out of the nursery window saw the soldiers in disarray, shooting in the air! Seeing Nadya was playing happily I went out to the hall of our flat where I saw three very young officers using our phone and asking for instructions as to how to cope with the soldiers who had refused to obey their orders.'

The youth and inexperience of the garrison officers in Petrograd was another factor that helped the Revolution. The three youngsters looked so alarmed that Rosamond felt very sorry for them, but a day or two later they might have looked more scared still, for on Red Monday, according to Stinton Jones, the mobs roaming the streets 'not only shot down the police, but stopped any officers met with, who were asked to give up their arms. If they agreed and handed over their arms they were allowed their freedom, but in cases where they refused they were shot down and their arms taken.' Not only individuals but all the ceremonial trappings of military rank aroused feelings of hatred: swords were seized, epaulettes torn from shoulders, and all distinctions of rank and forms of address completely abolished.

This abolition of rank applied to society as a whole. Everyone was now a citizen. Everyone was to be referred to as brother or sister, as comrade or friend. Here too it was the ceremonial trappings of social rank that aroused the most violent feelings. Louisette Andrews can remember people climbing up on top of clubs and other buildings, pulling down the coats of arms and emblems, and stamping on them; even the American eagle did not escape, for Stinton Jones has a photograph of one being burnt by the crowd, obviously because it bore too great a resemblance to the Imperial eagle that was so bitterly resented. Some of the palaces and grand houses of the capital were looted and burned, others commandeered for public use. Short of open defiance and its consequences, their owners had no choice but to accommodate themselves as best they could to the conditions of the new regime.

For families like the Rozhdestvenskys these must have been anxious months, though Emma Dashwood was never aware of it. 'Until I heard those shots being fired,' she recalls, 'I had no idea there was anything brewing—ignoramus that I was.' Like her pupil, she was sheltered from the full impact of outside events. She accepted them as a matter of course and was not curious; and even if there were a few guns being fired in the streets, how privileged she was to be living well in Russia, when life was so difficult for all of them back in England!

In April Emmie was more excited than disturbed to learn that the family was making hasty arrangements before leaving to spend the summer in the south of Russia. One of the last scenes she saw in Petrograd was the public burial of victims of the Revolution, which took place on April 5th. Because the ground was still frozen, huge mass graves had been dynamited in the Champ de Mars, the famous ceremonial parade ground of Tsarist times. Throughout the day a very long procession of soldiers and citizens carrying coffins made its way there from all parts of the city. No religious service was held, and contrary to usual practice, the coffins were draped in red, not white, and had their lids closed. As the Champ de Mars was just at the end of the Troitsky Bridge, Emma Dashwood met the procession when she was out with Oleg on their daily walk—for the daily walk must go on, Revolution or no Revolution.

Rosamond Dowse remained in Petrograd. When life became quieter after the Revolution and she was given some time off, she put a shawl over her head, peasant style, and mingled boldly with the crowds to get the feel of what was happening: a far cry from the young girl who less than three years before had been so scared by the drunken peasants lurching along those same city streets. Her reaction to what had happened was in general sympathetic. She noted that people now seemed happier and more carefree, and that there was a feeling of freedom in the air, though she was not sure that the Russians understood by 'freedom' quite what she did:

When the trams started running again, people got on them and clung on outside like a bunch of grapes or swarm of bees. In Russia one had to get on at the back, pass through the car, and get off in front, paying the conductor when you saw him. Once when looking up at a tram to see how I could get in, two burly Russian soldiers who were standing on the step invited me to join them and each put an arm round me to hold me on, so I felt reasonably safe and glad of the ride as I had some way to go. When I descended and thanked them I gave them my fare and asked them to give it to the conductor when they saw him. 'Oh, don't bother,' said one, 'you needn't pay now we have freedom.' 'Oh, indeed not,' said I, 'I am English and we are free but we still pay our fares on buses and trams.'

Rosamond also found herself a reluctant participant in the new style of Russian justice:

One night the nursery maid, Tania, came knocking at my door begging me to go and intervene as the two Maries (maids) were fighting each other! A few minutes later they both also came to my door, each with hair streaming and one with blood flowing from a wound on her head. One was a Pole, the other Russian (never friends) and after I had told them I had had my bath and the room was free they had argued as to who should go first and then fought with a flat iron! Well, the outcome of this was that Marie, the Pole, brought an action against the other Marie —and gave my name as the only witness. The first I heard of it was a summons to appear on a certain day at a court nearby. As all the usual courts had been closed, new ones were set up with three judges—one from the Army, one from the Navy and a third representing the people. I asked Madame to go with me for I was only twenty, but she refused and told me if I didn't go I would be fetched. So wondering very much what I was in for, I attended as instructed and was shut up in a tiny room until called for. On hearing my name shouted out I went into a large hall along the sides of which were seated fully armed Russian soldiers with rifles, with three men seated at a table on a platform and a scattering of ordinary people sitting on benches below. I wasn't required to take any oath but was asked to state what the case was about. So as I knew I had to live in the same house as these two women I told the story which sounded so childish that the soldiers began to laugh. And I made out that the quarrel was six of one and half-a-dozen of the other, so the case was dismissed with a caution to each woman. Afterwards the Pole, who had brought the case, thanked me so warmly for what I had said in helping her!

When Madame decided to return to the Caucasus in June, Rosamond asked to stay behind, as she was still desperately anxious to reach England. Through the British & American Chapel her aunt and uncle had become very friendly with a Mr Boyd and his Russian wife. He was a Scottish engineer working in Russia for Coats of Paisley, the cotton people. The firm had chartered a ship to cross from Aberdeen to Bergen in Norway and pick up the wives and children of their Scottish engineers, and it was arranged that Rosamond should accompany Mrs Boyd and help look after six-month-old Andrew. Then came a frantic rush to prepare all the necessary documents: a visit to the photographer's for passport photos, repeated visits to Russian police headquarters—come back tomorrow, they kept saying, right up to Saturday, the day before she was due to leave; from there to the British Military Mission, where the wounded young naval officer gave her his sister's address in England and asked her to write, and finally to the British Consul's office, which Rosamond and an extremely flustered Aunt Margaret reached just ten minutes before it was due to close at lunchtime on Saturday for the weekend. But at last all was in order, and very early on Sunday morning Rosamond Dowse left Petrograd's Finland Station at the start of her journey to England.

The Finland Station: does it ring a bell? Here, two months before, Lenin had arrived back in Russia from Germany, after twelve years of exile. The Bolsheviks, bent on seizing power from the Provisional Government after the February Revolution, had taken over as their headquarters the home of the ballerina, Kschessinska, who had once been the mistress of the Tsar. Her palace was 'only just down the road' from Louisette Andrews at the Korniloffs. Ignoring the objections of Madame, Louisette and Nina, the elder daughter, put on maid's clothes just as Rosamond had done, and went out one evening soon after Lenin's arrival to hear him address a huge crowd from the palace balcony. Louisette's Russian was not good enough to follow him closely, but seventeen-year-old Nina was impressed: he had a way of rubbing in his message so that you found yourself agreeing with him, even though you didn't want to.

He spoke for a long time and received a marvellous ovation, and when it was all over, Louisette and Nina quickly made themselves scarce. But that was the only occasion on which Louisette heard Lenin speak, for Mme Korniloff absolutely forbade them to attend any more political meetings.

19

The Promised Land

Edith Kerby did not feel entirely happy with her life in Shanghai, where she had arrived at the end of January 1917 to stay with her married sister. Of course, it was wonderful to have proper food again, to feel her strength returning, and to know that she did not have to worry about where the next day's meals were coming from; yet still there was something wrong. Not surprisingly, perhaps, the earnest young girl who had once taken down sermons in shorthand and diligently transcribed them into piles of notebooks was not very attracted to the colonial way of life, with its continual round of tea parties, dinner parties and visits to the club. But there was more to it than that. She could not help contrasting this frivolous, self-indulgent life with the seriousness of what she had left behind in Russia: with the colossal war casualties, the bread queues and the impassioned speeches in the Duma, where she had felt herself in the very thick of events. And the people of Shanghai did not know, and could not imagine, anything of all this suffering and drama.

From China she set off on a long visit to Japan. They were in a Russian ship, sailing along serenely in the Pacific Ocean and about to enter the Inland Sea, when a message came through over the wireless: the Tsar had abdicated and a Provisional Government had been set up. I wonder how many of the passengers reflected on the irony of hearing this news aboard a ship whose name was the *Empress of Russia*? Edith decided there and then that the Russian Revolution was something she just could not miss. The fall of the Tsar caused her no regrets. The Kerby philosophy of self-help and self-reliance had never had much time for the privileged idleness engendered by the Tsarist autocracy. Influenced also by the democratic outlook of her brother Harry and by the speeches urging reform that she had listened to with Mr Wilcox in the Duma, she felt elated by the turn events had taken in Russia.

It had been her intention to spend the whole of 1917 in China and Japan—but not now. She would complete her Japanese tour as planned, and then return to Petrograd at the earliest opportunity. On reaching Nagasaki, she at once phoned up Thomas Cook. Remembering her difficulties in the autumn, she asked with some trepidation what chance there was of a booking on the Trans-Siberian Express. An amused voice at the other end replied: 'Madam, you will have the train to yourself. No one wants to go to Russia today.'

When Edith's sister in Shanghai heard of this change of plan, she begged her not to be so foolhardy, but Edith's mind was made up. The Trans-Siberian Express starts at Vladivostok and Edith was due to join it on May 1st at Harbin, the Russian-Chinese frontier town. The warm weather had arrived and she was looking forward to the fortnight's journey. She thought back with pleasure to the charming little coupé of her outward trip, with its sofa bed, washstand, wardrobe and folding table, and to the friendly attendant who made up her bed every night with clean sheets; she recalled the comfortable Restaurant Car where main meals were served, while elevenses, teas and evening snacks were available in your own compartment and you could invite a fellow passenger in for a chat. At Harbin she had a sudden brainwave. Flour was still easy to obtain in that part of Russia, so she bought a 40 lb. sack to take home to her mother.

The train rolled in and Edith asked to be directed to her reserved seat in the Wagons Lits International First Class.

The guard looked at her oddly and laughed: 'There's no first class,' he said, 'get in wherever you can.' 'So much for Thomas Cook' might have been Edith's first reaction, but that would have been unfair. The amused man at Nagasaki could not have guessed that the train would be chock-a-block with soldiers returning to Moscow and Petrograd. After the February Revolution they had deserted from their units in great numbers and trickled back to their remote villages, but Kerensky, Minister of Justice in the Provisional Government, had recently announced an amnesty: all those who returned by or on May 15th would be pardoned and not shot for desertion. So at every station there were hundreds and hundreds of soldiers trying to board this last train. Bayonet fights broke out frequently on the platforms. Many soldiers travelled all the way back on the train roof, where in winter they would have frozen to death in no time.

Edith scrambled aboard and was lucky to find an upper bunk. She hurled her sack of flour up and climbed up herself, and on that sack of flour she slept for the next fortnight, resting her head on the small Russian *doomka* or 'thinking pillow' that she always carried with her. On the bunk opposite was a woman dying of T.B., on her way to a relative in Siberia to try the mare's milk cure. About half way through the journey they suddenly heard a terrible commotion and the train came to a halt in a densely wooded area. The Restaurant Car had caught fire and was burning fiercely. Without further ado, it was uncoupled, toppled over and left to burn itself out by the side of the track. This meant that for the remaining week they were dependent on the simple food that the peasants brought and sold at the wayside stations. It became almost a battle for survival, but often a kindly disposed soldier from her compartment would bring Edith back something, while she sat tight on her sack of flour.

Yet in spite of all these privations, the experience was one she would not have missed for anything—and certainly not for all those teas and dinner parties in China! She sat talking politics with the soldiers by the hour, listening avidly to every word they had to say about the Revolution, all of which was quite new to her. The days seemed to flash past. On May 15th the train arrived in Petrograd. They were two days late, but the soldiers were still in time to meet Kerensky's deadline.

It was only 5 a.m. as Edith left the station. Her luck seemed to be in, for she found a *drozhky* straight away. The driver was surly and demanded a fantastic price, but she was so anxious to reach home that she would have agreed to anything. She asked another man standing nearby to give her a hand with her luggage. As soon as he picked up the sack, he seemed to know what it contained.

'Flour?' he said.

'Yes, I've brought it ten thousand versts for my old mother.'

'Well, half of it's mine, or you'll get this'—and so saying, he took out a revolver and held it to her head.

In retrospect, what seems puzzling about this story is that the man did not pinch *all* the flour; but these were early days yet. As she stood there, silently watching him pour it into a kind of sheet he produced from a bundle, Edith only had time to reflect: 'so this is what a Revolution means, this is what I've let myself in for'.

Uncertain of when she would arrive, she had not warned anyone in the family that she was returning from China. She rang the bell of the flat, expecting their old Russian maid to come to the door as usual, and was very taken aback when the door was opened by Mother herself. Nothing like so startled, however, as Mrs Kerby—when she found standing on the doorstep the one daughter who was supposed to be safely out of the way in China! She looked pale and old and worried. Edith asked in bewilderment why there was no one else in the flat so early in the morning. They're out queuing for food, Mother explained, 'and they don't wear hats any more, they wear kerchiefs, because the Cossacks race up and down the streets cracking their whips at all the bourgeoisie. . . . Oh, Edith, whatever made you come back? You just don't understand what a Revolution means!'

No, but she was beginning to learn. Finding a job, she realised, must be her first priority. She made an appointment with the Ambassador, Sir George Buchanan, who knew of her work with the *Daily Telegraph* and offered her a similar post, compiling reports on the Russian daily press for the recently formed Anglo-Russian Commission. One of its members was Paul Dukes, who later became well known for his cloak-and-dagger exploits in Russia, while her immediate boss was the writer, Hugh Walpole. Then in his early thirties and already a famous author, he had been in Russia since shortly after the war, and the first of his novels with a Russian theme, *The Dark Forest*, was the fruit of his experiences at the front as an orderly with the Russian Red Cross. Edith came to know him quite well. He was generous and had a great sense of humour, but she never really took to him. She wished he didn't seem to be scrutinising her all the time and watching out for her naivetés. She felt sure he was going to put her into one of his novels.

In the evenings Edith resumed her voluntary work with the Ambassador's wife, Lady Georgina, helping to feed and clothe the thousands of refugees then pouring into Petrograd. Clothes were collected for this purpose in Britain and sent out by Lady Muriel Paget's organisation. Edith's job was to interview refugees and report on their needs. It could be a heartrending business. As she walked one evening through the rows of sleeping people in the huge dormitories on her way to speak to some new arrivals, her eye was caught by two lighted candles. A tiny emaciated little boy had just died and his body had been laid out, partly covered by a few dirty rags. One woman came to her for clothes, as she had just had a baby and didn't have a stitch for it. She described how she had fled from the advancing Germans, and not being able to keep up the flight with three small children, had thrown them all under a passing train. There was one girl she had come across earlier,

who had a most terrible expression on her face and looked as if she would strangle anyone who approached her. She had lost both parents, sisters and brothers, and stood alone. In her loneliness she made friends with a boy who had lost his leg in the course of his flight from the front. We placed these two in a family and gave them work that they could do. The boy was taught to be a cobbler and the girl took in repair work. Imagine my horror when I visited them on Christmas Eve with presents and a hamper of food—to find them cuddled up in one bed!

Quite out of the blue Edith heard one day that Mrs Pankhurst and Jessie Kenney, sister of Annie, were coming to Russia to study the contribution of Russian women to the war effort. What an opportunity! Would Sir George agree to release her for ten days to act as Mrs Pankhurst's interpreter in Petrograd? Sensible Sir George was quick to agree. Edith had read only vaguely about Mrs Pankhurst and the suffragettes, but was sick with excitement at the thought of being the shadow for ten days to such a celebrity.

Now Miss Kerby had never been one to make concessions to fashion or elegance. Her old-fashioned skirts nearly touched the ground, her dresses had high necks, and she wore her hair screwed up in a plait and coiled round her head in Edwardian fashion. So it came as quite a shock to her when she first saw Mrs. Pankhurst: for she was old (just under sixty in fact, though perhaps her prison experiences had made her look older), quiet, and what surprised Edith most of all—dressed in a style that seemed fastidious to the point of fussiness. Edith was struck at once by the elegant hat and gloves, by the lace and the frills and the little net that kept in place the carefully crimped hair. But behind this fussy, la-di-da exterior she sensed a very strong personality and was relieved to find they got on well together.

By a strange chance Mrs Pankhurst's visit coincided with the formation in Russia of the first Women's Battalion. An illiterate peasant woman from Siberia, whose husband, a butcher, had been killed at the front in the early days of the war, disguised herself as a man and volunteered for the army. After two years' service she was recommended for the St George's Cross. Kerensky, by this time Minister of War, sent for her and presented the decoration himself, asking if she had any special request to make. Your permission to form a Women's Battalion, was the quick reply. Seeing a chance to shame the Russian soldiery into greater efforts, Kerensky jumped at the idea, and Bochkareva, the former peasant woman, was made into a General. The highlight of Edith's ten days with Mrs Pankhurst was the time spent watching Bochkareva's recruits, who were taken from all walks of life, being put through a hard day's programme of training.

As the weeks went by and tension increased between the Provisional Government and the Bolsheviks, even a short walk could be dangerous. Lenin had made an unsuccessful bid to seize power at the end of June. The Kerbys' flat was on the Malaya Posadskaya, and to reach her work she had to pass the Bolshevik headquarters and cross the Troitsky Bridge. The Ambassador sent someone to escort her, but even so they often had to dodge machine-gun fire, and once she managed to keep out of trouble only by hiding behind a huge tree in the Summer Garden.

Then one fine morning in July, Sir George asked Miss Kerby to look in to his office to see him. She wondered what it could mean. Life in the city, he began, was becoming more and more dangerous, and it had been decided that Hugh Walpole would shortly be leaving Petrograd. There was similar work that he could do in the Russian Department of the Foreign Office . . . and how would Miss Kerby react to the suggestion that she too might be transferred at the same time to the Foreign Office in London?

The Promised Land! The Promised Land! And to be invited there, to be paid for working there! How would Miss Kerby react . . .? Her first impulse was to give Sir George a great big hug. It would have been a pleasant sight: demure, long-skirted Miss Kerby throwing her arms round the frail figure of His Majesty's Ambassador, dislodging his monocle and perhaps even disturbing a few strands of that distinguished silver-grey hair. But she contented herself with rushing home to break the glad news to her mother. It was the proudest moment of her life.

Within a short space of time Edith was in London, her elder sister and mother in China (they travelled on the last train to reach there in safety), and her younger sister in Stockholm with her husband and baby. Only their old Russian maid, because of her nationality, had to stay behind in the flat in Petrograd, together with all the family furniture, three pianos and that pile of thick notebooks into which the young Edith had transcribed the Rev. Orr's sermons.

And what of the five Kerby Aunts? They all chose to stay on in Russia.

20

The Last Glimpse

If the English governess had assumed a role of greater importance with the disruption of normal family life in Russia during the war years, this was bound to be even more true of the period of social upheaval that followed the February Revolution. Desperately anxious about their own futures, parents could console themselves with the thought that at least their children were in safe hands and shielded from unpleasant realities by a governess who might well, like Emma Dashwood, be enviably unaware of what was going on around her.

There were seven people in the Rozhdestvensky family party which left Petrograd in April 1917: five adults and two children. Madame was accompanied by her parents, whom Emmie met for the first time at the station, and by her sister, who was to help look after the little girl. They formed part of a very large exodus at that time of upper-class families to the south of Russia, where the Revolution had not yet taken such a complete hold, living conditions were easier, and they could wait in relative comfort to see what was going to happen in Petrograd and Moscow. Emmie was advised not to pack any winter clothes and left all her heavy luggage behind in the flat at Petrograd, which was to be lived in during their absence by Mr Rozhdestvensky's sister.

At Rostov, where they had to change stations, the river Don had overflowed and flooded the streets, and they had to be ferried by rowing boat from one station to another. Their destination was Gelendjik, a small resort on the Black Sea not far from the port of Novorossisk and situated, according to Baedeker, 'on a crescent-shaped bay, with 1800 inhabitants and good bathing'. No mention here of what struck Emmie as easily the most attractive feature of the little place: its splendidly appointed public baths, for which she was given a month's supply of tickets. Each week, in a deep sunken black bath with pale green tiled walls, she luxuriated in the pleasant warmth of the salt water, and as soap was useless, a warm paste of fuller's earth was provided which made her skin beautifully soft.

The season had not yet begun when they arrived in Gelendjik, and the whole place had a strangely neglected air about it. Before they could move into their very modest guest-house, all the beds had to be brought out into the open and anointed with methylated spirits to kill off the bedbugs. It was the evenings in Gelendjik that Emmie remembered best of all. Most of the day must have been spent on the beach with Oleg, for the sticky red clay underfoot made long walks impossible. But the evening had its own magic. Emmie had made friends with another Russian family who had travelled from Petrograd; the daughter was a student of English at the University. In the evenings the two of them sat talking English together on a stile at the far end of the family's large garden facing the sea. Emmie was fascinated by the green roses—green because of the glow-worms gleaming brightly inside the flowers. The air was delightful, and their hair was made to crackle and stand on end by the phosphorus in the mist coming off the sea. When they finally went indoors, and the others had all come in from the beach or a late evening swim, Emmie would be invited to stay on and drink tea with the family, taking her place in the cheerful noisy group round the samovar, which stood on a table in a room otherwise almost devoid of furniture.

She was sorry to say goodbye to Gelendjik. With very little warning they were on the move again. They travelled first to the port of Novorossisk, where they boarded quite a small boat. It had a strong unpleasant smell of smoked fish but it was comfortable. It took them across the Black Sea to 'the most fashionable and most expensive of the Crimean bathing-resorts . . . a district town with 30,000 inhabitants . . . picturesquely situated on an amphitheatre rising from a large bay of the Black Sea'—in other words, to Yalta. And what a contrast between the run-down little guest-house in Gelendjik and the luxurious Hotel Dzhalita at the far end of the promenade, with its oleander plants by the entrance and its tennis courts in the grounds!

At Yalta, in the summer of 1917, we glimpse for the last time the traditional world of the English governess and her Russian charges. For the last time they leave their hotels regularly every morning and make their way down to the beach. The lucky ones, like Oleg and Miss Dashwood, do not have far to go: the best part of the beach is almost opposite their hotel. The pavements are already hot, and the governesses are wearing white shoes and stockings, and thin light-coloured frocks. Miss Dashwood is wearing white buckskin shoes, her white piqué dress with the blue sailor collar ('they were quite fashionable then in England too') and a little white piqué hat from Wells, the hatters in Norwich. Oleg is also wearing a white sailor suit. Unlike Volodya Rahl with his military ancestors and his sentry box, there is naval blood in Oleg's veins, and his sailor hat is perched at a jaunty angle. To enter the beach they have to pass through a turnstile, for which they have previously bought a supply of tickets. Beneath the wall of the promenade there are fixed seats where the governesses install themselves, safe in the knowledge that nothing can be washed away by the tideless Black Sea.

'Not so many of us here this morning,' one of them remarks.

Some of the governesses are Emma Dashwood's age, others considerably older. They seldom know one another's surnames and even less often Christian names, but occasionally closer friendships are formed. Oleg has a jolly expression and is well liked by the other children and by Emmie's governess friends. Further along there is another paying beach used as a sun-bathing centre with a doctor in charge, where Oleg acquires by degrees a tan without scorching himself. The doctor also gives him massage to reduce his weight, for nautical Oleg is already in danger of acquiring a nautical paunch.

The sun still seems to be shining on Yalta beach in the summer of 1917; but if the storm cloud has not yet moved up, already it has cast its shadow before it. How strange, thought Emmie, that the beaches and boulevards seemed to be peopled almost entirely by Russian children and their governesses. Where were the parents? Why did the Rozhdestvenskys seldom even set foot outside the hotel? It must be to do with the heat, she supposed; or perhaps life was always like that in Yalta. One evening she was invited to visit a Russian girl living just off the far end of a fashionable boulevard running inland from the promenade. The girl was a semi-invalid not allowed out in the evenings—no doubt one of the many T.B. sufferers to be found in Yalta. Returning along the boulevard later that evening, Emmie was surprised to find it quite empty. And yet Yalta was said to be full; you couldn't find a hotel room anywhere. The explanation, of course, is that the situation then in Yalta *was* unusual. The usual holiday atmosphere was missing; no one knew what tomorrow would bring, and people preferred to keep themselves to themselves. 'All round and everywhere there is only anxiety,' wrote the well-connected compiler of *The Russian Diary of an Englishman*, who was also in Yalta that summer.

Within walking distance along the coast was the small white palace of Livadia, which had been built in 1911 and where the Imperial family spent many happy times during the spring and summer. It was quite a long uphill walk from Yalta. Between the road and the sea far below there was an uninterrupted expanse of vineyards. Very mouthwatering the grapes looked too on a hot day . . . but they were protected by a high fence and by armed watchmen in towers specially built at intervals. Emmie found herself thinking of the anthem about the watchmen who 'lifted up their voices together': these men, alas, would not 'break forth into joy' but with a loud cry of 'Woe betide you if you touch those grapes!'

They turned off on to a sandy track which cannot have been open to the public during Tsarist times. It led down steeply towards the beach through the gardens right in front of the palace, which was then being used as a hospital. Surrounded by roses and heliotropes, convalescents lay basking in the sun on beds dotted about all over the sloping gardens. To Emmie Livadia beach 'never seemed absolutely real, it was like a dream beach—the sand was so white and even now I can still feel that balmy air'. Bathing and picnics were much more fun at Livadia than at Yalta. It was there that Emmie met another English governess of her own age, with a pupil the same age as Oleg; 'no, I don't remember her name, we were just ships that passed in the night'. They lived not far from the palace. Unlike Yalta there were no turnstiles or fixed seats to bother about, and very often the four of them had the beach entirely to themselves.

Emmie had been given a room of her own on the ground floor of the hotel with a door leading to the garden, in which there were several individual chalets. After the midday meal everyone took a siesta. Emmie took hers in a shady spot just outside her garden door. One day, dozing in her chair, she became conscious of an unusual sound. Half-opening her eyes, she beheld a young man at the foot of the chalet opposite, playing a ukulele. . . . Then a young girl appeared on the chalet balcony. No, thought Emmie, I'm not dreaming, it must be something to do with that film they were making on the beach . . . and was about to close her eyes again when another young girl appeared round the side of the chalet. She had pretty dark hair and was smartly dressed in a pale blue frock with a large white chiffon hat. It was a curious thing but she bore a striking resemblance to. . . .

'*Gertie!*'

'*Emmie!*'

A few siestas must have been disturbed that afternoon.

It turned out that Gertie Kirby, who had nothing to do with the film, if film it was, had stopped off unexpectedly in Yalta for a few hours with her Russian pupil and his mother en route for their holiday home at Novo-Semeis, a small resort further along the coast.

'They're waiting for us in the garden of the hotel next door,' said Gertie.

Emmie spoke quickly to Madame and was soon sitting in the garden of the Hotel France. A very tall glass full of iced chocolate and other delectable things stood on the table in front of her. Before the glass was finished Emmie had received and accepted (since she knew there was holiday due to her) an invitation to join them later in Novo-Semeis for a fortnight.

The open wagonette jogged along the winding road from Yalta. There were about a dozen passengers, seated back to back facing the roadside. The sun beat down, the air was full of changing perfumes and the eye feasted on all kinds of exotic fruits. A Tartar village they passed through reminded Emmie of a colourful fairground in the brilliant sunshine. The wagonette set her down some way from the appointed rendezvous with Gertie. She immediately changed from her good shoes into a pair of light sandals. Shoes had become unobtainable and she kept well supplied with sandals which could still be bought in the market place at Yalta.

Those two weeks passed very quickly. They shared a room and often sat up talking until the early hours. Gertie, like Rosamond, had heard that her brother had been killed in the war but they did not talk about that.

When Emmie returned from her holiday, most of the familiar faces were still to be seen on the beach. She had one special friend in Yalta. Mabel Morris was a teacher of English who had been in Russia for some years. She lived in Moscow at St Andrew's House, the governesses' hostel, where she had two comfortable rooms, and took summer holiday jobs in the south: for teachers of English, like laundresses, had to go where the work was in the summer. Some ten years older than Emmie, she was very English in appearance and a stalwart member of the choir of St Andrew's Church in Moscow.

Emma Dashwood was always happy to be given good advice in Russia. 'If you want to return to England,' advised Mabel, 'you should come back to Moscow with me and not stay on in Yalta for the winter, even if it does mean paying your own fare.'

The Rozhdestvenskys were loath to part with her, Oleg especially, but they had no plans for returning north. If separate accommodation was not available at St. Andrew's House, Emmie could have the use of one of Mabel's rooms.

Mabel made all the arrangements. Round and round the mountain went the post horses taking them from Yalta to the railway station at Simferopol, where they were to start their journey to Moscow.

It would soon be the month of October 1917.

PART THREE

21

Cranberries and Potato-flour

'Are you going to write about the cranberries? I think that's the best story of all. If it hadn't been for those cranberries . . .'

'And the potato-flour . . .'

'Yes, the cranberries *and* the potato-flour . . .'

Mabel had brought the cranberries—a pound of them—all the way from Yalta to Moscow. Emmie saw them first when Mabel was unpacking in her sitting-room at St Andrew's House. But the story of the cranberries must not be rushed. As the imperturbable folk of Norfolk say: all in good time, my dear, all in good time.

Though St Andrew's Church, even down to the boiler-room where she had found her mislaid woollen jacket, was familiar to Emmie from her Moscow winter of 1912–13 with the Rahls, she had never before been to the nearby St Andrew's House. As the name suggests, it had been built by the same rich Scots lady, Mrs McGill, living in Moscow in the nineteenth century, whose donations were chiefly responsible for the building of the church. It was a pleasant building with accommodation for about thirty English governesses or teachers. Some, like Mabel Morris, might be permanent residents who had their own suite of two rooms and went out each day to give lessons; they always seemed to be in a hurry and were not often seen, except at mealtimes. Others were birds of passage, perhaps breaking a long journey there, or taking up temporary residence while they looked round for a new living-in job. The house had the abstemious atmosphere of a working community. There was a communal sitting-room and a dining-room with long tables: since many of the residents were out for meals, each meal was charged individually, at cost price. Emmie did not need to share with Mabel after all, as there was a cubicle available. She moved into a very large room containing four of these cubicles: curtained-off areas like small bedrooms with their own dressing-tables and wash-stands. In the centre of the room stood a table and chairs, and there was a large communal dressing-table over by the main window, where the light was strongest.

So that part of Mabel's plan had worked out well; but as for returning to England—'you haven't a hope,' they were told at the British Consulate, 'you'd have done far better to stay put in the Crimea.' And to think that Emmie had paid her own fare all the way back from Yalta! Later she received from the Consulate a 'safe-conduct', which stated in Russian that 'the bearer of this document, a British subject, Miss Emma Dashwood, is resident in Moscow and is under the protection of the British Consulate General'. This document, still extant, is signed by O. Wardrop, who had recently replaced R. H. Bruce Lockhart as British Consul in Moscow.

By this time the five who had been in Petrograd at the beginning of 1917 were widely scattered. Rosamond, of course, was safely back with her parents in Norwich; Edith too had reached her promised land and was working in the Russian Department of the Foreign Office in London; while Louisette, having left Petrograd with the Korniloffs not long after the February Revolution, was living in the south of Russia. Scottie had stayed on longest in Petrograd, long enough for the sight of Lenin and Trotsky haranguing the crowds to become a familiar part of her daily life during the summer of 1917. But the firm of Vickers, realising that the situation in Petrograd might become too dangerous for them to stay on there, had taken the precaution of reserving rooms for their staff at the Hotel Metropole in Moscow, and late that summer they decided to move out. But who was going to be responsible for taking all the drawings of guns and howitzers down to Moscow? The chief asked for volunteers among the men in the office. None was forthcoming. 'Eventually,' relates Scottie, with splendid lack of fuss, 'they asked me, so I packed up and caught the midnight train, complete with all the hampers and drawings.' The remark is characteristic: quiet, self-confident, and so full of Scottish matter-of-factness that she seems to be unaware of any dangers involved. After a few days at the Metropole, Scottie left to make way for the staff arriving from Petrograd and moved into a room on the ground floor at St Andrew's, where she had stayed several years before while working for the Siberian copper company.

She was probably already there when Mabel and Emmie arrived from Yalta.

On the first Sunday after their arrival, Mabel and Emmie went to St Andrew's Church and sang in the choir together. Emmie understood that this was not a special tribute to the beauty of her voice: 'I was dragged into it, the choir was so depleted then.' After the service several of the governesses started chatting in the churchyard before going back to the hostel. Among them was a friend of Mabel's called Miss Baldwin. She was elderly and very correct, and wore a hat at all times. She could not find a job and longed to return to England, though she had no relatives there. 'If the worst comes to the worst,' she said—and the remark was to stick in Emmie's memory—'I'll go back and open a little toffee-apple shop on the corner of one of the poor streets, and get a living that way!'

Although St Andrew's was not an official agency, it was an obvious place for anyone seeking an English governess to make enquiries. An Englishman living in Moscow, Mr Wilton, was looking for a resident governess, and Emmie went for an interview. Thanks to Mrs Russell (Dorothy Cooke), it has been possible to identify this Mr Wilton as her maternal uncle, Robert Wilton, who was for some years Moscow correspondent of *The Times* and one of the best informed of all Englishmen on revolutionary events in Russia.

When she was shown into Mr Wilton's study, Emmie could not help exclaiming at once: 'Norwich Cathedral!' There was a picture of the Cathedral hanging behind his desk, and she learned that he had been brought up on the Earlham Road in Norwich, only a stone's throw from Emmie. Yet in spite of this coincidence she did not get the job. Mr Wilton's Russian wife had recently died, but he was still quite a young man, and propriety demanded that his children's governess should be someone older than Miss Dashwood.

At her second attempt, however, she was lucky. Her youth must on this occasion have been an advantage; in those difficult times an elderly governess could well be more of a liability than an asset. Within a fortnight of her arrival at St Andrew's House, Emma Dashwood had been engaged as resident governess to the eight-year-old son of Judge Teslenko.

One morning near the end of the fortnight, she was sitting before breakfast in front of the large communal dressing-table by the window, combing out her very long hair and chatting with an acquaintance from the next cubicle: a middle-aged governess of very smart appearance who had not been able to find a job.

'Yes, you *have* been lucky,' said the latter. 'You know, I've always wanted to meet a Dashwood. Such a good name. I expect you're connected with the ——shire Dashwoods?'

'Well, if I am,' replied Emmie, 'it must be at the very tail end of that family.'

Only now does the implication strike her: that it was good connections which had enabled her to find a job so quickly.

'If it hadn't been for Miss Morris,' Emmie went on, 'I'd never have come here at all. Still, that's Fate, I suppose.'

'Not Fate, but surely a Wise Providence.'

A Wise Providence. . . . Yes, but what about that pound of cranberries?

Mabel had brought the cranberries from Yalta for a definite purpose: to make *kissell,* a Russian cross between a blancmange and a jelly. Unfortunately she had no idea how to make it. Governesses and teachers, used to being cooked for by others, are often quite hopeless in the kitchen. Emmie was only slightly less ignorant in this respect than Mabel but had picked up a little from Nanny on the estate at Pervitino.

'Do *you* know how to make it?' asked Mabel, reclining on the comfortable chaise-longue in her sitting-room.

'Well,' I said, 'cranberries, potato-flour and sugar—simple enough.'

She didn't need me to tell her how to eat it because she loved it both ways—hot or cold. I preferred it hot.

'But where can I get hold of potato-flour?'

'I can ask for it,' I said—I was used to asking for things in the shop on the estate. 'Half a pound of potato-flour: *polfoonta kartofelnoi mooki.*'

'But is there a suitable shop near?'

'Well, why don't we take a walk down to Yeliseyeff's one afternoon?'

Mabel was somewhat alarmed by the thought of going into such a grand shop to buy potato-flour—it was rather like going into Harrod's or Fortnum & Mason's and asking for a box of matches—but there was no alternative; Mabel had scarcely learned to speak Russian at all in her job as an English teacher, and Yeliseyeff's was the only shop that Emmie knew from her previous winter in Moscow.

It was the afternoon before I was due to move in to Judge Teslenko's. We had a lovely walk along the Tverskaya. . . . I rather think it was on that walk Mabel told me how someone had had a watch stolen at the hostel and it had turned up in the lavatory bowl. . . . Anyway, I spotted the right counter straight away.

'*Polfoonta kartofelnoi mooki*,' I said in my best Russian. '*Skolko?* How much?'

They handed me a little chit.

'I'll let you pay over at the desk,' I said to Mabel in English in quite a loud voice.

Then all of a sudden two tall, smartly dressed ladies, who must have heard me speaking English, came hurrying over towards me.

'*Nasha Miss Emmie!*' they exclaimed in great excitement. 'Our Miss Emmie! We've found you at last!'

They hugged me and kissed me, and then I realised who it was: Volodya's two aunts! I tried to explain that I was just going back to the hostel with my friend, but they simply wouldn't hear of it.

'Miss Emmie's coming to tea with *us*,' they said, and that was that. 'We'll see she gets home safely.'

Oh, they were so *thrilled* to have found me!

The aunts were staying in the hotel above Yeliseyeff's. Emmie could tell that they had only recently come from the south, because they were still wearing tall hats and had not realised that such hats were no longer socially acceptable. It turned out that while Emmie had been living with the Rozhdestvenskys in Yalta, having lost touch with the Rahls after the February Revolution, the Rahls themselves had actually been living 'next door' to Yalta in Theodosia, another Crimean port further to the north. After the Revolution they had been forced to leave the estate at Pervitino, and like so many families had sought refuge in the Crimea. During that time they had even been trying to find out Emmie's whereabouts in Petrograd, where they had last heard of her, in the hope of persuading her to join them again. 'Somehow the two of them took it for granted that now they'd found me, I'd be going back to the family—and I seemed to take it for granted too.'

When Emmie met them again a few days later they were certain that arrangements could soon be made for her to be fetched and taken south. In the meantime they had a very good friend in Moscow with a husband and small son, who would be happy to engage her as governess until the right moment came for her to leave Moscow. But there was still Judge Teslenko to be considered; Emmie had already started her job there. However, the Judge could not be sure of staying in Moscow—not surprisingly, perhaps, when one remembers what happened to the Law Courts in Petrograd—so Emmie was able to make this her excuse for giving notice. White-haired Miss Johnson from the hostel, who had been looking for a job for ages and felt quite hopeless about finding one, was only too happy to step into Emmie's shoes.

'To think of going into a shop like that to spend a few kopecks and receiving such a reward. And on the very day before I was due to leave St Andrew's. I think that's the best story of all. Not Fate but surely a Wise Providence. . . . If it hadn't been for those cranberries . . .'

'And the potato-flour . . .'

'Yes, the cranberries *and* the potato-flour—I'd have been with Judge Teslenko and who knows what might have happened to me? I'd never have met Volodya's aunts and I'd never have gone to stay with their famous friend . . .'

And Mabel's *kissell*?

'You know, I never thought to ask her whether she made it or not.'

22

The Battle

Imagine at the top of this page the curved, swooping wings of a sea-gull, Chekhov's *Seagull*, the emblem of the Moscow Art Theatre.

The story of the Art Theatre, founded by Stanislavsky and Nemirovich-Danchenko in June 1898, and especially of its early ups and downs, is a whole drama in itself. By that first December, when the Theatre was due to put on *The Seagull*, its finances were already dangerously depleted. The play had flopped badly when first produced at another theatre in 1896 and there were fears that an unsuccessful revival might damage Chekhov's by then precarious health. But in spite of everything the opening night of the new production was a great triumph and was always looked back to as a turning-point in the Theatre's history.

The very good friend of Volodya's aunts, with the husband and the small son, turned out to be a remarkable person. Her name was Maria Gérmanova and she was one of the Moscow Art Theatre's most celebrated actresses in the years before the Revolution.

Germanova's association with the Theatre must have begun at an early age, for by October 1905, when she was only twenty-one, she had already been given an important part in the première of Gorky's new play, *The Children of the Sun*. This première, as Nemirovich-Danchenko recounts in his memoirs, was the occasion of a quite extraordinary tragi-comic episode in the Theatre's history. It was a time of great political ferment in Moscow. On October 17th the Constitution had been proclaimed; people's thoughts were only of politics; the première had to be put off until the 24th. There were rumours that members of an extreme right-wing group known as the Black Hundred would actively intervene to stop the performance of a new play by this notorious revolutionary, and that the Theatre was going to be disbanded in any case by the Tsarist authorities. Nevertheless the play went ahead as planned, though the audience seemed to be on the *qui vive* all the time, listening for sounds beyond the walls of the theatre.

In the last act of the play, the professor is attacked by a group of workmen, presented by Nemirovich-Danchenko, stage-manager of the scene, as 'an association of plasterers, all soiled with white lime, and provided with scrapers and small spades'. The professor retreats before them swinging a handkerchief, his young wife (played by Germanova) runs out on to the steps with a revolver, and the yard porter very methodically beats up the offenders by striking their heads with a board.

At the dress rehearsal, the audience reaction to this scene had been one of unceasing mirth. Gorky was unperturbed. 'Let them laugh,' he said. But on the night itself events turned out very differently:

When from behind the wings became audible the first voices of the advancing crowd—and, of course, we gave a very lifelike representation of the scene—the audience was at once on its guard. With the approaching din, it became perturbed, began to drone, to look around, to rise from their seats. And when with retreating back, swinging a handkerchief, Kachalov appeared, followed by a group of plasterers with threatening gestures, a clamour arose and outcries. And scarcely had Germanova with an extended revolver in her hand sprung out on to the steps when hysteria broke out in the parterre, then in the upper tiers, then somewhere in the depth of the auditorium. A part of the public, thrusting out their elbows, rushed toward the exits; another section raised an outcry to persuade the timid ones that the scene was not reality but part of the performance. Someone shouted, 'Water!' Others shouted, 'Stop the play!'—'You dare not make sport of our nerves!' A woman's voice screamed brokenly: '*Seryozha! Seryozha!*' A celebrated ballet dancer writhed with hysteria. There was jostling in the corridors, some tried to fight their way to the cloakroom, others fled as they were—with no other thought than to save themselves. . . .

The truth is, the public took my association of plasterers for members of the Black Hundred, who had come to break up the Theatre and had begun with artistic personnel.

The most diverse shrieking din filled the theatre. And Kachalov and Germanova and my plasterers and Shadrin—the latter was a man of the people playing the part of the yard porter—all stopped playing and in perplexity gaped into the auditorium. The stage-manager's assistant had the curtain rung down.

The really remarkable thing was that the confusion continued for some time. Many who had not had time to escape remained on being persuaded that the men on the stage were real members of the Black Hundred and that they had entered into negotiations with the management. The auditors . . . were ready to swear that they had seen several revolvers in the hands of the Black Hundred intruders aimed at Kachalov.

When calm was restored the performance continued, but the theatre had been emptied of more than half of its audience.

It must have been about the middle of October by the Russian calendar that Emma Dashwood joined the Germanova household. Volodya's aunts had told her, of course, that their friend was an actress at the Moscow Art Theatre, but of her reputation Emmie knew nothing; and there was no chance to acquire that knowledge before they were all, Germanova included, having to play their parts in a drama of real life. If at the time of the February Revolution there had been street fighting and bloodshed in Petrograd, in Moscow no fighting at all took place and not a man was killed. This situation was reversed during the Bolshevik Revolution of October. On October 25th/November 7th two shells grazed the side of Petrograd's Winter Palace, where members of the Provisional Government were still in session, but nothing more violent than that was needed to put an end to Kerensky's regime; whereas in Moscow fighting continued for almost a week. The opposition to the Bolsheviks came mainly from five thousand young officer cadets who took possession of the Kremlin.

The cast for this drama is a small one, as follows:

Maria Germanova, an actress, aged thirty-three. Tall and graceful. 'A beautiful woman with a caressing voice and innate qualities of a great actress' (in the words of the critic, Marc Slonim), whose 'figure, eyes, tone, her whole manner suggested Anna Karenina' (Nemirovich-Danchenko).

Germanova's husband, also in his thirties. Tall and thin.

Andryusha, their six-year-old son. A happy child and (fortunately) easily amused.

Emma Dashwood, an English governess. Twenty-seven years old but does not look it; of less than average height.

(The inevitable maids and servants who normally fill up the lower part of the cast list are absent; two maids did usually live in, but neither was on the premises when the Battle started. There is however one other character whose presence at that particular place at that particular time seems at first so unexpected that he might well be thought of as a playwright's whimsical invention, but for the fact that he is described in a recent edition of the letters of Chekhov's widow, Olga Knipper, the Art Theatre's most famous actress.)

Suhravardi, a young Indian. Graduate of Cambridge University. Writing a thesis on the history of nineteenth-century Russian literature. Frequent attender at the Art Theatre and on friendly terms with many of the actors and actresses. (Was he in the middle of a social visit to Germanova when the Battle started and trapped him in the flat?) Speaks perfect English with a cultured accent, so that Emma Dashwood can only think of him as an unusually sunburnt Cambridge graduate. Smartly dressed in a very light grey English flannel suit; also below average height.

The setting is Germanova's comfortable third-floor flat above shops on a street off the Arbát, one of Moscow's best known and busiest thoroughfares, clearly visible less than a hundred yards away when you look out of the large bay window in the dining-room. The Arbat leads to Arbat Square, a strategic point from which heavy artillery can be directed by the Bolsheviks against the cadets in the Kremlin.

Not far from the flat guns suddenly begin firing and all the dining-room windows rattle ominously.

There follows a lightning change of scene: to the vestibule of the flat, opposite the lift. 'We shall be safe in here,' someone remarks, 'even if the windows are blown out.' The vestibule contains a large table and chairs, and in normal times serves little purpose except as a place where visitors can be asked to wait. Now it comes into its own. There is much scurry and bustle as the various characters exit left, right and centre and return laden with armfuls of rugs and cushions. The vestibule has no windows, so the doors have to be propped open for ventilation. They will remain in this vestibule for the next six days. Each person has his or her own private sleeping area against the wall: 'rather like travelling on a comfortable train', comments Miss Dashwood, never at a loss to see the bright side.

The dialogue alternates between Russian and English. Madame Germanova speaks perfect English, her husband only Russian.

Andryusha speaks a little English at the start, and quite a lot more by the end of the week. Unfortunately none of the script has survived in Miss Dashwood's memory, but it might have borne some general resemblance to the Arabian Nights; for it was Suhravardi's idea to pretend they were in the Orient by spreading cushions round the floor and telling one another stories. He himself told amusing tales of his life in India, and Emma Dashwood, I imagine, was also able to make her contribution. So in striving to keep Andryusha amused, they also succeeded in keeping up their own spirits. Did Germanova tend to be the centre of attention? Not a bit of it, apparently. She was mainly concerned for her son and there was never anything at all of 'the actress' in her behaviour.

To be honest, the action of the drama is lacking in development: 'sitting it out' did not prove very eventful. Off-stage there was little let-up in the terrific din of gunfire coming from the Arbat area. They would have liked to take a glimpse from the dining-room window to see what was happening, but did not dare go in. All the dramatic interest centres on a single prosaic theme: food. The Battle was not very old before the food in the kitchen began to run out, and they were reduced to a diet of sugar, black rusks made from rye, and as many cups as they liked of China tea—so the water supply must have continued to function normally. Yet it would be wrong to over-dramatise this theme, for Miss Dashwood cannot remember that any of them suffered greatly from their privations.

And the dénouement? At last there came a time when another lull in the firing seemed to have gone on much longer than usual. Madame Germanova decided to take a look from the dining-room window; her husband thought it was still too risky and tried to dissuade her. Germanova turned to Miss Emmie for moral support. The two of them—tall Russian followed by short Englishwoman—walked gingerly across to the large bay window and looked out towards the Arbat. It was quiet and completely empty, though the state of the buildings bore witness to the battle that had raged there.

Fortunate indeed that the Battle came to an end when it did, for they had almost exhausted the supply of black rusks. From sub-sequent enquiry they learned that casualties in their block of flats had not been heavy: a cook on the top floor had lost a thumb!

But what a relief after those six cramped days to be able to walk without fear to any part of the flat, and to go out again on the first

Sunday after the Battle into the streets of Moscow! The wide pavements were thronged with Muscovites who had come to inspect the damage to the buildings. Though there was nothing unusual in her dress, the tall and graceful Germanova could not help being a distinctive figure. As the five of them—four adults and Andryusha—walked along in a line, Emmie became aware of fingers pointed in their direction. Then she caught the words:

'*Vot Germanova!* Look, there's Germanova!' They were friendly, excited voices—well, you know the Russians, they don't say things softly —and I thought to myself: good gracious, she *is* well known, and I hadn't realised! I think people were reassured at seeing her. Look, they seemed to be saying, there's Germanova, *she's* all right.

Lucky Miss Emmie too! At a time when those associated with the old regime went in fear and trembling, she walked without thought of danger, for the Bolsheviks had no quarrel with the Moscow Art Theatre; though Miss Emmie, I suspect, would have walked like that in any case, with or without Madame Germanova.

Scottie saw the Battle of Moscow in quite a different light: literally, for as she lay awake in her room on the ground floor at St Andrew's House, she could see the sky suddenly lit up by flashes of gunfire, or glowing from the light of houses that had been set on fire and were burning themselves out. An expert in such matters since starting work for Vickers, Scottie had no difficulty in identifying the 9-inch guns firing on the Kremlin, or the 3-inch guns which fired day and night down a boulevard parallel to the little street in which the hostel was situated. St Andrew's was packed with governesses of every description, and the sitting-rooms, like that of Mabel Morris with its comfortable chaise-longue, must all have been turned into bedrooms by this time. Food was short there too, and no one turned up her nose at being offered a stale crust soaked in water with Oxo added to it.

When the situation became calmer, Emma Dashwood's thoughts turned to the trunk which she had left behind that spring with Oleg's aunt in the Rozhdestvenskys' flat in Petrograd. It contained all her heavy winter clothing, and with the thermometer falling rapidly, she determined to retrieve it at the earliest opportunity. Madame Germanova provided her with sufficient food to last for the return journey and she caught the night train from Moscow.

In Petrograd she spent what was to be her last day at the Aunts' flat in Kronverksky Prospect. Perhaps it would have been better if she had not done so, and retained only memories of the cheerful, well-run flat of the past, where in winter a fire was always burning in the English-style grate in the hall, and domesticated Aunt Jane would go down on her knees in front of it to warm the visitors' coats before allowing them to step out into the cold of the street. Now, just to keep the kitchen stove alight, they had to go out in all weathers in search of logs and drag them back through the streets of Petrograd, running the gauntlet of onlookers like the one who stopped and jeered: 'Look at the bourgeois horses!' They were still in good heart and pleased to see her, but made no secret of their relief on seeing that she had brought all her own food with her.

The Aunts sent their maid, Polya, with Emmie to fetch the trunk. They were able to take the short cut that Emmie had used so often before, from Kronverksky Prospect to the back entrance of the flats on the Kamenno-Ostrovsky. Oleg's aunt was living in a single room of the flat, furnished as a bed-sitter. She was glad to help Emmie with the trunk and watch them drive away by sledge, thankful no doubt to see the back of it at a time when searches of private accommodation were frequent and everyone had to be able to give a good account of all their possessions. Though she had a second-class ticket, Emmie travelled back to Moscow in the luggage-van, sleeping as best she could on top of her trunk. She was not the only one to take this precaution. The luggage-van was full of passengers sleeping on the floor or on top of their luggage; or rather not sleeping, but making sure that their belongings were not stolen during the night.

Germanova was very relieved when she arrived back safely, and life returned to a relatively calm routine.

In his memoirs Nemirovich-Danchenko tells how the woman guard of the theatre in St Petersburg,

when we first arrived there, could scarcely believe that these most ordinary mortals were the actresses of our company. 'What sort of actresses are these?' she asked with scorn, having expected bright, loud costumes, coiffures, hats, a special bearing, a special mirth. . . .

'Theatricality' was a dirty word in the vocabulary of these theatrical crusaders, with their fervent belief in the theatre of 'authentic emotion', and this anti-theatricality was well exemplified by

Germanova. She never attempted to draw attention to herself in any way. In the flat she usually wore a blouse and skirt, and the sealskin coat that she wore out of doors, though simple and elegant, was not at all modish. Only in her movements might it have been possible to detect the actress, though still an actress of the Art Theatre; for all her movements were easy and fluent, and seemed to Emmie 'always to be expressing something unconsciously—like a dancer, and yet she *wasn't* a dancer'.

Nor was there any question of her leading a riotous life of theatrical parties or failing to spend enough time with her son, to whom she was devoted. With all her Russian pupils Miss Emmie strove hard to inculcate the spirit of punctuality (wisely, when we recall how frustrated Marie Russell Brown was by the absence of this quality in the adult Russians she had to deal with), and once the breakfast things had been cleared away from the dining-room table, she and Andryusha started promptly on their first lesson of the day. Germanova meanwhile was still in bed. Since the most tiring part of her day was the evening performance, she did not get up early the next morning. At about eleven o'clock she would call out from her bedroom: '*Andryusha, kotoryi chas*? What time is it, Andryusha?' This was the regular cue for Miss Emmie to announce their mid-morning break, which Andryusha loved to spend with his mother.

After the October Revolution the Moscow Art Theatre continued to function, and Miss Emmie was invited by Germanova to attend a performance of Griboyedoff's *Woe from Wit*, one of the best known works in the Russian classical repertoire. Germanova was celebrated for her role in this play as the young heroine, Sofia, and Emmie felt greatly honoured by the invitation.

I was accompanied by Germanova's husband—no, I don't remember much about the theatre or the audience—and we were shown to reserved seats in the front of the stalls. I was so *astonished* when the curtain went up—for there was a large room with a bedroom leading off it, and from the bedroom came the sound of Germanova's voice singing out to her maid: '*Kotoryi chas*? What time is it?'

Well, you know how I am, I just *live* in anything that happens to me, and when I heard that voice I was so staggered, it was so vivid to me, I felt I'd got to turn to Andryusha and say to him: 'Run along to your mother now, Andryusha, it's time for your break!'

One Saturday afternoon a few weeks later, when Germanova was at the Theatre, Miss Emmie was sitting at the dining-room table with Andryusha when the maid came in and delivered the classic line:

'A gentleman to see you.'

The gentleman followed close behind. It was Uncle Vasya, who brought with him a letter from Mme Rahl in Theodosia.

'Uncle Vasya has come to fetch you,' Emmie read. 'We're all dancing round the table here, we've found our Miss Emmie and she's coming back to us.'

'Can you be ready by tomorrow morning?' asked Uncle Vasya.

It was short notice but she had been warned to expect this and so had Germanova. She felt sad to be leaving the flat near the Arbat, where she had lived through six days of history, and to have to say goodbye to Madame Germanova, who had been unfailingly thoughtful and generous. Apart from the Rahls there was no one among her Russian friends whom she would later recall with greater affection.

On the Sunday morning she drove happily by sledge with her luggage to the station. By a strange chance she caught sight of some of her English friends just as they were coming away from morning service. At church the previous Sunday she had spoken to Mr Stephens, the man who had once said to her on the boat going to England: 'They all come back to Russia. They always do.' Now, like everyone else, his only thoughts were of how to get away.

'Are you *off*?' the other governesses called out, catching sight of her luggage. 'Oh, you *are* lucky!'

'And you know,' comments Miss Dashwood, 'it gave me such a terrific surprise when they said that to me, because I hadn't realised till then how worried they all were and what a bad time they were having. . . . It's true, I *was* lucky, all the time I was in Russia. Meeting Volodya's aunts again like that and staying with Germanova made me feel coming back to Moscow from the Crimea hadn't been such a mistake after all.'

But fate was less kind to the elderly Miss Baldwin, who had no relatives in England and always wore a hat. Before the Battle she had not been taking meals at St Andrew's and perhaps had been too proud to admit she was not having meals elsewhere either. She never had a chance to open her toffee-apple shop in one of the poorer streets, for soon after the Battle she was taken ill from malnutrition and did not recover.

23

Trains

'Of course travelling in Russia is no longer what it was.'

The words echo down the years because they are the opening sentence of Mackenzie Wallace's famous book on Russia, first published in 1877. The tone is typically tongue-in-cheek, the ironical understatement suggesting a contrast between the conventional poetry of Russian travel (snow, troikas, padded coachmen, jingling bells) and the modern reality of a railway network already in the 1870's beginning to spread over a vast country.

But to the foreign visitor even a prosaic railway journey had a flavour of its own in Russia. You might be charmed or irritated by the way in which the train would stop in a forest or among fields to enable the wood-burning engine to get up steam again, whereupon lots of passengers would get out to stretch their legs until warned by the engine bell that they were about to move on again; or by the mystifying way in which Russian stations were often miles distant from the towns they were meant to serve. The trains were not very fast but comfortable; at least, first and second class were. If you happened to be the children of a railway giant like Nikolai Karlovich von Meck, they were very comfortable indeed, for then you had your own private family carriage with a separate children's compartment and meals prepared specially for you at railway restaurants along the line. Third class was neither clean nor comfortable, but it was companionable. When Tolstoy travelled by railway (which was not more often than he could help, since he had an aversion to trains, and in his fiction train journeys are regularly associated with some disaster in the characters' lives), he shunned the bourgeois second class and either travelled first in aristocratic seclusion, or third and hobnobbed with the peasants.

But how ominous Mackenzie Wallace's words sound if we transpose them to the context of Russia after the Revolution! After the Revolution travelling in Russia was indeed no longer what it was. After the Revolution it became a waking nightmare.

There are 'real' nightmares in which we find ourselves setting out on a long train journey. We know there is a train that we are desperately anxious to catch; there may not be any others. With growing impatience we await its arrival; will it never come? When at last it appears, we scan the carriages; already the train is full to overflowing! Panic gives us the strength to scramble aboard somehow. The crush is unbearable, but even in its midst we find ourselves asking: what am I doing here? where can I be going?

All these feelings and many more were experienced in reality by the railway fugitives in Russia after the Revolution, and the nightmare did not end with their awakening. A home after all is still a home, even if you have no food, even if it is searched or pillaged; it is still there, even if you are arrested or imprisoned. Such horrors seem bearable. It is not to them but to those terrible train journeys that we should look to appreciate the disruption and dislocation of day-to-day life in post-Revolutionary Russia. Homes had been abandoned, almost certainly for ever. Behind the fugitives lay a shattered past and the future was unknowable. What am I doing here? Where am I going? Why can I not wake from this waking nightmare?

Such must have been the feelings of Helen Clarke and her Russian companions when they travelled from Bakmout to Kharkov in January 1918.

Helen was a young Englishwoman living in the Ukraine, in the south-west of European Russia, on the estate of a Russian family whom she had known well since before the war. In the spring of 1914 she went out to stay with them as usual, never dreaming that on this occasion her visit would last for five long years. The estate was doubly prosperous: beneath its twenty thousand acres of fertile soil there lay rich deposits of coal, for it was situated in the Donets Basin, Russia's principal coal-mining area. One of the young men employed at the mines, remembered because he used to come to the house to collect subscriptions, later became well known to the world: his name was Nikita Khrushchev.

Distances were vast in that part of Russia, but for Helen, brought up in the English Fens, there was nothing alien about those limitless horizons. More than any of the other Englishwomen we have described, she responded deeply to the poetry of her surroundings. In a passage already quoted, from the introduction to a private account of her Russian experiences written soon after her return, she evokes the atmosphere of a Russian country house, with its large, cool rooms, wide corridors and comfortable nooks, where 'you would feel yourself no stranger; for your welcome would be so sure that in less than no time you would be wondering if by any chance you had been there before'. She responds to the pattern of the seasons in Russia: to the white pall of winter and the sudden arrival of spring, when you can lie in the long warm grass looking up at the trees and imagine the leaves are moving, so fast do they seem to be growing; and to the great vast stillness of summer, when the corn waves and shimmers for mile after mile like a sea of swaying gold. And she remembers the distinctive sounds of life on that Ukrainian estate: the music of the nightingale—'some people have an idea that nightingales sing only at night, but that is quite a mistake'; the comforting little song of the toad, so quiet and persistent, and the more dramatic music of the frogs—'there will be one long note and then the whole orchestra will break out into the most bewildering music; it will get wilder and madder till it reaches a perfect pandemonium, only to die down as suddenly as it began'; and the song of the peasants, 'low, sweet and harmonious, but sad, so sad. Why should their music be sad?', she writes at the end of her introduction. 'All nature in this glorious country is so gay, and seems to impel happiness. Are not the people also meant to be happy? In this vast and grand country, is there no room for happiness? At present, I fear not, for this country is Russia.'

The Donets Basin had long been a centre of political unrest, but for the first two and a half years of the war life on the estate changed very little. Their first real intimation of trouble came on New Year's Day, 1917,

in the shape of a very abusive, illiterate letter, addressed to the lady of the house, demanding that the sum of three thousand roubles should be ready and would be called for by a certain date about a month hence; if this demand was not complied with, the whole household should pay the penalty with their lives. The letter was signed by 'a party of three hundred strong'. Not a very pleasant greeting for New Year's Day! and one which could not easily be forgotten.

Although the lady of the house, Vera Petrovna, and her husband, Vladimir Petrovich, did not feel in immediate danger, they were aware of a strange undercurrent among the servants and workmen, and decided to move with their five children to the nearest centre of population, the small town of Bakmout, several hours' journey away. Bakmout was a miserable little place lying in a deep valley, full of soldiers being drilled. After more than a fortnight when nothing was heard from the outside world, news finally came through of the February Revolution, and great was the excitement in Bakmout: 'people ran about the streets crying for joy, shaking hands and congratulating one another'. A number of sailors arrived from Kronstadt, bringing with them Bolshevik literature and holding large open-air meetings; their propaganda soon made great strides.

In the summer of 1917 Bakmout became almost unbearable and three of the children sickened from the heat and poor sanitation. Though the parents did not dare to return to their estate, it was thought safe enough for Helen, whose role by this time has become in effect that of the loyal English governess who identifies her own interests entirely with those of her Russian family, to go back there with a nurse and the three sick children.

We found our house in order, but the garden very much spoilt by the peasants and miners, who already considered it theirs by right; and we were obliged to stay near our home or run the risk of being insulted. On Sundays our garden was the chosen spot for picnics, and men, women and boys came in front of our windows playing concertinas and dancing with the very evident intention of annoying us. It was indeed irritating, but quite useless to interfere. We knew we were entirely in their hands; any movement on our part would have given them the incentive for which they were waiting. They broke down the beautiful fruit-trees and tore up the flowers by their roots.

By the autumn life on the estate had become impossible again, and they returned to Bakmout. 'We left with the sad feeling that we looked for the last time upon the dear old place. And so it was, for a few months later it lay in a heap of ruins.' After packing all the silver, plate and trunks the night before, they slipped away unobserved in two cars early the next morning; they could not travel by train, as all baggage was being searched at the mines which were already in the hands of the miners. As they sped along, they came upon a flock of wild turkeys, a most beautiful sight. About a hundred of these huge birds had been forced down, the frost having made their wings too heavy for flying.

But in Bakmout life quickly went from bad to worse, with a complete breakdown in law and order.

In the town there was a large store of spirit which belonged to the Government, and as all sale of spirit had long since been prohibited, the store was considerable and the Town Council, knowing it to be a great danger to the community owing to the lawlessness of the soldiers, decided to let the spirit leak away gradually down a drain. This was soon discovered by the soldiers, who were very quickly in a state of intoxication by sucking the mud into which the spirit had leaked. It also so infuriated them that they rushed the spirit store and fired into one of the reservoirs. This naturally caused an immediate explosion, and flames leapt up sky-high. It was a grand, though terrible sight. The sky was a lurid red, and all through the night, the fire roared and crackled. The following day it had somewhat abated, and the streets were alive with men, women, and even children, running with every conceivable vessel to procure the spirit. The soldiers rushed out in flames from the burning building, rolled themselves on the ground or threw off their clothes. Many fell, cutting themselves terribly with the glass bottles which they had filled with spirit; and the most horrible sights were to be seen in the streets, chiefly owing to the breakage of glass. After the fire had burnt itself out, the bodies of two soldiers and a baby were found drowned in one of the reservoirs. Without doubt, a woman holding her baby had gone to dip in her bottle, and in doing so, had let the child fall.

When the Bolsheviks arrived and took over the town, Helen and her friends quickly had to find places in which to conceal their valuables: not such an easy task when living in a second-storey flat in a modern house. Fortunately most rooms in the Ukraine are whitewashed, so they bored a hole in a bedroom wall, plastered it over and whitewashed it. There was also a large space between the ceiling and the roof, reached by a tall ladder and a trap-door. The problem here was what to do with the tell-tale ladder once their work was finished. Someone would have to pull it up into the roof space; but how could the person then get down again, since the trap-door was fully twenty feet above the ground? At last they hit upon the idea of collecting four tables, three of which were placed on top of one another. Then one person went up the ladder into the roof, another climbed on to the third table, the one above pulled and the one below hoisted. It was nervous work, for outside the town was in an uproar and they never knew when their door might be burst open. But finally the ladder disappeared into the dark recesses of the roof, and the fourth table was hoisted into position. This was just high enough for the person in the roof to jump down and close the trap-door behind him, and when he reached the floor, they all laughed nervously and felt thankful it was over.

About 130 miles north-west of Bakmout lies Kharkov, second city of the Ukraine after Kiev. It too was in Bolshevik hands. At great risk Vladimir Petrovich travelled there to collect from one of the banks his wife's papers, jewellery and money, returning safely with the jewels sewn into his clothes and money into his shirt. But each day in Bakmout brought new fears and dangers. Vera Petrovna received a demand for 50,000 roubles (£5000), but when the man came up the front stairs, she fled down the back, leaving Helen to confront a very excited and voluble individual who failed for some time to appreciate that *she* was not Vera Petrovna. That same evening Vladimir Petrovich was due to return from another journey. Afraid that the house was being watched and that he would be arrested, Helen went out into the street to intercept him; at about nine o'clock he came along, driving fast; she waved him down and sent him on to his wife's hiding-place.

But about midnight both husband and wife returned to the flat. They had decided there was no point in trying to hide, as the children might be taken as hostages. Next morning the two of them went out into the town. Half-an-hour later came news that Vladimir Petrovich had been arrested; this could mean either imprisonment or death on the spot. But within an hour Vera Petrovna returned. To ensure her husband's release she had signed a cheque for 70,000 roubles (£7000) and rushed back for another 5000 roubles in notes: the contents of the hole in the bedroom wall that had been whitewashed over.

Vladimir Petrovich now lost no time in leaving for Kharkov. The day after, a message came that his wife was to join him there immediately, but on no account to go to her sister's house. As ill luck would have it, there were no trains running from Bakmout next morning, so Vera Petrovna had to travel a considerable distance by sledge across the steppe and catch a train by another line; fortunately the mining area was served by a complicated network of railways. Left in Bakmout with the children, Helen at once set about the task of packing what was essential and selling what was not, prior to leaving with the children for Kharkov. Just as it was getting dark, to her great surprise, Vladimir Petrovich walked in quietly by the back entrance, looking cold, dirty and very pale.

'Has my wife gone?' were his first words.

'Thank God!' he exclaimed, on being assured that she had.

The Red Guards were now hunting for Vera Petrovna and her two sisters, the joint owners of the mine, in the hope of using their private fortunes to pay the high wages being demanded by the miners.

Next morning, without regrets, Helen Clarke said goodbye to the little town of Bakmout. She was one of a party of ten: the five children, their father, herself, nurse, and a man and woman to help with the considerable amount of luggage. They rode on and on across the snow-covered steppe, constantly afraid that their cavalcade of four sledges would attract attention. They ran into a blinding snowstorm and the horses began to tire, but at about five o'clock they reached their destination: a country railway station, where the kindly station-master provided them with a small room, a samovar and one bed. The children fell asleep immediately without a murmur . . . and it was not until the next morning that the nightmare began in earnest.

Our train was due at 5.30 a.m., so about 4.30 we dressed, fed the children, and set out for the station on foot, it being only a few minutes' walk from the station-master's house in which we had spent the night. It was a bitter morning, the snow lay thick on the ground, and the twilight of the early morning struck a note of desolation into one's heart. We trudged along, holding a child by each hand, the eldest being twelve years old and the youngest two; and as we crossed the rails, an old white-haired man came up to me, bareheaded, and bowing low said: 'God help you!'

'Thank you, Grandfather,' I replied, 'we need his help, and may God help you also.'

I shall never forget the impression that old man made on me; his simple prayer and reverent mien; we did indeed need help that day. We knew there might be difficulties, but, thank God, we did not know what we had to face.

After about half-an-hour the train came in. It was packed, people riding on the roofs of the wagons, and on the steps. In those days it was impossible to travel anything but third class, the first being occupied by the soldiers. A third-class carriage in Russia in normal times was anything but pleasant, but at the time of which I am writing, it was a hell. To leave by this train seemed an impossibility, but as it was an absolute necessity, there was nothing to be done but push in. Vladimir Petrovich, the father of the children, although not far away, could be of no help to us. His presence only enhanced our danger as he was too well known, and we were fleeing, perhaps for our lives. I took the baby under one arm, the little boy of six I put in front of me, the three girls and nurse followed hard behind. The floor of the wagon was literally covered with bundles and baggage of every size. The boy pushed his way in, and I after him, and after falling several times, we worked our way almost to the end of the wagon. The wagons are divided into compartments with shelves arranged from the floor to the roof, and on these the passenger lies. Every shelf on this occasion was full to its uttermost, some of them holding as many as four men. The atmosphere was indescribable, the heat unbearable even at that hour of the morning, and we knew we had ten hours of it in front of us. After standing for about an hour, I managed to get the children up on to one of the higher shelves, and there they sat with their legs doubled under them for ten solid hours, the perspiration streaming down their faces, not a bite or sup the whole time, and not a murmur or complaint from them. I knew that one of them had a high temperature, for she had developed chicken-pox the day before we left home.

These compartments are supposed to hold thirty persons at the most, and in ours, over a hundred were crowded, the men smoking, spitting, verminous, the women as bad; not a window or ventilator open, and the adjoining wagon empty save for a few railway officials who insisted upon keeping the door closed. Once, when they passed through, I asked one if he would kindly have the ventilator opened; by way of reply, he swore and banged the door to. At last, there were some men who said they could bear it no longer. Two of them banged on the door and shouted that if the door were not opened they would break it in. As there was no response, a man who sat next to me took out his pen-knife, twisted the lock, and the door flew open. A whiff of fresh air came in, much to the relief of all, but the officials were furious, and threatened us with terrible words. The man whom I had asked to have the ventilator opened was especially brutal. He saw that we belonged to a different class, and took advantage of the occasion to make us conspicuous. He pointed me out as being the woman who had incited the men to open the door, and finished by saying: 'You wait till we get to the next station. I will call the Red Guards and then you will see what you will get.'

The next few minutes seemed like leaden hours. I repeated over and over again that old man's prayer. My fear was that our identity would be discovered, for I was carrying Vera Petrovna's passport since she had travelled with a false one, and I knew that there was no justice in such a crowd. At last, the train stopped, and in came the Red Guards, boys of nineteen or twenty, armed to the teeth. They demanded: 'Who opened the door?' No one answered. Then the same official came forward and said: 'It's that woman's fault that the door was opened,' pointing to me. It was an awful moment, but I remained perfectly quiet and appeared quite uninterested, though I had vivid visions of being dragged out of the train. Fortunately, the Red Guards took no notice of me, but again demanded who had opened the door. Again, no one replied, so they ordered the three men to get out of the train. After a space of five minutes, two of the three men re-entered the train. The Red Guards put the man who had actually opened the door against the wall just opposite our window and shot him. It was terrible, and seemed to freeze one's very blood; that poor man, alive and sitting by my side one moment, and the next a lifeless corpse. But the danger was not over. The temper of such a crowd is very fickle, and may turn at any moment. I felt my safest plan was to keep perfectly silent. I had been pointed out by the official as being the one to blame, and although quite innocent, I was aware that at such a time and in such a company, it would have been useless to protest.

So I sat on feeling bewildered and horrified, expecting to be arrested at the end of our journey which I knew was almost over. As the train drew into Kharkov, our destination, the passengers clambered down from their shelves; consequently, the crush was very great. I told the children to sit perfectly still until I should give them permission to move, and I did the same. Directly the train stopped, there was a rush, but an order was shouted from the other end that no passenger would be allowed to leave the train until an arrest had been made. The nurse with the two younger children was very little distance from me, but being divided by the crowd, became hysterical and cried for help; the two children naturally became frightened and screamed also. Then the crowd began to move towards the door, and I quickly lifted down the three girls, dressed them, and to my astonishment and relief, we all walked out of the train. Vladimir Petrovich met us at the door, his face drawn and haggard. As we stepped out of that awful train, he exclaimed: 'My God, I thought you were all dead.' I could not speak, I could scarcely breathe, being so choked for want of air, and nervousness.

No wonder that the details of this journey were still fresh in Helen's memory almost sixty years later.

24

French Luck

'Of course, it was foolish to take any chances. If you heard a shot in the streets, you were *ventre à terre* before you could say Jack Robinson.'

Thus the bi-lingual Louisette Andrews, using a pleasant mixture of French and English idiom to comment on life in Petrograd at the time of the February Revolution. Like Emma Dashwood's family, the Korniloffs soon had their car commandeered—they heard it being driven off in the middle of the night—and it was not long before they received a visit from a Bolshevik search party. Since the Bolsheviks were not in power, these search parties were in theory still answerable to the people's militia set up by the Provisional Government, and were supposed to confiscate only arms and ammunition, but it was well known that they would not scruple to lay their hands on anything else of value that might catch their eye.

The concierge had warned the Korniloffs early one morning that a search party was expected. They hastily collected together all the family jewellery and hid it about their persons. Louisette was given a diamond brooch, and a pearl necklace which she wound round herself. The Korniloffs were having breakfast when four men carrying guns burst in. They had obviously been drinking and were in an ugly mood. First the staff were herded into the breakfast-room along with the family, and they were all made to put their hands up. Then, leaving one man behind on guard, the other three went off to search the rooms of the flat.

The door to the next room was left wide open. This room was Madame's boudoir. Watching in the mirror through the open doorway, Louisette could see the three men setting about their work. Suddenly she noticed that in her haste Madame had left several *écrins*, or jewel-cases, lying on her dressing-table. One of the men had also spotted them and was moving in that direction. Supposing he opens one of them, thought Louisette, and finds it empty—what then? With horrified fascination she watched him go up to the dressing-table, reach out furtively for the jewel-cases—and scoop them all quickly into his pocket. Louisette breathed again. Once the men had gone, the Korniloffs felt safe, for the searchers could not complain of being cheated out of jewellery they were not supposed to be looking for anyway.

Not long after, like so many other families, the Korniloffs left Petrograd for the south of Russia. They travelled via Simferopol to their large house at Gurzuff, nine miles to the north of Yalta. Gurzuff is described in Baedeker as 'an attractively situated bathing-resort, which may be recommended for a long stay'. It had close links with the poet, Pushkin, who had lived there for a time at the start of his southern exile in 1820, and whose first lyric poem of that period was begun one night on a steamer taking him to Gurzuff. The 'Pushkin Grotto' still remained a tourist attraction. But for Louisette and the Korniloffs the pleasure of that Crimean summer was clouded by threatening letters which forced them to engage a Tartar as a body-guard.

Very soon after the October Revolution, Louisette's brother, Emile, arrived in Petrograd to stay with the Tamplins, intending to bring her back to England as soon as possible. From Petrograd she received a wire telling her to join him there immediately, as there was a chance for English people to get away at last. So Louisette Andrews set out alone on *her* unforgettable journey through post-Revolutionary Russia.

When she first arrived in Russia, Louisette had often written home to her mother saying how glad she was that she found it easy to mix with people, and never had any inhibitions about getting into conversation with complete strangers. This quality of sociability had served her well in her jobs in Russia, especially when she was with the gregarious Korniloffs. But never did it prove more useful to her than on that long journey from south to north, for without it her journey might have turned out very differently.

At Simferopol she ran into her first difficulty. The porter whom the Korniloffs knew well was nowhere to be seen. She had a special permit from the Bolsheviks authorising her to travel, but no ticket, and without this porter's assistance there seemed little chance of getting one. The station was swarming with drunken soldiers brandishing pistols. Just when it seemed that all was lost, she happened to overhear in the crowded waiting-room three nuns speaking together in French. At once she engaged them in conversation and explained her problem. They were travelling in quite another direction, but by a great stroke of luck one of them had a ticket as far as Moscow, and was quite happy to hand it over to Louisette.

By this time she could already hear her train approaching and needless to say, it was packed out. A helpful porter managed to bundle her aboard with her light luggage, including precious food for the journey, but all her heavy luggage had to be left standing on the platform. (Remarkably enough, she was able to recover it later through Westinghouse, her brother's employers.) Picking her way carefully between the bodies of drunken soldiers sprawled in the corridors, she eventually found a seat in a crowded first-class compartment. The compartment gradually began to empty until her only companions were one Russian lady and two men. The men were talking French. As with the nuns in the waiting-room at Simferopol, Louisette boldly started up a conversation, for she felt sure from what they were saying that she knew the identity of the older of the two companions, a distinguished looking man in his forties.

'*Excusez-moi, monsieur*,' she began, 'but I believe I have the pleasure of being acquainted with your nephew.'

'Really, *madame*?'

'Yes, I am a great friend of the Korniloffs, and their son, Vsevolod, was at Law School with him. . . .'

'Ah, the Korniloffs! But of course!'

This broke the ice. Louisette had been right in her supposition. The man into whose compartment she had unknowingly stumbled —in retrospect it seems as if that Wise Providence must have been at work again—was the composer Rachmaninov, then on his way to Moscow and shortly to leave Russia for what was to be the last time.

Without the help of Rachmaninov and his companion, Louisette wonders how she and the Russian lady would have managed on that dreadful journey. The two men did everything possible to help them and make the journey tolerably comfortable. During much of the long trip they had to lock themselves into their compartment for safety. At Kharkov, the destination of Helen Clarke's journey from Bakmout a few weeks later, two men were murdered on the train and their bodies thrown out onto the platform. When they reached Moscow, Louisette needed to buy another ticket to take her on to Petrograd. Before saying goodbye to the two ladies, Rachmaninov and his companion saw to all this for her, and wished them both a safe journey.

At Petrograd they found the station strangely deserted. Louisette shared a taxi with the Russian lady. Compared to the St Petersburg she had known before the war, with its colourful night life, and even to Petrograd after the February Revolution, it seemed like a dead city.

Not long after her arrival at the Tamplins, Louisette and her brother left Petrograd as members of a large party of English refugees. They were one of the few English groups to cross the border by train to Finland, where civil war was soon to break out, making this route impossible. More than five years had passed since she first left England and started her 'six-month holiday' with Emile; almost four since she embarked so unexpectedly on her career in Russia as a reluctant chaperone.

When I came to check Miss Andrews' story with the known facts of Rachmaninov's life, I made a surprising discovery. There have been several biographies of the great Russian composer and pianist, the most detailed, by Bertensson and Leyda, first appearing in 1956. What I read there did not appear to tie in at all with what Miss Andrews had told me. In 1917 Rachmaninov and his family spent a troubled summer together in the Crimea, and on September 5th, in Yalta, he made his last public appearance in Russia. Soon after this the family returned to their Moscow apartment, where Rachmaninov remained for the duration of the Battle. Then, at the end of November, after receiving a telegram from a Swedish concert manager inviting him to appear in Stockholm, Rachmaninov went on ahead with his sister-in-law to Petrograd to obtain permits for the family to leave Russia, and on December 23rd the Rachmaninovs, accompanied by the composer's best friend, Nikolai Struve, all left Russia for good.

Nothing here to make one think that Rachmaninov was in the south of Russia *after* the October Revolution. But when I suggested to Miss Andrews that she might have been mistaken in some way, she stuck stoutly to her story and left me in no doubt that the man on the train had indeed been Rachmaninov. At some time therefore between November 14th, the last day of the Battle, and the end of November when he left Moscow for Petrograd, Rachmaninov must have made a visit to the south; presumably a very short visit, since in normal times this journey took three days each way, and at that period was taking much longer.

But what reason could he have had for undertaking such a very unpleasant, if not dangerous, journey? To fetch something, perhaps? When the Rachmaninovs left the south in September, the composer is unlikely to have imagined that within a very short time he might wish to leave Russia for good. He might well have left behind something of importance that was not immediately required. But what? Surely not money or valuables? Could it have been music? Miss Andrews had the impression that like herself, Rachmaninov and his companion (perhaps not a secretary, as she assumed, but the composer's best friend, Nikolai Struve) were travelling very light.

All of which is pure speculation; but if the reason for his sudden dash south was to salvage the material for future musical compositions, it is pleasant to think that he successfully combined this errand with giving timely help to a young Englishwoman in distress.

25

A British Subject

When Volodya's aunts told Miss Emmie that while she had been staying in Yalta in the summer of 1917, the Rahl family had been living 'next door' in Theodosia, they were using 'next door' in a very relative sense. The Crimean port of Theodosia was a good seventy miles north-east of Yalta. After starting life as a Greek colony in the sixth century B.C., it had been refounded by the Genoese (a Genoese tower still remained a landmark), had reputedly grown to the astonishing size of 100,000 inhabitants by the fourteenth century, and in 1475 was captured by the Tartars. Earnest Victorian travellers made a point of going to study its antiquities. Before I knew of this colourful history or that Miss Dashwood had spent some time there, I had been intrigued by the unusual name of Theodosia, which occurs in Chekhov's famous short story, *Lady with a Dog*, where he describes how the lovers drive out in the early hours of a summer morning to Oreanda, a beauty spot not far from Yalta on the road beyond Livadia, and looking down at the sea from the cliffs, watch the passenger steamer, 'lit up by the warm glow of the dawn and with its lights already extinguished', arriving at Yalta from Theodosia.

Theodosia was slightly bigger than Yalta—its population in 1914 was 38,000—and Baedeker writes that 'its excellent sandy beach has made it a popular sea-bathing resort'. But unlike Yalta it did not give the impression of existing primarily for the sake of its tourists and permanent visitors. It had a life of its own. It was cheaper, less fashionable and less self-conscious than Yalta. Its hotels were neither so numerous nor so expensive, and moreover—a very strong point in its favour so far as Miss Emmie was concerned—you could walk straight down to that excellent sandy beach just as you pleased and not have to bother with tickets and turnstiles.

Tsar Nicholas, anxious to preserve his quiet family retreat at Livadia, had decided that the railway was not to be taken as far as

Yalta, which meant that travellers from the north had to go by train as far as Simferopol and continue their journey by road. Theodosia had been more fortunate. Not only did it have its own station but it was possible to travel all the way from Moscow without changing. On that train Emma Dashwood celebrated her twenty-eighth birthday and (a day later) the English Christmas, and somehow or other her travelling companions—Uncle Vasya and Lydia Ivanovna, a Russian governess who had been with the Rahls for several years—managed to procure some cold chicken for her, which she ate sitting up on her top sleeping berth. With frequent stops for fuel and food, the journey lasted much longer than the three days which Emmie and Mabel had taken from Simferopol to Moscow a few months earlier, but as they neared the south, food started to become slightly more varied and plentiful. Compared to the journeys of Helen Clarke and Louisette Andrews it sounds a peaceful affair.

Approaching Theodosia, the railway swung abruptly to its right and ran along for a short distance between the road and the sea. Beyond the station was the main shopping and residential area, and then the harbour. The Rahls' new home was in the opposite direction, in a quiet area on the outskirts of the town about a mile from the station, and to reach it meant going back along the road by the railway and crossing the bridge at the point where the railway turned inland. On the right, between the road and the beach, stood a small collection of datchas. In one of the first and biggest of these, Emmie later discovered, there lived a large Russian family with an English governess, Olive Barnwell. Then came a pair of smaller houses, the second of which was known after its owner as 'Gorokhovatsky Datcha'. Here the Rahls had been renting the first floor flat since some time in the spring or summer of 1917.

In what circumstances the family had been forced to leave the estate Emmie never found out. Very little was ever said on the subject, and it was almost as if Pervitino and the life there together had never existed. Only once did Emmie learn in passing from Uncle Vasya that before leaving the estate, he had taken the precaution of emptying all the vodka from the distillery into the river. Miss Emmie, it must be admitted, took this story with a large pinch of salt: Uncle Vasya liked his joke. Even though she never touched spirits herself, it did seem to her thrifty English nature a most appalling waste of vodka, especially after all the hard work that had gone into planting and harvesting the pink potatoes. That the peasants were likely to seize the vodka at the first opportunity, and in their drunken condition to smash up the estate, did not enter her head.

But there was one piece of news of which she could not be left in ignorance. Mr Rahl was no longer alive.

Just when and how he had died were likewise never explained to her; perhaps the details were not known even to his immediate family. We can only guess that since he was in charge of a Red Cross train based at Kiev, he may have been too closely identified with the unpopular policy of continuing the war against Germany. His charm and kindness were to be long remembered by Miss Emmie. It was Mr Rahl who had declared so emphatically when the Kovalskys tried to reclaim her in 1913: 'Miss Emmie's with *us* now!'; and who had insisted, quite rightly, that since she was living in Russia, she must do as the Russians do and face up to a proper thick Russian soup, instead of being indulged by their chef in Moscow with a characterless French bouillon. It was he who on one of his last visits that she could remember to Pervitino during the war had brought with him a new car: an open Ford.

'Will you be the one to try this out with me, Miss Emmie?' he asked. 'I expect the others will all refuse.'

As they lurched along the bumpy Staritsa road, dry but dusty in the summer heat, it was almost impossible to remain seated, and a horse in one of the fields was so scared by the noise that it reared and upset its load of hay. And it was Mr Rahl, they explained, who had been looking for her that summer in Petrograd, while all the time she had been 'next door' to them in Yalta.

Yet it was strange how soon Emmie felt as if she had never been away for those two years and had simply returned home after a long holiday to find the family in different surroundings but otherwise very much the same. Volodya had grown, of course, and was shortly to start attending the local school, while Irina was now having lessons from the Russian governess, Lydia Ivanovna, who also spoke English. Uncle Vasya was good company, just as he had always been. As for Mme Rahl, she still seemed young and pretty and cheerful, and enjoyed Miss Emmie's cheerful company—'but oh the ignoramus that I was, I can see now that they were *forcing* themselves to make the most of it, whereas being British I was living naturally, I had such great faith in my own country. I didn't realise there were such horrors going on . . . and perhaps it was a jolly good thing I *didn't* realise.'

None of the servants from the estate was still with them, but two maids who lived with their parents in the town came in daily to look after the house. All the shopping was done by Lydia Ivanovna. 'Whether they were spending a small fortune on food I don't know —they never did bother me with things like that. I remember Lydia Ivanovna telling me once she'd had to pay 17/6 for half a cabbage in the market, but it was one of those great big cow cabbages which were very hard and lasted us for ages.' At breakfast they had a coffee substitute: ground roasted barley mixed with chicory. Bread was a sandy shade of brown with a lot of crust. Lunch usually consisted of cabbage soup and meat rissoles, sometimes followed by rice-cakes with a sweet raisin sauce. Sunflower oil was used for all the cooking: dirty-looking stuff which made a terrific smell.

On the ground floor of 'Gorokhovatsky Datcha' lived two more Russian families with whom they had little contact, but Emmie soon made friends with the young Russian girl who lived very quietly with her father in the small datcha next door. There was a covered-in tepid swimming pool which served both houses, and the entrance to it was just opposite the Rahls' garden gate. They met frequently either at the pool or on the beach. The girl reminded Emmie of the Russian friend she had made at Gelendjik, for she was in her twenties, very jolly, and probably a recent graduate as her English was so good. She did not seem to have any friends and was always glad of a chat in English, inviting Emmie to enjoy the shade of her parasol.

Unlike the Rahls, who were only renting their datcha, the girl's father must have been an owner-occupier, for their house was known as 'Ulyanoff Datcha' and the girl was Miss Ulyanoff: not a very remarkable name in Russia, but for the fact that it happened to be Lenin's real surname; and in Theodosia the story was current that this Mr Ulyanoff was none other than Lenin's brother, desperately trying to lead a life of quiet obscurity. Lenin himself was then forty-seven. Miss Dashwood cannot remember where she first heard the story, but almost certainly it came from knowledgeable Miss Barnwell, the English governess in the large datcha further up the road leading into town.

A not-to-be-missed opportunity for Emma Dashwood, who never

came anywhere near meeting Rasputin and failed to bump into Rachmaninov on a train, to squeeze her way into the history books; but was the story true? The mysterious Mr Ulyanoff certainly gave the impression of being a hermit, but there was nothing unusual in those days about people keeping themselves to themselves. Emmie was never invited into the 'Ulyanoff Datcha' and caught sight of its owner only once: a fleeting impression of 'a fairly elderly gentleman standing in front of the mantlepiece with his hands behind his back, wearing a black smoking-cap and with a little grey beard like the Tsar's'.

A smoking-cap? A little grey beard like the Tsar's? As a description of Lenin's brother it sounds so delightfully inappropriate that it has to be true! But unfortunately it does not take much research to establish that whoever else he might have been, this man could not have been Lenin's *brother*. The elder brother, Alexander, was executed in 1887 for his part in an unsuccessful plot to assassinate the Tsar, while the lives of the two younger brothers, politically both above criticism and too young in any case to match our description, have also been fully documented by Soviet historians.

There remains the possibility that the man might have been Lenin's cousin. Russians distinguish less sharply than we do between 'cousin' and 'brother': a male cousin is a 'once-removed brother' and may often be referred to loosely just as 'brother'. Moreover, Lenin's family background was bourgeois rather than proletarian. His father was a Director of Schools, his mother the daughter of a doctor who had retired from practice and bought an estate. Bruce Lockhart thought that at first glance Lenin might have been taken for a provincial grocer. There were certainly cousins growing up alongside Lenin in the provincial town of Simbirsk, now Ulyanovsk, where he spent the first seventeen years of his life: older cousins too, the children of an uncle who was nine years senior to Lenin's father. But here the trail quickly grows faint. These cousins fade into the background after Lenin's adolescence, presumably pursuing their own middle-class careers—perhaps purchasing their own small datchas in the Crimea?—and deliberately cutting themselves off from Lenin's revolutionary activities.

That Mr Ulyanoff was indeed Lenin's bourgeois cousin, the black sheep of the revolutionary family, skulking away in Theodosia and acceptable neither to Reds nor Whites, with a daughter shunned by everyone except an English governess who knew no better, seems to me quite possible: partly on the 'no smoke without fire' principle and partly because such coincidences seem to happen so frequently in Russia as to be no longer surprising. But whether this painstaking piece of research on my part will have earned Emma Dashwood even so much as a footnote in the Lenin biographies still seems open to doubt.

The alarming face of revolutionary history did however come uncomfortably close even to Miss Emmie in the early months of 1918.

The Crimea was then in the hands of the Bolsheviks. At Sevastopol, according to Obolensky, 'the revolutionists had opened all the jails, taken the convicts into the fleet, given them uniforms and used them to terrorise the population'. In Yalta Bay, which Miss Dashwood and Oleg had visited every morning the previous summer—he in his white sailor suit and she in her white piqué dress with the blue sailor collar—the water is unusually clear. On sunny days early in 1918, under the water of the tideless Black Sea, you could easily make out a number of corpses, waving their hands with the currents: fifty officers, some dead and some alive, had been thrown into the bay by the Bolsheviks with stones attached to their feet. Was it because Yalta symbolised so overtly the idle and privileged life of the aristocracy that it witnessed this reign of terror from the middle of January 1918?

How fortunate then that the Rahls had chosen to establish themselves not in Yalta but in Theodosia, that much further away from Sevastopol. Miss Emmie's luck had held again. If there was a reign of terror in Theodosia, she was not aware of it. 'I do seem to recall seeing some sailors once driving through the streets and firing their rifles into the air, but I just said to myself—they must have been drinking, pay no attention to them. I never thought that kind of thing had anything to do with *me*—I felt so safe because of being *British*.'

There was however the 'slightly unpleasant' incident of the Bolshevik search party.

Most of the rooms in the Rahls' flat were facing the sea, but Miss Emmie had a room of her own at the back of the house with a pleasant view of the almond and apricot trees in the orchard. The two parts of the flat were joined by a communicating door, but otherwise it was like having her own flat with a separate staircase entrance from the garden.

The search party was expected. They went first to the main part of the flat. Emmie learned later that the search there had passed off without incident: 'we didn't seem to be people of any special importance—they didn't pay more attention to us than to anyone else'. In any case, Mme Rahl and Uncle Vasya had had plenty of time in which to conceal whatever they wanted to conceal. Miss Emmie knew of only one hiding-place. The toilet beyond the kitchen was small but had a very lofty ceiling. Once when the two maids from the town were unable to come and Lydia Ivanovna was doing all the cooking, Emmie saw Uncle Vasya making a false ceiling in the toilet and hiding Mme Rahl's furs inside it. From then on, whenever she had to use the room, she always felt uncomfortably aware of what was lying just above her head.

The search party had not been told of the connecting door, and Emmie first saw the three armed men as they came round through the garden.

'Now remember,' Uncle Vasya had said to her, 'you are a British subject. Tell them they have no right to search your room.'

She knew that the searchers were looking for such things as jewellery, weapons and Bibles. Her conscience was easy as regards jewellery and weapons; as for her Bible—she was quite determined not to let anyone take that away from her. Going out on to her small balcony, she closed the door behind her and took up her position in front of it.

'Open that door,' demanded the leader of the group on reaching the balcony, while the other two men waited watchfully down below.

His tone was polite but firm.

'No, no,' replied Miss Emmie, 'you cannot go in there.' And stood her ground.

'Hands up!' ordered the man, less politely, and moved to push past her.

Miss Emmie did not put her hands up, she was too busy trying to think of the words she wanted in Russian.

'No, no,' she tried again, with the confidence of one who is unaware of danger, and thinking only of the precious Bible on the table in the room behind her. 'You cannot go in there. You have made a mistake. I am a British subject.'

'A British subject? Show me your passport.'

Emmie always kept her passport in a special large pocket stitched on to a pyjama girdle inside her skirt. Unfastening her skirt at the side, she brought out the passport straight away.

My Russian couldn't have been *perfect*, but he could see I wasn't a bit frightened. Ooh, I wouldn't let him *have* the passport! I opened it out and showed him where my name was and my photo. He looked at me, then he looked at the photo, and then he looked at me again. '*Izvinite, barishnya!*' he said (and when Miss Dashwood tells the story, these words are always spoken in a tone of the utmost deference). '*Izvinite, barishnya!* Beg your pardon, Miss! Good day to you!'

And off the three of them went.

'*Molodets, nasha Miss Emmie!*' exclaimed Uncle Vasya, when they were comparing notes about their experiences later on. 'Well done, our Miss Emmie!'

26

The Governess Takes Risks

At the time of the February Revolution the English were still popular in Russia. Challenged by the crowd and asked why he was not wearing a red ribbon, the English businessman, Stinton Jones, replied by showing them the small Union Jack that he wore under his greatcoat in the lapel of his jacket, whereupon they immediately gave three cheers for England and allowed him to proceed on his way. But after the October Revolution things were very different. Whereas the Provisional Government had been in favour of continuing to support the Allies in the war against Germany, the Bolsheviks were strongly opposed. Nor were they concerned to make any fine social distinctions: for them all English people in Russia, whether diplomats, businessmen or governesses, were tarred with the same capitalist brush as the Russian upper classes. Their nationality, of course, still gave them some protection. 'How we wish we had a passport like yours!' Volodya's aunts had confided to Emma Dashwood shortly before the Battle. But though our governesses may have derived some comfort from the belief that they belonged to a country which would always come to the protection of its subjects wherever they might be, in reality their position became increasingly vulnerable after October 1917. If the Bolsheviks stopped just short of complete hostility towards British residents in Russia (during the period from 1918 to 1920 a number of British civilians, including governesses, were arrested and imprisoned, but none, so far as I know, was ever shot), this was only because they dared not run the risk of provoking massive British intervention.

No, life after the Revolution cannot have been very pleasant for the English governess in Russia! Yet it is precisely at this time of crisis that her qualities show up to best advantage. Loyalty and reliability had long been her trademark. To these were now added a courage and resourcefulness that are very remarkable and provide a fitting climax to the story of her century in Russia. The days of gracious living had become a distant dream. Like everyone else she was engaged in a constant battle to keep body and soul together. But it was not just her own welfare that she had to think of. She might easily find herself the only able-bodied person left in a family where the parents were dead, imprisoned or in hiding, and the remaining members were too young, too old or too sick to fend for themselves. She rose to the occasion. All her reserves of physical and mental toughness were called upon to cope with the exhausting, never-ending task of foraging for fuel and provisions.

But her close association with upper-class families in Russia also placed her in a position of considerable danger, especially if she chose to identify her own interests entirely with those of her family. Loyalty might often be taken to the point where she acted with complete disregard for her own safety. Not every governess would have gone so far as May Griffiths, who, when the members of her Russian family were lined up to be shot, is supposed to have insisted on lining up to be shot alongside them, and was only restrained by a younger sister in whom the taste for self-sacrifice was not so highly developed. But this kind of *spirit* seems to have been the rule rather than the exception. Even the Daughters of Albion came into their own, for self-discipline, a cool nerve and a sense of superiority to all those around her were just the qualities needed for the highly risky and confidential tasks entrusted to the English governess.

Miss Neame was one of the many English governesses who must have been caught up in the dangerous business of helping high-born Russians to flee the country. Her story is told by Nadine Wonlar-Larsky, the aunt of Vladimir Nabokov, in *The Russia That I Loved*. Miss Neame was governess to Georgie, son of the Tsar's younger brother, Grand Duke Michael, who had refused the throne after the abdication, and to Tata, his wife's daughter by a former husband. (A royal scandal had followed Michael's clandestine marriage in 1912 to a commoner already twice divorced.) In October 1917, after steadfastly refusing even to consider leaving Russia, the Grand Duke finally agreed to a plan whereby he and his wife, Miss Neame and the two children, and Mme Larsky's daughter, were to escape by car from Russia to Poland. The jumping-off point was to be the estate of Nabokov's father, a member of the Provisional Government, at Batovo. Mme Larsky, Miss Neame and the two children arrived there safely on the morning of October 25th in the Grand Duke's Panhard, and were to be joined during the night by the Grand Duke and his wife in their Rolls—not the most inconspicuous vehicle for such a venture!

But it had all been left just too late. October 25th was the day of the Bolshevik coup in Petrograd. On reaching Batovo, Mme Larsky learned that the car's arrival had been spotted, that the local Commissars intended to arrest its occupants, taking them for members of the Provisional Government trying to escape, and that the telephone wires had been cut. Her first thought was how to warn the Grand Duke. 'Leaving the children in the hands of brave Miss Neame, I managed to get a horse and rode to the hospital where I found one line still working. I rang up the Grand Duke, explaining to him in English what had happened, knowing that should we be overheard no one could understand the language.' From then onwards the Grand Duke and his wife were kept under house arrest, but shortly before Christmas they agreed to send the two children abroad under the care of Miss Neame. This was not easy to arrange, but the plan 'was carried through successfully, unnoticed by the Bolsheviks'.

In the last months of 1917, all over Russia, on country estates and datchas, in palaces, town houses and apartments, upper-class Russians were engaged in a feverish activity: either digging holes in remote corners of the grounds, or drilling cavities in the obscure angles of walls, so as to secrete therein the family jewels and valuables. Elderly ladies were ingenious with balls of wool. It was important to conceal these activities as far as possible from the Russian servants, who could not always be relied upon. Nabokov has described how their doorman, who had earlier been an agent for the Tsarist secret police when Nabokov's father was a political suspect, 'in the winter of 1917–18 heroically led representatives of the victorious Soviets up to my father's study on the second floor, and from there . . . to the south-east corner room . . . to the niche in the wall, to the tiaras of coloured fire'.

But who better at keeping a secret than that model of loyalty and discretion, the English governess? Members of the family might be shot or imprisoned, but the secret would still be in safe hands. One governess at least, according to Professor Elizabeth Hill, 'was the only survivor for years who knew exactly under which tree the family jewels and silver were buried on the estate'; and for all we know, they may be lying there still.

Being entrusted with the precious secret of the family jewels; helping to smuggle high-born children out of Russia from under the noses of the Bolsheviks; as we look back now, it is easy to surround all this in a colourful, romantic haze, to see in it the material for an exciting tale in the best tradition of *A Tale of Two Cities*. But to those involved at the time these activities were too commonplace to be colourful: there was no excitement, for living in a state of constant apprehension soon became the normal state; there was no drama, but only a grim reality lit by occasional flashes of grotesque comedy.

These are impressions gained by reading *From A Russian Diary 1917–1920*. Its author is an anonymous Englishwoman whom I shall reluctantly have to call Miss X. She seems to have been in her late thirties, possibly older, had been living in Russia for some years and made a number of Russian acquaintances, and spoke the language fluently. In 1917 she was living with a Russian family in a town on the main railway line from Moscow to the west. The father occupied the same position as Mr. Rahl, as a Marshal of Nobility for the district, while his wife, the owner of three estates, was 'the daughter of a well-known and much-loved member of the first Duma'. There were three children—a girl of eighteen, a boy of nearly fifteen and another boy of eight; also a number of rather elderly dependants. Judging by the enormous exertions that she made and the terrific risks that she took on their behalf, Miss X. must have known this family very well indeed and identified her own interests with theirs entirely. We hear of her going out into the provincial town to give private English lessons, but I assume that she was, or had been, a governess to the children. She seems particularly close to the teenage son, Nikita, whom she refers to as 'the dear old boy', and might easily have first joined the family as his governess. But it is strange that she never makes this explicit, and I do not think the word 'governess' occurs once in the whole diary, not even towards the end, when she is writing about the residents of St Andrew's House. Did she feel that there was something socially degrading about having to admit to that title, with its Victorian stigma? Is it significant that her woollen jersey and raincoat were bought at Harrods?

She was certainly no lover of the new social regime in Russia.

When she sees some soldiers run over a woman and not even stop to find out if they have hurt her, she does not hesitate to tell the other onlookers what she thinks of their 'magnificent' revolution. She is convinced that all the Bolsheviks, including Lenin, are Jews in German pay. 'Lenin's father,' she writes, 'was a Jew who married a Christian named Ulyanoff; soon after his marriage he changed his name from Zederbaum to Lenin; the children used the mother's surname.' Garbled, of course—Lenin's father was in fact a Russian named Ulyanoff, Lenin being the son's political pseudonym—but Miss X. in her provincial town, and for that matter in Moscow too, where she joined the family in the autumn of 1918, was constantly picking up rumours true and false. 'Yesterday we heard that Mirbach (the German Ambassador) was killed; today they say Lenin has been murdered. Is it true?' Of Mirbach, yes; Lenin, no.

Miss X. is tough and she is resourceful; in her quietly determined way she must have been quite a formidable character. In Moscow she does not think twice about travelling by train to their provincial town in appalling winter conditions to collect food for the family, returning with over ninety pounds to carry;

it would have been easy enough to carry on my back, but I had it in two packets which I had to carry in my hands; the train was so long that our truck, one of the last, was far out past the signal-box. I staggered along as best I could, but rather slowly. My slowness, however, had a good side: when I got up to the barrier the searchers had already gone and I passed unmolested, my precious provisions safe. How relieved I was!

It is she who in the spring of 1918 cultivates single-handed a large kitchen garden, on the produce of which they later live almost entirely. The diary entry for May 20th, Trinity Sunday, begins:

Yesterday I got up early, as usual, and was at work in the garden before 4.30. I worked until 9, then came into breakfast; there was no bread, no potatoes, nothing except coffee. Luckily there was milk, so had three cups of coffee. Went to work again; had to dig beds for my cucumbers, which needed to be planted out. Worked till one.

She is afraid of cracking up but does not, though the strain, mental more than physical, is apparent in entries such as that for September 17th, when they were making hasty preparations to leave for Moscow, with the immediate threat of searches and arrests hanging over them:

I only hope I shall not lose my head with all I have to do; when I am tired and at table look up and see Tatiana Nicolaevna, with her head shaking as it has done ever since she was in the Moscow firing, it irritates me dreadfully.

Before this departure for Moscow she has to sell certain items on the family's behalf and to hide or jettison others that should not have been in their possession. 'We had no leave from the Bolsheviks to sell, and might find ourselves in prison for so doing, but I meant to take the risk.' On September 21st she writes:

I had not a second today. I sold much. After dark I threw into the pond four big copper samovars, one small silver samovar, four big candlesticks, three candlesticks of the old Russian pattern, the Count's candlestick, the big brass ewer, the big brass pot. Buried two boxfuls of coins belonging to either Nikita's or his father's collection.

On September 23rd 'threw more copper into the pond'; later that same day 'must get into bed . . . am dead tired. Have just been throwing more things into the pond.' Next morning men from the Soviet arrive to make an inventory of the furniture. 'When they first came they had no order with them; we very politely begged them to return for it, as we wished to be quite sure of their being authorised to inspect the house.' Miss X. is not slow to seize her opportunity: 'whilst they were gone I sold a big mirror'.

Soon afterwards she reaches Moscow safely with three trunks and her hand-luggage, but not without an unpleasant cross-examination at the Moscow station, where her Bolshevik interrogator asks what she thinks of a portrait of Karl Marx. Very interesting, she replies; is he one of their leaders? 'Of course Marx was long dead. This amused him very much, and evidently convinced him that I was a fool.'

But only a couple of days later she is returning to the provincial town to dispose of still more family possessions! She hides the bronzes from the garage and scares the lodgers out of their wits by depositing three of the heaviest pieces in their bath, which they beg her to remove—'very foolish of them, for their rooms have not once been searched'—but she does finally consent to take the bronzes upstairs with the help of Franz, an Austrian prisoner-of-war, and somehow they manage to hoist them through the trap-door in the roof.

But the last and trickiest operation was still to come. Some time previously the family jewels had been hidden underneath the ground in the cellar. At 3 a.m. Miss X. is woken by the Baroness, another prominent member of the family due to leave shortly for Petrograd.

I went down to the cellar, covered all the air-holes, then lit a candle and started digging; but, although I worked until 5 a.m., I could not come on the glass jar—I only used a trowel. I was afraid to use a spade. . . . Overhead slept our lodger's nephew, who only the night before had screamed because he heard a noise on the verandah.

Next evening Miss X. went and called Franz, whom she had told to be ready for her.

He came; I had a spade ready. I think he fancied I wished to bury something, and was a little surprised when I told him to dig until he struck glass. He worked hard, the sweat streamed down his face; but not until he had made a huge and deep hole did he at last find the bottle— a big one, some fifteen inches high and six or seven in diameter . . . I went up to my room and opened the jar. The stench was awful; water had in some way got in, or perhaps some vile gas had helped. I undid all the little silk bags, some of which were so rotten that they fell to pieces; then I started sewing. Row after row of pearls went round the bottom of a long pair of stays, quite at the bottom went two or three rows of golden chains. All the top was filled with brooches and parts of the dismounted diadems, and carefully covered with cotton-wool so that they would not stick into me and hurt. Then four boot-polishers were produced; on to two of these jewel after jewel was sewn, then came a layer of marl and cotton-wool, then the other two were sewn down over them. From time to time the Baroness came up to see how I was getting on; at 3 a.m. I told her I had nearly finished, she need not come up again, but would she wake me at 6 a.m. At 3.30 I had finished; at least I thought I had; but as I rose to my feet a ring fell to the ground and rolled some distance, then lay like a drop of blood. I bent and picked it up, there was no place left for it. Since the day of my arrival I had been wearing two of the late Countess's rings on a ribbon round my waist; it was put with them. I went to bed. At 6 a.m. the Baroness woke me and took away the pail full of that dreadful black, stinking water and all the little pieces of silk and had them done away with. They had spent the night on the verandah. Dressing was a tedious job; everything had to be sewn to everything else with stout twine. I would be on my feet all day and perhaps all night too; there must be no accident.

That evening the Baroness and Miss X. at last got away. They walked to the market-place, then took a cab; Miss X. was afraid of walking further.

I went to the station. I was too late for the 11.40 train and had to wait for the 2 a.m. . . . Our baggage was examined by three men at Y—. I was not the least nervous, even though one man said he had heard the ring of metal and told the other to look carefully; I knew he had heard the medical syringes which I was taking to Maria Petrovna. . . . Our baggage was again examined in Moscow. I got through all right . . . got to the house about two or three o'clock, took off all the jewels, including that blood-red ring which had been hurting me dreadfully, bundled them under my pillow, and went fast to sleep. . . . In the evening we made the jewels up into as small a parcel as possible and next morning they were taken out of the house.

* * *

Of course, house searches under the Bolsheviks were not so perfunctory as they had been at the time of the February Revolution, when the search party at the flat of the Misses Chamot in Petrograd, where Scottie was staying, had not dreamed of looking further on being told by the old butler that there was an English lady in the bedroom who was not well. One of the problems about these searches was that you never knew what someone else might have concealed before you. The head of Miss X.'s family, Alexander Alexandrovich, had gone to live in Moscow, and unknown to the others had left behind what amounted to a small arsenal of weapons hidden in different parts of the house. Turning out a cupboard in his room, Miss X. 'had a pleasant surprise': there was a revolver lying among a pile of shirts. 'Just like him,' she complains to her diary. Although the penalty for keeping firearms was death, she took it up to her room, for, true to her English principles, she still had 'qualms of conscience as to throwing other people's belongings into the pond'. A week or two later a search party came to the house. 'Luckily, they went into the Countess's room first. I had time to run into mine and put the revolver inside my dress.' (Sounds simple, but what kind of dress was it that hid a revolver with so little difficulty? Old-fashioned and voluminous? Anyway, Miss X. had no fears that the revolver might be detected about her person.) Returning boldly to the Countess's room, she invited the searchers 'to visit the attic and go through the trap-door on to the roof; they did not consent to either'.

Miss X. sends a note to Alexander Alexandrovich asking what he wants done with his revolver. He tells his son to hide it, but the son botches the job, the maid comes upon it, and Miss X. finds it on her hands again. Not long after, noticing a hard lump on the side of an armchair, they fish out another revolver and some cartridges. 'The cartridges are in the pond; the revolver in my room. Now I have two.' It could not be left in the armchair because, apart from anything else, the Bolsheviks were requisitioning armchairs. A week later they discover more cartridges in the armchair. Persuaded by a Russian friend of the family that if the revolvers are found in her room, she really will be shot, Miss X. at last buries them. The same friend tells her that if she looks hard enough on top of the stove in Alexander Alexandrovich's room, she will find something else. She does: a rifle, three swords and several packages of gunpowder. She hides the rifle and swords 'under a piece of iron which ran the length of my balcony and one end of which was loose so that I could just force the things under'. No mention of where the packages of gunpowder went: into the pond, presumably. That same afternoon new lodgers arrive to take possession of the room, and the first thing they do is to heat the stove: 'how pleasant for all if the gunpowder had still been on the top!'

Two days later a search party comes to the house. They search thoroughly, room by room, and stay over three hours. Awaiting her turn, Miss X. sits in her tiny cell wondering where to place a bottle of liqueur. 'Out on the verandah? Dangerous; for, if they found it, they might go on searching; then the swords would come to light. Between the double windows? Not good enough. Behind the door stood my high dark-blue water-jug; into that I stowed it.' She allows herself to be discovered with a Greek grammar open in front of her, as if studying. The searchers are not rude, and their haul for a long evening's work is negligible. 'Poor things,' comments Miss X. with an unexpected note of commiseration, 'they have two more houses to do tonight', but quickly recollects herself and adds: 'They wished us "Restful night" and we them a restless one.'

But the most nerve-racking incident of all took place one morning just before Miss X. was due to leave the town for the second time. Before breakfast the yard suddenly filled up with carts, men swarmed into the house, and Jacov, the Commissar, informed them that he was going to take away all the furniture, leaving one bed, one table and one chair for each person. As the men were lifting a pile of things which had been taken out of the late Countess's room, something fell to the ground with a metallic ring.

I knew what it was; wherever I had turned the last few days I had come across bullets; Alexander Alexandrovich even had two little bombs in the attic. I thought I was done for, Jacov was just behind me. Luckily, two clumsy fellows were trying to remove the grandfather clock; Jacov thought the clock pendulum or weights had been responsible for the noise, and he angrily told them to be careful. I bent and picked up a little bag which had fallen; it was heavy. Going into the next room where only Franz, quite aghast, was staring his eyes out, I examined my find—bullets. I handed them to Franz with—'Into the pond at once.'

That pond must have been quite full by the time Miss X. had finished with it!

27
Scottish Pluck

At the start of 1918 there were only two girls remaining in Russia of the five who had been in Petrograd a year earlier: Emma Dashwood and Scottie. Apart from the summer of 1912, when she accompanied Galina von Meck to England, Scottie had been in Russia continuously for six and a half years. Like Emmie she had lived through the Battle of Moscow, lying awake in her room on the ground floor at St Andrew's House and watching the night sky suddenly lit up by flashes of gunfire. She spoke Russian without a trace of accent and felt quite capable of taking care of herself; but how she longed to see her native Scotland again!

One of the Bolsheviks' first priorities after the October Revolution had been to make peace with Germany, but when negotiations at the peace conference of Brest-Litovsk, where the new Soviet Government was represented by its fiery Commissar for Foreign Affairs, Leo Trotsky, broke down in February 1918, the Germans immediately began advancing into Russia. Afraid that they might reach Moscow, Scottie's chief at Vickers, Colin Anderson, decided that the two of them should try to get back to England via Archangel. In fact, the Soviet Government was quickly forced to accept the German terms, and the Treaty of Brest-Litovsk was signed on March 3rd; but by that time Colin Anderson and Scottie had already left. In any case, with Russia out of the war, Vickers' presence in Moscow was obviously pointless.

There has been much reference in previous chapters to the far south of European Russia: to the Black Sea and the Crimean Peninsula, where grapes and huge water-melons grow in abundance, and where the ports and seaside resorts, like Yalta and Theodosia, are on a latitude only slightly to the north of Nice and Menton. Now with Scottie and her boss we leave Moscow and travel in exactly the opposite direction. There are wolves howling round the train as it makes its way due north through the bleak February landscape to the White Sea port of Archangel, which is free of ice only from May to October. Archangel has strong historical links with Britain, for it was in that area that Sir Richard Chancellor landed in 1553 and was summoned to Moscow by Ivan the Terrible. This led to the formation of a British trading company in Russia, whose activities were for many years centred on Archangel, until the foundation by Peter the Great of St Petersburg at the beginning of the eighteenth century; and there still remained in Archangel a British Consulate, and an English Church on the main street.

The town itself, which in 1914 had a population of 38,000 (the same size as Theodosia) was spread out along the right or northern bank of the Dvina delta, about thirty miles from its outlet to the White Sea. The railway station, however, was on the left bank, and to reach the town took one hour in summer by steam-ferry. Scottie and Colin Anderson arrived in winter to find masses of snow everywhere, and reindeer sledges waiting to convey the passengers across the frozen river. These sledges were driven by Samoyeds, a non-Russian people native to the area; and flying down the river in a reindeer sledge, three reindeer abreast, was to become one of Scottie's chief delights in Archangel.

But there seemed very little chance of a speedy return to England. Colin Anderson's idea that they would be able to travel by sledge across the frozen White Sea and round the Kola Peninsula to Murmansk was obviously quite absurd. (Murmansk, founded in 1915, was the port well within the Arctic Circle, which remained free of ice all the year round because of the proximity of the Gulf Stream.) It would be another three months before the river at Archangel broke up. And to make matters worse, neither of them had any money; in order to earn some, Scottie began giving English lessons, and worked in a greenhouse in exchange for a meal.

A further complication then arrived in the persons of an English mechanic, his wife and son, who had travelled all the way from Tsaritsyn on the Volga, where Vickers had started the first gun works. Scottie haunted the Consulate in her efforts to find some way of getting these three back to England. At last the Consul told her that an icebreaker was due to cross the White Sea to the port of Kem, from which it would be possible to travel by rail to Murmansk. It was decided that Scottie should go with them. They set out in two

sledges for the winter port of Ekonomia, near the mouth of the
Dvina, and from there walked out across the ice to the icebreaker. It
was not a large boat and all the accommodation provided for them
was one small officer's cabin. The wife and Scottie slept on a tiny
bunk, the husband on a bench and the son on the floor.

After a day or two they had an influx of school children travelling
to their homes round the White Sea. Then a Commissar came to
inspect them and to check their passports. He passed Scottie without
any bother, impressed perhaps by her fluent Russian, but did not
seem so happy with the other three. Later Scottie saw the Captain.
He told her there had been a hitch, and that a wireless message had
been sent off to no less a person than Trotsky himself. Back came
the answer that all four English people were to be arrested. So in the
middle of the night they were marched back across the ice, with Red
Guards in front and behind carrying fixed bayonets, and taken to a
military barracks where they were detained until morning ('and what
a filthy place *that* was . . . the sanitary arrangements were so primitive I told them I preferred to go out to the road'). Afterwards, when
they had been released and had returned to Archangel, Scottie went
to see the Commissar, who apologised for arresting her, but said that
in any case the boat had never reached Kem, as it had turned back
after ten days with its bows broken. Reading Bruce Lockhart's
Memoirs of a British Agent, one wonders whether the apparently
pointless arrest of Scottie and her companions was an indirect result
of those 'minor frictions' which took place at the time between
Britain and the Bolsheviks, and which provoked Trotsky to sudden
outbursts of anti-British feeling.

Like the ports in the far south, Archangel soon became crowded
with foreign and Russian refugees from every part of the country.
Then at last the frozen river broke up, a British boat arrived, and the
British refugees were taken off. Alas, poor Scottie was not among
them! As had happened to her in Petrograd in the spring and summer
of 1917, when the chance of returning to England had passed by
because Vickers could not find anyone to replace her, she was paying
the price of indispensability. This time it was the British Military
Mission, for which she had recently begun working, that found
itself quite unable to manage without her efficient services. To see all
the other British folk leaving was almost too much to bear! There
was one English family that stayed on. The Carrs had lived in

Archangel for many years and Mrs Carr was a good friend of Scottie's. She had given her a loaf and a cooked *ryabchik* (handsome presents in those days of near starvation) when Scottie set off for the icebreaker; and Scottie was never to forget the bunch of flowers that Mrs Carr now brought her as a consolation for being left behind.

Between April and June small detachments of British troops and an Allied squadron had been arriving at Murmansk, and towards the end of July the situation in Archangel became very tense, with well-founded rumours circulating that the British were about to seize the town. An ugly situation for those British people already in Archangel; and Scottie was felt to be in particular danger, for she had been handling the secret dispatches between Archangel and Murmansk, and might easily be taken hostage by the Bolsheviks. So it was decided that she should disappear quietly to a village on an island in the Dvina delta, opposite Archangel itself, called Keg Island. Mr Carr also arranged for his family to stay there until the situation became clearer.

Scottie lived on Keg Island with an old peasant woman. Here life went on as it always had done, and one wonders what the old woman made of this unexpected visitor who spoke Russian fluently but whose pink cheeks looked so un-Russian, and whether words like 'English' (let alone 'Scottish'!) or 'Bolshevik' meant anything at all to her. To reach her living quarters,

you went up a rickety outside stair to her kitchen and barn. She had a cow below and when the river broke up they had to bring their livestock up to these barns. She asked me where I wanted to sleep; I went and looked at the barn and came back and said it was too cold, so she said she just wanted to know where I would like to sleep on the *floor*. She slept on the top of the stove. It was very primitive—just little benches to sit on and a little table. I had taken some food with me, but when I had finished it I was very hungry. I thought I could get eggs but my old peasant said that if they had hens, they would all quarrel about who the eggs belonged to. She was having some porridge, so I said 'Is it good?' She filled a bowl and invited me to join her, eating out of the same bowl.

But this simple life was not to last for long. From her island Scottie watched the allied squadron sailing up the river. The British troops landed without opposition and there was very little fighting in Archangel. Faced by the combination of British troops and anti-

Bolshevik elements within the town, the Bolsheviks fled south along the railway and river. But to Bruce Lockhart in Moscow it seemed 'an unbelievable folly' that having committed themselves to a policy of intervention, the Allies had landed with a force no more than twelve hundred strong.

Next morning Scottie asked some men from the village to row her back to the mainland. Her old peasant was very sorry when she left. She said they had been so happy together: 'just like two dolls'.

Back in Archangel, Scottie began working at the new Military Headquarters under General Poole, compiling the General's reports. She was the only girl on the staff. But just when it seemed that she was in danger of becoming indispensable again and that her stay in Russia was going to be prolonged indefinitely, she was at last given permission to return home on a troop ship, the *Oporto*, which was taking wounded soldiers back to Britain. This time there were no hitches; though they had to wait for three weeks at Murmansk and then sailed far up into the Arctic Ocean to avoid German submarines. She finally reached Edinburgh a few weeks before the Armistice.

From Colin Anderson some thirty years later there came a long letter recalling the old days. He wrote of their times in Moscow together, especially visits to the Moscow Art Theatre, listening to the beautiful voice of the actor, Kachalov (the Professor in the ill-fated 1905 première of Gorky's *Children of the Sun*), and watching the performances of Chekhov's widow, Olga Knipper: 'the finest actress I have ever seen'. He recalled the wolves howling round the train taking them to Archangel. 'And I shall always remember,' he wrote, 'what a brave and loyal friend you were.' Words that we can echo: brave, loyal, and surely one of the most capable and versatile of all the young girls who went out as governesses to Russia.

28

The Occupation

Uncle Vasya and Miss Emmie saw plenty of one another in Theodosia. He always seemed to be up to something: like roasting sunflower seeds or making his own kind of toffee over a small spirit stove. He and Miss Emmie spoke only Russian together, and he was helpful in correcting her mistakes and pronunciation. As for Uncle Vasya's English, it seemed to consist of no more than four lines of song, delivered in a strong Russian accent:

> 'Yankee Doodle went to town
> To earn a little ma*w*ney,
> They put a feather in his cap
> And called him macara*w*ni!'

'It's not macara*w*ni, it's macar*oh*ni!' Miss Emmie would correct him, all prim and proper, but soon gave up the struggle: this pupil was obviously incorrigible.

He was also a dreadful tease. It must have been in Theodosia that he announced his intention of hiring himself out as a coachman, and Emmie was in two minds whether or not to take him seriously. Then one spring morning in 1918 he came in with a very straight face and told her that Theodosia had been occupied by the Germans, and that the white flag of surrender was flying there. If that was Uncle Vasya's idea of a joke . . . but could she be sure that he *was* joking? There was nothing else for it: she would have to walk along as far as the bridge over the railway and take a look for herself.

What she saw from this vantage point more than confirmed Uncle Vasya's report. German soldiers seemed to be everywhere: some were sitting in the gardens of houses, others simply resting on the pavements, while still more were streaming towards the centre of the town from the station. It was fortunate that the Rahls were living so much on the outskirts, for many of the larger houses closer in were soon requisitioned, and at the home of Olive Barnwell's Russian family further down the road they even had German soldiers sleeping on top of the grand piano.

The seizure of the Crimea by the Germans was a direct violation of the Treaty of Brest-Litovsk. To the north their occupation of the Ukraine had more semblance of justification, for the Soviet Government had recognised the Ukraine's independence, and the German intervention was ostensibly in answer to the émigré Ukrainian Government's call for help against the Ukrainian Reds; but both in the Crimea and the Ukraine the underlying German motives were in fact economic.

In Kharkov, second city of the Ukraine, Helen Clarke had been leading a life of great tension under the Bolsheviks ever since her nightmarish journey there from Bakmout with the five children in January 1918. As the children's mother was being eagerly sought by the Red Guards, it was decided that only the youngest child should remain with her, while the other four were entrusted to Helen. Thanks to the help of the British Vice-Consul two rooms were hired in her name and a notice put up on the door saying that the rooms belonged to an English citizen and that no one had the right to enter. But they dared not apply for ration cards, so early each morning Helen used to walk to the market about a mile away. When it was dusk, the parents would steal in to spend an hour with their children.

But the hours of darkness were the worst of all. 'Night after night one heard running feet, screams and revolver shots, and in the morning on going to the market, one saw pools of blood; the result of the night's work.' This terror was intensified when news came through that the Germans were advancing from the south. The night before their entrance, cannonading was heard, but next day they entered Kharkov without firing a shot.

It was an extraordinary change. The shops were all closed, and the whole of the inhabitants seemed to be in the streets. German bands were playing in all the principal squares, motor cars with German officers in smart uniforms were flashing up and down the streets, German artillery lined the roads, and the town seemed to have put on holiday garb. They certainly gave us a feeling of security, and after the terror through which we had lived during the previous six months, I must be forgiven when

I say we felt safe. We no longer had to hide like rats, we could come out of our various hiding-places and live once more *en famille*.

Any fears that Emma Dashwood may have had about the German occupation of Theodosia were likewise quickly dispelled. All that the British subjects had to do was to report together once a fortnight to German Headquarters. There were only three of them: Olive Barnwell, Emma Dashwood and a Mr Wisdom, who gave English lessons, had a Russian wife and lived at quite the other end of town. The Germans even offered to help arrange for Olive and Emmie to return to England, but Olive said no: the Germans were not to be trusted. Emmie agreed with Olive, of course, but could not help thinking to herself that the Germans' behaviour towards them showed the greatest charm and courtesy.

They settled down to an unexpectedly normal summer in occupied Theodosia. Emmie had a chance at last to give some thought to her wardrobe. Clothing coupons were issued by the Germans to enable each woman to buy enough cotton material for two dresses. Olive had found out about this, and she and Emmie went along to the depot together. By now the famous white piqué dress with the blue sailor collar had become worn out from frequent wear, although the collar was still good. Emmie picked out one length of cotton print in a creamy shade with a pale blue speck, and another with a navy stripe of better quality material on to which the blue collar could be transplanted.

In Kharkov at this time, where children's shoes and boots were almost unobtainable, Helen Clarke was busy emulating Tolstoy by taking lessons in boot-making; in less than a week she was able to finish a little pair of shoes for a girl of seven, and before long had fitted up all five of the children. Emma Dashwood also had problems with shoes and stockings. In order to save her best pair of white buckskin shoes, she had been wearing canvas sandals, bought from the market, as often as possible, while in very cold weather she wore her skating boots bought in Petrograd (having first, needless to say, unscrewed the skates). The only snag with the boots was that they rubbed holes in her black stockings more quickly than ordinary shoes. Darning cotton was impossible to find, so the gift of a reel of white cotton from Uncle Vasya came as a very welcome surprise. She was able to darn her black stockings with the white cotton and then paint the darns over with black ink. No matter that the ink came out each time she washed them: she just had to paint them over again.

With the arrival of the fine spring weather, they took most of their meals on the balcony at the front overlooking the beach, but in summer they spent the hottest part of the day indoors or sought out the shadiest spots in the garden. The walks in Theodosia were less varied and attractive than those of Yalta—'it was rather a straight sort of place with no rambles'—so that much of Miss Emmie's time was spent at the swimming pool which they shared with the Ulyanoffs, or on the beach where Volodya often played with Olive Barnwell's Russian pupil.

'I expect you realise,' Uncle Vasya had said to her at the start of the bathing season, 'that there's a German part of the beach and a Russian part?'

I wondered whatever he could mean. Was he pulling my leg as usual? So I asked him what the difference was.

'Oh, that's quite simple,' he replied, 'you see, on the *German* part of the beach they wear bathing costumes . . .'

I went out on to the balcony to have a look for myself—and it was *true*!

Miss Emmie decided there and then that she and Volodya would use the German part of the beach, even if this did mean fraternising with the enemy. As it turned out, the Germans could not have been nicer. 'You are a little frog,' one of the young German officers said to Olive's pupil in very broken English, 'I will throw you into the sea'; but it could not seriously be claimed that this amounted to terrorising the local population.

But Miss Emmie had a problem. It was the same problem that some years before had confronted Miss Eagar, when she went on holiday with the Imperial family to the south of Russia without a bathing costume and discovered that it was impossible to buy one. How Miss Eagar resolved the problem—whether she followed the advice of the Yalta shopkeeper to 'go and bathe in her skin as her grandmother did before her'—we do not find out. Miss Emmie, however, soon came up with an answer. She had in reserve several unused chemises that had been made for her by the old seamstress at Pervitino whose chickens lived in the downstairs room. These garments were of white nainsook, 'softer than calico but the same texture'. Since Mme Rahl was the same size as Emmie, she produced a bathing costume as a pattern, and Olive Barnwell was also recruited to help in the task of conversion.

It didn't require much cutting. . . . We had to make two legs for me to get into, of course—well obviously, otherwise it would have been open at the bottom and the water would have come right up—and then with the material left over we were able to make a loose belt to go round the middle. . . . Yes, the legs came just below the knee. No sleeves, of course, but good wide shoulder straps and buttons down the front that you could do up like a shirt. . . .

'Like men's combinations, in fact?'

'Yes, I suppose so . . . but not as *ugly* as that. It was really rather nice. My old seamstress had made a wonderful job of the embroidery.'

The bathing season went on late that year in Theodosia, but then one autumn night the Germans disappeared as suddenly as they had arrived. Once again Miss Emmie walked along to her vantage point on the railway bridge to take a look for herself, and once again what she saw amply confirmed what she had been told. There was no longer a trace of a German to be seen anywhere. They had vanished completely. Emmie was thrilled by this unexpected development, but her Russian friends all seemed anxious.

29

Getting Away

For Helen Clarke the summer of 1918 did not pass so smoothly, though it was still a considerable improvement on the earlier months under the Bolsheviks. Ever since the Germans' arrival, great loads of corn and food of every description had been seen leaving Kharkov, obviously intended for Germany. In the town itself food was very scarce and the peasants could name their own prices. As the hot Ukrainian summer wore on, it became clear that the discipline of the German soldiers, undermined by skilful Bolshevik propaganda, was deteriorating rapidly, and the town was no longer so well controlled as before. Rumours were going about that the German soldiers intended to revolt; certain it was that German officers, like their Russian counterparts after the February Revolution, had been obliged to remove their epaulettes. Then came rumours that the Germans were about to evacuate the Ukraine altogether, and that the Allies would shortly be occupying Kharkov—a rumour that was so widely believed by the end of October that money was collected in the English and French colony for a Presentation Flag to be handed over to the Allies on their entrance.

The German evacuation materialised, but the Allies did not. For Helen and her Russian family, Kharkov was no longer safe. There seemed little hope that the Ukrainian soldiers could hold out long on their own against Bolshevik pressure from the north. Having fore-seen this danger, Vladimir Petrovich had rented a small house at Simferopol, to which they might flee in case of need. It normally took about ten hours by train from Kharkov to Simferopol, the capital of the Crimea. But trains were few and far between, and when they did run, they were nearly always stopped by gangs of robbers who stripped the passengers of everything they possessed. The stage is set once more for Helen Clarke, with the memory of that dreadful journey from Bakmout to Kharkov still fresh in her mind, to undergo another 'ordeal by Russian train'. All the by now familiar preliminaries to departure had to be gone through—the visits to the pawnshop, burying of silver and jewellery, anxious waiting for news of the arrival of a train from the Crimea (for if none arrived, none would leave), complicated arrangements for procuring tickets, crowded waiting-rooms—but at last they found themselves installed in relative comfort in the obscurity of a third-class wagon: a party of four women, five children and a dog. Though she 'looked forward to the journey with terror', it was a great relief to Helen that at least on this occasion she did not have sole responsibility for the children, since their mother and aunt were also travelling.

For the first ten hours their progress was slow but quiet. Then, at about nine in the evening, the train came to a sudden standstill, and hooligan-looking men in soldiers' uniform, armed to the teeth, burst into the wagon and demanded to search their luggage: 'they hunted through with a curiosity and greed indescribable, examining everything minutely, but took nothing from us personally'. A young man and his wife were sitting not far away. He was evidently an officer trying to escape from the Ukraine and concealing his identity. They turned his baggage inside out and confiscated various articles with much yelling; but when they came upon some cartridges for a revolver, there was uproar.

No one was allowed to carry a revolver. If it were found after its existence had been denied, the penalty was instantaneous death. The young man denied having a revolver. They shook their fists at him and shouted: 'For God's sake, give us the revolver or we will shoot you where you stand. What are these cartridges for if you have no revolver?'

It was a terrifying moment. Our little children began to cry quietly, and the elder ones to say their prayers and cross themselves. The Bolsheviks had also made a law that no one should be allowed to have more than two of every garment: two shirts, two pairs of boots, two pairs of trousers, and so on. Whilst this argument was proceeding in connection with the revolver, searching was in progress amongst the other passengers' luggage. All at once, there was a lull in the tumult. It had been discovered that one of the passengers had two pairs of trousers in his bag! One pair he was wearing and two in his bag! This important discovery came as a godsend to the poor young man with the cartridges. The ruffians threw themselves upon the unfortunate owner of the nether garments, quite forgetting their anxiety to procure the weapon they so much desired, if weapon there be. The poor man was very much distressed, and begged to be allowed to keep his garments, but all to no avail. They were torn from his trembling hands amidst yells of fury and with this prize the ruffians left us.

But we were not left in peace for long. They soon came back to make more inquiries of the young man and his wife. The former was very diplomatic and calm, which was the only thing that could save one at such times. He argued and reasoned with them very quietly, and offered to give them forty roubles if they would bring back the eau-de-cologne for his wife. This they agreed to do, whereupon the owner of the trousers offered a hundred roubles if they consented to bring him back his trousers. This they also agreed to, and he there and then pulled out his purse in which were nine hundred roubles in all, and took from it the hundred roubles. When they saw that amount of money in the purse, they snatched it from him, stamping and shouting that they were not to be bought, then rushed from the wagon, slamming the door behind them. So the poor man lost his trousers *and* the nine hundred roubles!

After a very long delay, they travelled on for a few more hours, but then the train came to another standstill. Again they were searched, this time more ruthlessly than before. Vera Petrovna and Helen had divided their considerable sum of money between them. One of the men came up to Helen,

and putting his dirty hand on my chest, asked if I had anything hidden there. He then touched my pockets and asked the same question. I replied: 'I have nothing.' Then, hoping to frighten me, he put his horrible face close to mine and whispered in a hoarse voice: 'Mind you, if you have anything, and it is afterwards found, it will be the worse for you.' I replied: 'All right, I have nothing.' A minute after, another man came and demanded to see my passport. I took it from my coat pocket and gave it to him. He then demanded my name. The name was, of course, written on the passport both in Russian and English, but he was evidently unable to read. So I replied in Russian: 'Yelena Ivanovna Clarke.' At this he began to shout, and say the passport was out of date. I replied quietly: 'Yes, of course it is, but what does that matter?' and drawing myself up to my full height I said: 'I am an Englishwoman.' He then folded up the passport and in a very insinuating voice said: 'Yes, we are looking for spies', but as I showed no state of alarm, he left me. Some of the children were asleep when this lot of men entered, but the noise soon woke them. They were lying above our heads on the shelves to be found in all third-class wagons. One of the little girls, about eight years old, lay on the top shelf, flat on her stomach. Below her stood a sentry, his rifle just reaching to the child's head, and she amused herself by quietly spitting down the barrel. After they had left the carriage, the baby girl of three exclaimed: 'Thank God I didn't bring my little white cock!' At the home we had just fled from, she had a little toy white cockerel which she loved very much, and I suppose it would have been the last straw if these men had touched her beloved cock.

Within two hours they had reached the safety of the Crimea, though their journey was still by no means over. Their passports were inspected yet again, but this time by soldiers of the anti-Bolshevik Volunteer Army, formed in February 1918 from army officers, cadets, university students and even schoolboys. The young man and his wife could now talk freely, and he told them that he *did* have a revolver, but at the entrance of the men at the first stoppage, he had handed it to his wife, who quietly slipped out of the wagon into the lavatory and put it in the water-tank which was then empty. Not long after arriving in Simferopol, they learned that their train, which had taken thirty-six hours instead of the usual ten, had been the last to get through: the bridges were blown up and the line destroyed, for the Bolsheviks had entered the Ukraine and cut off the Crimea completely.

December 1918. In Europe the Armistice had recently been signed, but in Russia the outcome of the Great War, once such a central fact in people's lives, ceased long ago to be a matter of much interest to anyone. The Crimea, where Helen Clarke and Emma Dashwood were both living, was controlled by the Volunteer Army, and much of the coastline by French troops. All the towns in the relatively small peninsula were swollen by refugees from every part of Russia. In Simferopol, where a Regional Government for the Crimea had been formed, Helen counted it a privilege to be able to get up at six in the morning and walk a mile and a half to market with a basket over each arm: for 'there were so many people who had been used to the same luxurious lives as ourselves, and who now had not the means to buy enough food to fill one basket, let alone two'.

In Theodosia, however, Emma Dashwood was no longer living
with her old friends, though she did go to see them from time to
time. To tell the truth, Mme Rahl was not very pleased by Miss
Emmie's defection, especially when they had recently nursed her
over a mild attack of Spanish flu (and she wouldn't have caught that,
claimed Mme Rahl, if she and Olive hadn't insisted on bathing in
the swimming-pool too late in the year). But the British Vice-Consul
in Theodosia, who was in fact a Scandinavian, had emphasised that
if she wanted to stand any chance of getting back to England, she
must be on the spot all the time near the harbour; and the Rahls'
datcha was more than two miles away on foot.

So Emma Dashwood, thanks to an introduction from the Vice-
Consul, began her last job in Russia: as governess to nine-year-old
Gayane (pronounced *Guy-arnie*, not *Gay-annie*), younger daughter
of Prince Iverico Mikeladze, a Georgian who wore Georgian-style
dress (Astrakhan hat, high boots and knickerbocker trousers) but
claimed English ancestors and had a fine English library. Her salary
of two hundred roubles a month, insofar as such figures still meant
anything, was the highest she ever received in Russia. It was paid
in the so-called Don money; Helen Clarke relates that more than
ten different kinds of currency were being used in Kharkov in the
summer of 1918, and one never knew which of them would be
acceptable. With his Russian wife and two daughters, Prince
Mikeladze was living permanently in the Central Hotel at Theodosia,
right at the corner of the harbour. (Emmie understood that he
owned the Hotel France in Yalta.)

The winter of 1918–19 was an exceptionally hard one throughout
the Crimea.

In Theodosia, where the previous year Emmie had seen blossom
on the fruit trees soon after her arrival at the end of December, there
were now icicles hanging from the beach-huts. 'This is not the kind
of weather we expect here,' said a sad-faced Russian lady of distinguished appearance when she and Emmie passed one another out
walking on the beach. She addressed Emmie in English, correctly
assuming that no one else but an English governess would be out for
a walk in such raw winter weather.

Inland, the winds in Simferopol blew fiercely and were bitterly
cold. Very heavy falls of snow occurred in February. The supplies of
food from the north of the Crimea slowed down to a trickle; they

came by train and there was not enough fuel for the engines. To make one's way through deep snow at seven in the morning to buy food from the market—and not always to find any—was no longer pleasant.

Emmie and Helen were both waiting.

There was great excitement in Theodosia after Christmas when the first British destroyer, H.M.S. *Tilbury*, came into the harbour bringing Prince Olaf on an official visit. He was entertained by the Vice-Consul at the nearby consulate, while the British officers were Prince Mikeladze's guests for dinner at the Central Hotel. Earlier that afternoon Emmie had been shown all over the destroyer and invited to play the 'Dulcitone' piano, a gift to the ship from the men of Tilbury Docks.

But unfortunately the *Tilbury* was not able to pick up passengers.

A few weeks after her arrival in Simferopol, Helen had taken the train south-west to Sevastopol, hoping to contact other English people, to send off messages home and find out the chances of getting back to England. It was not by her standards a particularly horrifying journey. True, the train was supposed to leave at eleven in the morning and did not come in until 7 p.m.; true again, it was hopelessly overcrowded, people were pushing and fighting for places, and Helen was already about to follow the example of many intending passengers and clamber up on to the roof; but then she decided to change her tactics and attached herself to a group of frantic ladies who, having cornered the unfortunate station-master, finally persuaded him to unlock an almost empty carriage for them.

Sevastopol station was under the control of the French, and next morning Helen found out that there were British ships lying at anchor in the bay.

After waiting a few minutes, I saw a motor-launch flying the white ensign making for the quay on which I was standing. It was the first time I had seen the sea for over five years—that in itself was a great joy—but to look once more on the British flag was almost too much for the moment.

On the quay she met two English ladies who had come to Sevastopol for the same reasons as herself and, it transpired, were actually living not far from Helen in Simferopol. The lieutenants in charge of the motor-launch were very kind, promising to send off any letters they might care to bring and inviting them to afternoon tea on board ship. One of the ships was leaving for England that very day, and it was with mixed feelings that they chatted to some of the lucky passengers. But the three of them left Sevastopol next morning in good heart, for the Embarkation Officer had promised that as soon as another boat was due to leave for England, they would all be notified in good time.

That had been in January. It was now March. No news from England, none from Sevastopol; but news from the north that the Bolshevik Army was within two days' march of the narrow neck of land joining the Crimean peninsula to the mainland.

There was no immediate panic in Simferopol, as it was understood that with the support of the Allies, the Volunteer Army would be able to hold the frontier for some time.

March 22nd, 1919. Helen Clarke receives word at last from Yalta that a British ship will shortly be leaving to pick up all British subjects. Much relieved, she travels next day to Sevastopol to make final arrangements for departure—only to be told at the Transport Office that no one knows if the ship will be arriving within a week or a month. There is nothing else for her to do but return to Simferopol, having arranged for a telegram to be sent to her as soon as the ship arrives.

A week later the Bolshevik Army broke the frontier.

The banks were all closed and the inhabitants fleeing. All motors and vehicles were commandeered by the Volunteers for their families, as they were the first to be evacuated, for at the entrance of the Bolshevik Army, the wives and children of the Volunteers were as a rule massacred. The next day the panic had somewhat subsided, for the Volunteers gave out that they could hold their position at least another fortnight; but in four days' time a worse panic ensued. We then packed our belongings, which by this time did not amount to much. The only place of escape was Sevastopol. I had previously received information from there that in case of panic all British ships lying in the harbour would stand by in readiness to take off all who wished to get away, but the problem was how to get there, with no trains and no motors or carriages available. We managed to hire a wagon and two horses at the bazaar, but on the way to fetch us, it was commandeered by the Volunteers; so we were forced to remain another day, during which time we scoured the town and neighbourhood for a conveyance of some sort, and at last found a man who had a wagon and three small horses, and for the sum of one thousand roubles was willing to come for us on the morrow at six a.m. and drive us to Sevastopol.

By five a.m. the next morning, all was in readiness. This time we were a party of ten: five children, their parents, aunt, nurse, myself and dog. We waited until seven a.m. and still no sign of the wagon. Our hopes began to die within us. Everyone seemed to be fleeing but ourselves. At last in despair, Vladimir Petrovich rushed out of the house to look for the man. He found him at the bazaar with a wagon full of saddles and accoutrements belonging to the Volunteers. These he quietly pitched out, and he and the man drove quickly away. As soon as he reached us, we packed in with our various bundles, and were off in less than five minutes. The wagon was minus any springs and before we had gone twenty versts, every bone in our bodies ached. After we had made fifty versts, one of the horses fell ill, and had to be left behind at a small inn; but we continued our journey at a slower pace.

When in Sevastopol a week before, I had hired two rooms in case of necessity. It was fortunate I had done so; otherwise we should have had to spend the night in the street, for when we arrived that evening, every hotel was packed. The town was naturally in a state of intense excitement. It was pitiful to see the plight of the fugitives. Vehicles of every description were pouring into the town. There was a continual stream of motor cars with the tyres worn to ribbons; carts, cabs, laden with women and children; horses ready to drop from exhaustion; hand-carts and perambulators. It was a sight never to be forgotten. After settling in and feeding the tired children and parents, I went at once to the Transport Office. . . .

Meanwhile, in Theodosia, oblivious of danger to the last and knowing nothing either of the Bolshevik advance into the Crimea or of the desperate evacuation of Simferopol, Emma Dashwood is still quietly biding her time, relying on Olive Barnwell and the Vice-Consul to let her know as soon as a boat is expected. 'No, I wouldn't say I was *particularly* anxious about getting away—though I wanted to, of course—because I was always living so much in the present.' Now that the weather is not so bad, she frequently takes Gayane on the two-mile walk to see Volodya and Irina at the datcha, and the children play some good English games together in the garden. There is however one minor tragedy. Brandy, the Mikeladzes' little fox terrier, dies. He had been suffering from distemper and they had made a coat of bright red velvet specially for him.

'Why, even their little dogs wear velvet!' jeered the peasant women in Theodosia market, where the husks of sunflower seeds crunched underfoot; and Miss Emmie and Gayane were careful to avoid the market-place on future walks to the datcha. . . .

When Helen Clarke reached the Transport Office at Sevastopol that evening, she found it surrounded by excited people, but as she already knew the officers in charge, she made her way in and was quickly handed an envelope marked 'Secret, On His Majesty's Service'. This she opened, after leaving the building, and found it was an order to be on board H.M.S.—— by 8 a.m. the next morning.

So she and her Russian family said goodbye, though it was not to be for the last time. Her friends had decided to stay in Russia and were also leaving next day on a boat for Novorossisk.

When the Black Sea is rough, it can be very rough, and for forty-eight hours the British cruiser taking Helen to Constantinople tossed about like a cork on the water. But none of this discomfort seemed to matter any more. Nothing was too much trouble for the Commander and his Lieutenants, and she soon found herself laughing at their kindly jokes. Her cheeks felt quite stiff from their unaccustomed exertion. All the tensions, the horrors and the nightmares of the previous two years had affected her in a way she had not realised: she had forgotten how to laugh.

The date of Helen's departure from Sevastopol must have been about March 31st or April 1st. At more or less the same time Emma Dashwood received news at last from the Vice-Consul that a British boat would be calling any day at Theodosia—and presumably going on from there to Yalta and Sevastopol—to pick up the three British subjects.

It might have made a neat conclusion if I had been able to describe how Helen Clarke and Emma Dashwood, unknown to one another, left Russia together on the same British boat from Sevastopol; but unfortunately the boat calling at Theodosia was not a cruiser but a destroyer, the *Northesk*—and quite apart from that, Miss Dashwood was not on it. Prince Mikeladze was hoping that he would be able to arrange through Emmie for his family to travel by British boat to Constantinople. Since his wife and daughters were travelling to Sevastopol on a French destroyer, it was agreed with the British Transport Officer at Sevastopol that Emmie should also travel on the French boat, which was due in any case to leave Theodosia before the British one.

But when Emmie presented herself at the Hotel Kist, overlooking the Bay of Sevastopol, Lieutenant Ashmore was quite adamant: however much he might like to help, there could be no question of any Russians leaving for Constantinople on a British boat. It was doubtful if the vessels available would be adequate to take care of all the British refugees. 'They can share your room here in the hotel for one night only, if you like; but that is all.'

So the four of them packed into a room intended for one, and while Princess Mikeladze and Gayane slept on the bed, Emmie and the older daughter, Olga, shared a mattress on the floor. 'It reminded me a bit of that time at Germanova's during the Battle, when we were all sleeping on the floor of the vestibule.' To make matters worse, there was a black-out in Sevastopol that night and no lights were allowed in the hotel.

Next morning, very early, four British sailors came to collect Emmie's luggage. Her trunk was all packed, and she had even remembered to roll up her umbrella and slip it underneath the strap.

The Mikeladzes walked down to the quay with her. A motor-launch was waiting, already crowded with British subjects. The boat they were to travel in lay a little way off shore. The *Chalkis* was quite a small vessel, captured from the Turks. All the officers' cabins had been given over to passengers. Just how seaworthy the *Chalkis* was, must remain in doubt; but as soon as they reached Constantinople, it immediately went into dry dock.

Looking back from the motor-launch as it pulled away from the quay, Emmie saw the two girls and their mother waving to her and weeping. What was to happen to them, she had no idea.

*   *   *

'And did you realise,' I asked Miss Dashwood, 'that the Bolshevik Army must have occupied Sevastopol only a few days after you left? There were still boats taking people off even then, and the Bolsheviks fired on them from the shore with machine-guns. . . .'

'*Did* they? And to think I never knew anything about it! I just thought how kind it was of Lieutenant Ashmore—Ashmore or Ashford? I'm not sure which but it doesn't matter—to arrange for me to leave so quickly like that. Well, how extraordinary! So I *was* lucky. . . . And come to think of it, I reckon I was jolly lucky all the way through—don't you?'

30
The Last Survivors

So ends the story of Emma Dashwood in Russia; but the final chapter in the story of the English governess in Russia still has to be concluded, for Miss Dashwood was by no means the last English governess to leave the country.

The anti-Bolshevik intervention by British forces that Scottie had witnessed at Archangel in the summer of 1918 had unpleasant repercussions for the British residents in other parts of Russia. Not even the women were safe from arrest. The redoubtable Miss X., who had been so zealous in filling up that garden pond with candlesticks, samovars, revolvers and bullets, and who was now living with her Russian family in Moscow, wrote in her diary on November 23rd, 1918, that a Miss ffrench (a governess, perhaps, and of good birth?) had been brought from Simbirsk and had already spent a month in Moscow's Butyrky prison, though 'as she is British, they can at least send her food'. With her Russian family Miss X. waited up to see in the New Year, but not surprisingly, 'we drank to 1919 rather dispiritedly. . . . Last night an unfortunate woman threw herself from a seventh story window of the house opposite on to the pavement. . . . There are cases of small-pox; typhus goes on. . . . More and more people are dying from heart failure caused by attenuation.' On January 4th, 1919, she writes that she 'was again nearly poisoned by eating frozen potatoes. . . . At night I lie awake and see all the things I should like to eat; simple things: meat, butter, milk— simple, yet unobtainable.' One night at a friend's house she is given three cups of real tea and a slice of raw bacon: 'Excellent; I feel quite a different person.' But at least there was no shortage of work, for English lessons were still in great demand. To return home had become impossible. 'How sick I am of it all!' she writes on May 30th, 'I want to hear only English, see pleasant faces, and leave all this miles behind me'; and on June 7th: 'it will end by nearly all, or even all of us, being taken as hostages'.

On July 12th Miss X. refers for the first time to St Andrew's

House, where she had been for a frugal dinner. The hostel had become so overcrowded, with Russians and Germans as well as English people, that it was impossible to obtain a room there, and to make matters worse the Bolsheviks now commandeered the whole of the ground floor. Then on Sunday, September 7th comes the following entry in the diary:

> On Friday night soldiers went to St Andrew's at 10 p.m. and left at 3 a.m., after having taken all the English, except some of the very old ladies, prisoners. Miss Martensen, the matron, was much surprised to see Miss —— and myself turn up for dinner yesterday; she thought we had likewise been arrested. I went straight back after dinner, washed some clothes, and packed a few things I should need in prison. Mr North went to the Foreign Office yesterday morning and hopes that the women will be let out to-morrow or the next day.

As chaplain of the English Church in Moscow, Frank North was the only British subject who could still claim any kind of official status in Russia, and he and his wife campaigned vigorously on behalf of the few remaining British subjects, especially the prisoners of war. But on this occasion Mr North was too hopeful. The Englishwomen, including a number of former governesses, some of whom must have been known to Emma Dashwood when she stayed at St Andrew's in the autumn of 1917, were not released, neither on the next day, nor the day after that. Miss X. was surprised to find herself still at liberty, if liberty is the right word to describe her life then: 'Usually I run from lesson to lesson from early morning until 9.30 or 10.30 p.m., then I go and get the pot which contains my supper from the O——'s stove, have supper, get my next day's supper ready, and then go to bed; so it goes on from day to day and week to week.' It was the city itself, glimpsed on walks between lessons, that helped to keep her sane: 'How beautiful Moscow is! Walking along at sunset, the air seems to tremble with light and colour; quaint spots become more quaint and in the gathering dusk the great, grand churches seem to loom out of the distance like giants.'

Meanwhile, for the Englishwomen in the Butyrky prison, days turned to weeks and weeks to months. Eight more Englishmen were arrested. Did it mean that the women were to be let out and the men taken instead, for 'true to English tradition, as soon as the women were taken the men offered themselves in exchange'? No, the women were not released, and now the cruel Russian winter had set in. Returning from her last lesson at about 9.30, Miss X. would snatch her supper of cold gruel without even taking her cap off and hurry to bed in the hope of getting undressed before losing the heat from her brisk walk home. In a friend's room the temperature was some degrees below zero: 'she is reserved enough, but even she could not hold out; she got into bed and gave her lessons, even to men pupils, in bed'.

Christmas Day, 1919, finds Miss X. at St Andrew's, where 'it was quite gay. We all stopped on after dinner, and at 4 we had coffee and cake.' Then, on the night of January 3rd, 1920, after four months of imprisonment, the Englishwomen were released at last, 'all except Miss McCarthy, who is in the prison hospital, and another whom they say died of typhus'. So ended a grim episode in the history of the English governess in Russia: how grim we do not know, for Miss X. says no more about it and I have not been able to contact any survivors; but it might easily have turned out far worse.

Resourceful Miss X. was to score one last triumph in Russia. She had always had a genius for concealment: one remembers the heavy bronzes deposited in the lodgers' bath, the revolver hidden in her dress, and the bottle of liqueur deftly stowed in her dark-blue water-jug. In March 1920 she finally left Russia as one of a trainload of British subjects. At Petrograd's Finland Station their luggage was searched on the train. 'Whilst the hand-luggage was being searched —mine was done first—I managed to get this diary from up my back and two books from my stockings; I threw them among my already searched belongings, so that when the girls passed their hands down over me there was nothing to detect.'

The diary returned safely to England with its owner and was published by John Murray in the following year.

Not only in Moscow, but in other parts of Russia held by the Bolsheviks during the Civil War, there must still have been a fair number of stranded English governesses to be found as late as 1919 and 1920.

One of the most remarkable was a young Irish governess, Rosa Houston, whose story takes us right out of European Russia to Tashkent. Captured by the Russians in 1864, Tashkent had become the main centre of Russian trade in Central Asia and seat of the Governor-General of what was then known as Turkestan. British subjects were rare in this semi-Asiatic city. There was an English teacher called Smales, who had been there for fourteen years and was married to a Russian; a very old widow of English birth, Mme Quatts, who had gone out to Tashkent some fifty years before as governess to the children of General Kauffmann, the Russian conqueror of Turkestan; and Miss Houston, living with a Russian family as governess to their three children.

In 1918 another Englishman, Col. Bailey, arrived in Tashkent, and it is from his book, *Mission to Tashkent*, that my information about Miss Houston is largely drawn. His mission was to establish contact with the Bolsheviks in the hope of persuading them to continue the war against the Central Powers, or at least not to liberate the very large numbers of German and Austrian prisoners of war being held in Central Asian camps. Suspected at once by the Bolsheviks of being a spy, Col. Bailey decided to go into hiding. Here Miss Houston's assistance was invaluable to him. The cloak-and-dagger atmosphere of their activities is well caught by a note in pencil written to Col. Bailey by Miss Houston: '. . . you will see a grey-haired lady coming along from our house direction with a bundle wrapped in a red tablecloth under her arm. She will stop at the Town Hall for a minute and light a cigarette, then go on walking. You must follow: then when she will go into her house you pass and afterwards come back and go in yourself.'

Early in 1919 Miss Houston was given an opportunity to leave Tashkent, but with the loyalty so characteristic of our governesses, she decided to stand by the three children. Some time later, however, she did decide to make her escape; and what an extraordinary escape it was to be! In September 1919 she had taken up a post as teacher of English at a Soviet military school. Registered as a Soviet worker, she was able to apply for a transfer from Tashkent to Askhabad, intending to escape from there across the frontier to Persia. But the Bolsheviks got wind of her plan and gave orders that after leaving Tashkent, she should be taken off the train at Samarkand. Friends on the railway arranged for her to travel a few days earlier on a special train, and once in Askhabad she immediately went into hiding. For the large sum of 240,000 roubles a Persian agreed to provide her with a guide to take her across the mountains to Persia.

'With her guide and mounted on a small pony, minus a saddle,' writes Col. Bailey, she travelled from Friday evening till Monday night through the mountains. She slept two nights in the open and after a third day's travel reached a smuggler's cave high up among the cliffs in the mountains. Here the guide, who had been exorbitantly paid for the job, deserted her, taking the pony and her knapsack which contained the few belongings she had been able to take out of Turkestan. The position looked terrible for her, left entirely alone in the heart of the mountains.

Luck was with her, however, for a party of fifteen cheerful smugglers turned up who eventually agreed, after putting her through a test of horsemanship, to take her on to Persia. The road was rough and things were not improved by a blizzard. At midday they halted to light a fire and melt themselves and she was given a dirty piece of bread which one of her rough friends produced from a knot in his not too clean sash. This with a sucked icicle was her meal.

The smugglers themselves could not eat as they were carrying out a Mohammedan fast. At last at dusk, on Monday, they saw the lights of the Persian customs post at Jiristan in the distance. 'There you are,' they said, 'there is the end of your journey.' She told them that one of them must come with her to get the promised reward. This was, to say the least of it, difficult and awkward, for in all countries the smuggler is the enemy of the customs official! However, she promised one of them a safe conduct and he trusted her word and influence and went with her. She was welcomed by the French-speaking Persian customs officer, but both he and his staff were horrified to see her accompanied by a noted smuggler whom they had been trying to catch for years. She smoothed things over and eventually her smuggler friend joined them at a meal and was given the promised reward and allowed to depart unscathed. The war between the smugglers and the customs was closed for those few hours to be reopened the next morning.

From Jiristan Miss Houston was able to get into communication with the British mission at Meshed, where she eventually arrived.

This colourful adventure might seem a suitable finale to the story of the English governess in Russia, but the last paragraph of all must belong to Miss Fellows.

When Fitzroy Maclean, then a young military attaché, discovered her in 1937 and wrote about her in *Eastern Approaches*, twenty years had passed since the Revolution and Miss Fellows was still living in Russia: as an English governess! She had first gone there in 1911, the same year as Scottie, Emmie, Gertie and a host of others who by varying routes and with varying degrees of difficulty had long since made their way back to England. The survivors of her once well-to-do St Petersburg family were now living in a single room of their former house in Tiflis, the capital of Georgia. Repeating a pattern that had been common before the Revolution, Miss Fellows was acting as governess to the small son of her original pupil. Like the governesses of earlier years she had 'stuck' in Russia with a single family, but in other respects how great a contrast! For their lives had been led against the secure background of privilege and luxury, whereas Mary Fellows had lived through Revolution, Civil War and Stalinist terror, had obviously *chosen* to endure all the privations of life with her family in one room, after having known the gilded apartments and countless servants of Tsarist times. Still very English in her ways—when Soviet officials tried to persuade her to change her nationality, she just told them not to be so silly—yet completely devoted to her Russian family, she personifies that spirit of selflessness which is perhaps the most attractive feature of the English governess in Russia: that willingness to dedicate her life to the well-being of others, no matter how great the hardships that she has to endure herself.

Sequel

Miss Fellows died in 1941.

Her death might never have been notified to the British authorities, had not Britain and Russia become allies that year in the war against Germany. There may possibly have been others like her, no longer in touch with England, living obscurely in distant Russian towns to which foreigners seldom came, who survived the Second World War in Russia as well as the First; but the death of Mary Fellows in 1941, on the eve of the German invasion, is a convenient point at which to close this account of the English governess in Russia.

There remain, however, a few loose threads. What happened to Edith Kerby after her return to London, to the five Kerby Aunts who had stayed behind in Russia, and to the Russians with whom Emma Dashwood had been so closely associated?

It was a Saturday morning in the summer of 1917 when Miss Kerby, after a hazardous wartime journey from Russian via Finland and the North Sea, finally reported for duty at the Russia Department of the Foreign Office. Hugh Walpole was there to greet her. He at once suggested that she should take three weeks' holiday before starting work. As her pay had been accumulating in London, she asked him if she could draw some money to go away on.

'Sorry,' he said, 'but it's a Saturday and the banks are all closed. But I can let you have something. How much would you like?'

'Well, about £75 will do.'

Walpole's face dropped. Then he burst out laughing and gaily handed her five pound notes, the total contents of his wallet.

Edith *revelled* in London! Her old friend, Mr Wilcox, of the *Daily Telegraph*, had arranged for her to rent his sister-in-law's furnished flat in Hampstead, while she was away nursing in France. It was very close to Christ Church, which had an adjoining school. Edith was one of the privileged few at the Foreign Office who did not have to sign in at a fixed time, and so every morning, over an unhurried breakfast, she listened to the very English sound of the children next door singing the morning hymn. The lunch hour found her eating sandwiches on top of an old-fashioned open London bus, avidly exploring new parts of her beloved city. Later the Zeppelin raids began and people tried to persuade her to go down into the Underground, but she waved them aside and sat by her window high up on Hampstead Heath, watching the Zeppelins burn over London. Winter came, and she thought she would die unless she bought herself heavy long-sleeved Wolsey combinations. She was thrilled to be wearing real English underwear (how envious she had been of the children wearing real English Patent Leather shoes at the Embassy celebration in St Petersburg of King Edward's coronation!) and as the material looked of such excellent quality, she could not resist the temptation to allow a little of the cuff to peep out of her sleeve.

And the Kerby Aunts? In the summer of 1917 they had chosen to stay on in Petrograd: all their life savings were invested in Russian banks, so how could they consider going to England now that it was impossible to transfer money there? When Emma Dashwood visited them for the last time in the flat on Kronverksky Prospect, their living conditions had already sunk desperately low. That was late in 1917. Aunt Kate, companion to the young Princess Beloselsky-Belozersky, had left earlier for England with the Princess and her mother, but it was not until 1919 that the other surviving members of the Kerby family were allowed to leave Petrograd.

Edith was at the station to meet them on their arrival in England. It was a pathetic group of refugees that dragged itself wearily from that train. The Aunts had shrunk so much that their dresses trailed along the ground. During the past months they had gradually lost their teeth, their hair and their nails, and their memories had become very hazy. Edith took them to the house in Muswell Hill which had been bought for members of the family by her brother Harry.

There were only three Aunts. Aunt Annie, several years older than the others, had died in Russia of starvation: Aunt Annie, who had been such a good friend to Emma Dashwood and to so many young English governesses before her, and who had celebrated the joint triumph of Emmie's engagement as a governess in the Rahl family by going into the pastrycook's to buy a good selection of cakes. Her death must have taken place during the harsh winter of 1918–19. Since there were no coffins to be had (all used up long ago as firewood), the other three wrapped her body in newspaper, put it on a sledge and dragged it as far as the cemetery. No one had the strength to dig graves any more, so the bodies, frozen stiff, were thrown on to a pile and left.

The doctor had given Edith instructions that the three survivors must be carefully nursed back to health by making them observe a very strict diet. Easier said than done! The sight and even the thought of food was too great a temptation. No sooner had everyone retired for the night than Edith would hear ominous shufflings and rattlings of doors, and on going downstairs to investigate would discover the three Aunts gorging themselves in the larder. But they all lived to a good age, and Aunt Jane—hospitable Aunt Jane, who always liked to warm the visitors' coats in front of the fire before allowing them to step out into the cold streets of St Petersburg— Aunt Jane lived to the age of ninety-nine.

And what of the Russian friends whom Emma Dashwood had left behind in 1919? Not long after her departure she learned that the Mikeladzes, whose weeping figures on the quayside at Sevastopol had been her last memory of Russia, were also safely out of the country. A card arrived for her from Gayane. It was postmarked Constantinople, and on it Gayane had carefully drawn a flag and printed underneath it the magic words: 'Onion Jack'.

Several more years were to pass before Emmie heard anything of Maria Germanova. Then, to her great excitement, she suddenly found out that Mme Germanova was in London, playing at the Garrick Theatre. (In 1919, during the Civil War, Germanova had been one of a group of fifteen members of the Moscow Art Theatre giving guest performances in the south of Russia who were cut off by the unexpected advance of the White armies. When the Whites retreated most of the fifteen followed and settled in Europe. Germanova became the leading figure in what was known between the wars as the Prague Group of the Moscow Art Theatre.) Emmie wrote off at once to the Garrick Theatre and received back a signed photograph, with a pressing invitation to come and visit Germanova in London. But Emmie's mother persuaded her not to go, being convinced that one word from Mme Germanova would be enough for Emmie to throw up her career in England as a teacher and be off on her travels again.

Not until the 1930's did Emma Dashwood have news of the Rahl family. Then she learned that they too had long since left Russia and were living on the Continent. Photographs were exchanged. 'How strict you look!' wrote Mme Rahl, after Emmie had sent them one of her school photographs. 'We hardly recognised you.' Volodya sent a fine photographic portrait of himself. He was then almost the age that his father had been when Emmie first knew the Rahls in Russia, and she was at once struck by the likeness. Of himself he wrote that he was 'no longer the First Gentleman of Staritsa but an ordinary engineer earning his own living'. How very fortunate, Emmie might have been forgiven for thinking, that I made such a point of letting him 'mess about' on his own in his workshop at Pervitino!

Mr Wilton, Mr Wilcox and Mr Walpole all published books about Russia soon after the Revolution. Mr Wilton, Russian correspondent for *The Times*, had been the man with the picture of Norwich Cathedral behind his desk who did not engage Emma Dashwood as a governess in the autumn of 1917. His book appeared in 1918 and was entitled *Russia's Agony*; Mr Wilcox, of the *Daily Telegraph*, followed a year later with *Russia's Ruin*. Hugh Walpole's novel, *The Secret City*, successor to his earlier Russian novel, *The Dark Forest*, came out in January 1919. The secret city was Petrograd and the story, which centres round the February Revolution of 1917, seems more interesting now for its first-hand descriptions of places and events than for its fictional intrigue. Amusingly he conjures up the atmosphere of 'demure English provincialism' which lay over everything in the large English Shop at the corner of the Nevsky Prospect: 'Here, indeed, I could fancy that I was in the High Street in Chester, or Leicester, or Truro, or Canterbury. . . . The air was filled with the chatter of English governesses, and an English clergyman and his wife were earnestly turning over a selection of woollen comforters.' He writes of the English Propaganda Office in Petrograd, with its 'colossal toy map of the London Tube, and a nice English library with all the best books from Chaucer to D. H. Lawrence'; and when he refers to 'several young women clicking away at typewriters', I immediately began to think that Edith Kerby's worst fears were about to be realised and that Hugh Walpole had indeed put her into one of his novels. But further reading disclosed, a trifle disappointingly, that the typists were all Russian and bore no resemblance to Miss Kerby.

Soon after her return from Russia Emma Dashwood came into contact for the first time with Rosamond Dowse, though they must have seen one another at the British & American Chapel in Petrograd early in 1917. Emmie had decided to resume her teaching career at the point where it had been so unexpectedly diverted in 1911. As it turned out, the years had not been wasted, for the knowledge she had gained in Russia of the psychology of one small boy was to stand her in good stead when dealing with many. She became a student teacher at Thorpe House, the private school in Norwich belonging to Rosamond's parents. Not that she and Rosamond ever talked much about Russia. . . . Louisette Andrews, the reluctant chaperone, went to America some time after her return from Russia and became social secretary to a millionairess. World War Two found her rolling bandages and preparing dressings just as she had done in Russia in World War One; but no longer was it necessary to stand up and curtsey whenever the Empress came into the room. . . . Nikolai Karlovich von Meck, Scottie's first employer in Russia, refused even to contemplate the idea of leaving his native country after the Revolution and threw in his lot with the new regime, but after being arrested on a number of occasions he was finally shot by the Bolsheviks for alleged counter-revolutionary activities in 1929, at the age of sixty-six. His daughter Galina also spent many years in prisons and labour camps before reaching England in 1948. Later she and Scottie were guests of honour at the première of a new production at Glyndebourne of Tchaikovsky's opera, *Eugene Onegin*. . . . As for Helen Clarke, she had only been back in England a few months in 1919 when she was again caught up in the drama of Russian life. A pathetic appeal arrived from her Russian family: life is impossible, they wrote, every day we are besieged by robbers, the children have fallen ill, do please come and save us. So back she went without hesitation to Constantinople, then teeming with refugees, and after about a week the family turned up from Russia on a cattle boat: the familiar complement of mother, father, five children and the dog. Greatest disaster of all, the dog had to be left behind at the British Consulate, but the family came back safely to England under Helen's supervision.

As for the author of this book, he has enjoyed the company of his governesses, both past and actual, and still looks forward to another meeting with an alert octogenarian or nonagenarian who will say to him:

'You know, Mr Pitcher, I really have had rather an *interesting* life. When I was in Russia . . .'

Sources and Acknowledgements

This book may be described as a joint enterprise, for I have been helped by a great number of people who put information at my disposal.

Among written sources I must start by mentioning *A Memoir of an English Governess in Russia, 1914–1917* by Rosamond Dawe, *née* Dowse, originally published in 1973 by Bishop Otter College, Chichester, and now under the imprint of Unwin Brothers. This is the first in a series of 'reminiscences and personal documents from the past', edited by John Fines, with the general title of *Looking Back*. Mrs Dawe generously allowed me to make free use of her memoir which I was able to supplement with further information gathered on visits to her in Wallington; the memoir, I hasten to add, contains much fascinating detail not included here. Then I was also fortunate in being able to incorporate other written material that had not previously appeared in print: in 1948 Mrs Bangham (Edith Kerby) wrote an informal account for family consumption of her life until that time, of which she kindly lent me a copy; Mrs Thomson (Scottie) gave me her scripts of two broadcast talks on Russia, and Mrs Whitley (Helen Clarke) the typewritten account which she compiled in 1921 describing her Russian experiences from the start of 1917 until her departure in the spring of 1919. As in the case of Mrs Dawe, this written information was considerably augmented by a number of visits which I paid, notebook in hand, to Roehampton, Chorley Wood and Brancaster respectively, where I was received with much kindness and hospitality. Finally I am most grateful to John Vaughan, Tutor Librarian at the School of Education Library in the University of Liverpool, who first wrote to tell me of the existence of Marie Russell Brown's unpublished book, *This Was Russia*, to Iain Campbell for his letters describing Miss Brown, and to Mrs Edna Campbell of Oxford for allowing me to quote extensively from Miss Brown's manuscript.

As far as Miss Andrews and Miss Dashwood were concerned, almost all the information was provided orally, although Miss Dashwood at my suggestion courageously undertook to compile her own memoirs, which served as a basis for later elaboration and discussion. Miss Andrews entertained me on several occasions in Kensington, but it was the immediate accessibility of Miss Dashwood in Cromer that first made me think a book of this kind might be possible, and I soon lost count of my weekly visits on Monday afternoons to Cabbell Road to drink tea and talk Russia. Without Miss Emmie's patient and enthusiastic participation the book would not have been realised.

The reader may wonder, as I did, to what extent one can rely on the memories of people in their eighties and nineties. (The oldest former governess in Russia whom I met, Miss Dunnett, 'ninety-five and a good half' when I visited her at Angmering in the summer of 1974, apologised for not being able to recall more of her time out there, but explained: 'You see, I've grown old since then. Very foolish of me, but I couldn't help it.') In Miss Dashwood's case I had ample evidence of her remarkable memory in fields quite unconnected with Russia. It was fortunate none-theless that Russian history between 1910 and 1920 has been so fully documented, since this enabled me to check the historical accuracy of information given and to establish dates with reasonable certainty. In general, I have been cautious; have taken with a grain of salt some of the stories told me; and can say with a clear conscience that there is very little in this book of 'author's decoration' and certainly nothing so irresponsible as a flight of fancy.

My thanks are also due to the following people who gave me information that was used directly: Mrs Edna Bird (*re* the Sinclair family); Mrs Elsie Brown (*re* Rosa Houston); H. L. Carr; Miss Mary Chamot; Mrs Anna Collingwood; Dame Professor Elizabeth Hill; Marvin Lyons; Mrs Tatiana Minorsky; Mrs Dorothy Russell, *née* Cooke; Anatole Theakstone and Miss Sophie Theakstone (great-grandson and great-granddaughter of Helen Pinkerton); Miss D. F. Wallace (*re* Miss Winkworth); and Mrs Sonya Witter (*re* Prudence Browne). My thanks are no less due to all the other people who took the trouble to write to me, often at considerable length, and whose information enabled me to build up a general picture. I am also grateful to the courteous staff of the B.B.C.'s Script Library, where I was able to consult the script of the programme about Mrs van Doren and her sister, Miss Judge, broadcast in 1959, and to the Secretary and staff of the Governesses' Benevolent Institution, who not only allowed me to comb their records and to copy out Dr Edward Law's letters about Miss Handcock, but also gave me free tea and biscuits.

Finally, acknowledgements are gratefully made to the authors and publishers of the following books from which quotations have been taken:

Asquith, Cynthia. *Married to Tolstoy* (Hutchinson) 1960.

Baedeker, Karl. *Baedeker's Russia 1914* (first published 1914, reprinted 1971 and jointly published by David & Charles, Newton Abbot, and George Allen & Unwin).

Bailey, Lt.-Col. F. M. *Mission to Tashkent* (Jonathan Cape) 1946.

Cross, Anthony (ed.). *Russia Under Western Eyes, 1517–1825* (Elek) 1971. Includes extracts from the letters of Mrs Disbrowe.

Dobson, G. *St. Petersburg*, painted by F. de Haenen, described by G. Dobson (Adam & Charles Black) 1910.

From A Russian Diary, 1917–1920. By an Englishwoman (John Murray) 1921.

Howe, Bea. *A Galaxy of Governesses* (Derek Verschoyle) 1954.

Jones, Stinton. *Russia in Revolution: being the experiences of an Englishman in Petrograd during the upheaval* (Herbert Jenkins) 1917.

Lockhart, R. H. Bruce. *Memoirs of a British Agent* (Putnam) 1932.

Meck, Galina von. *As I Remember Them* (Dennis Dobson) 1973.

Nabokov, Vladimir. *Speak, Memory*, rev. ed. (Weidenfeld & Nicolson) 1967.

Nemirovich-Danchenko, V. I. *My Life in the Russian Theatre*, translated by John Cournos (Geoffrey Bles) 1937.

Obolensky, Serge. *One Man in his Time* (Hutchinson) 1960.

Percival, Alicia. *The English Miss To-day & Yesterday* (Harrap) 1939.

Slonim, Marc. *Russian Theater from the Empire to the Soviets* (Methuen) 1963.

Stanislavsky, K. S. See *A. P. Chekhov v vospominaniyakh sovremennikov* ('A. P. Chekhov Recalled by his Contemporaries'), Moscow, 1960, which contains Stanislavsky's description of the English governess on the neighbouring estate; the translation is my own.

The Russian Diary of an Englishman. Petrograd, 1915–1917 (Heinemann) 1919.

The Story of the Governesses' Benevolent Institution, 1962. (For private circulation only.)

Vorres, Ian. *Last Grand Duchess: The Memoirs of Grand Duchess Olga Alexandrovna* (Hutchinson) 1964.

Walpole, Hugh. *The Secret City* (Macmillan) 1919.

Wonlar-Larsky, Nadine. *The Russia That I Loved* (Elsie MacSwinney) 1937.

Miss Dashwood with the author

About the Author

Harvey Pitcher was born in London in 1936, and educated at Merchant Taylors School and St John's College, Oxford. During National Service he qualified as a Russian interpreter. In 1963 he was invited to start the Russian department at the University of St Andrews. He published his first book in 1964, and since 1971 has been a full-time writer and translator, with two main areas of interest: Chekhov and the British community in Russia before the Revolution. His Chekhov publications include a study of the plays, and a biography of Chekhov's wife, the actress Olga Knipper. With Patrick Miles he translated Chekhov's early stories. *When Miss Emmie was in Russia* (1977) was followed by two other 'Anglo-Russian' books: *The Smiths of Moscow* (1984), about a family of British boilermakers, and *Muir & Mirrielees* (1994), the story of two Scottish families who created Moscow's most famous department store. In *Witnesses of the Russian Revolution* (2001) the events of 1917 are presented through the eyes of British and American observers.

Harvey Pitcher lives in Cromer on the North Norfolk coast, and it was there that he met Miss Dashwood.

Index